# DOMESDAY BOOK

## Cheshire

*History from the Sources*

# DOMESDAY BOOK

### A Survey of the Counties of England

*LIBER DE WINTONIA*

Compiled by direction of

## KING WILLIAM I

Winchester
1086

# DOMESDAY BOOK

general editor

**JOHN MORRIS**

26

# Cheshire

edited by

**Philip Morgan**

*from a draft translation prepared by*
Alexander Rumble

PHILLIMORE
Chichester
1978

1978

Published by

PHILLIMORE & CO. LTD.,
London and Chichester

*Head Office*: Shopwyke Hall,
Chichester, Sussex, England


© John Morris, 1978


ISBN 0 85033 139 0 (case)
ISBN 0 85033 140 4 (limp)

*Printed in Great Britain by*
*Titus Wilson & Son Ltd.,*
*Kendal*

# CHESHIRE

History from the Sources
*General Editor:* John Morris

The series aims to publish history
written directly from the sources
for all interested readers, both
specialists and others. The first
priority is to publish important
texts which should be widely
available, but are not.

# DOMESDAY BOOK

The contents, with the folio on which each county begins, are:

Domesday Book is termed *Liber de Wintonia* (The Book of Winchester) in column 332c

# INTRODUCTION

## The Domesday Survey

In 1066 Duke William of Normandy conquered England. He was crowned King, and most of the lands of the English nobility were soon granted to his followers. Domesday Book was compiled 20 years later. The Saxon Chronicle records that in 1085

> at Gloucester at midwinter ... the King had deep speech with his counsellors ... and sent men all over England to each shire ... to find out ... what or how much each landholder held ... in land and livestock, and what it was worth ... The returns were brought to him.[1]

William was thorough. One of his Counsellors reports that he also sent a second set of Commissioners 'to shires they did not know, where they were themselves unknown, to check their predecessors' survey, and report culprits to the King.'[2]

The information was collected at Winchester, corrected, abridged, chiefly by omission of livestock and the 1066 population, and fair-copied by one writer into a single volume. Norfolk, Suffolk and Essex were copied, by several writers, into a second volume, unabridged, which states that 'the Survey was made in 1086'. The surveys of Durham and Northumberland, and of several towns, including London, were not transcribed, and most of Cumberland and Westmorland, not yet in England, was not surveyed. The whole undertaking was completed at speed, in less than 12 months, though the fair-copying of the main volume may have taken a little longer. Both volumes are now preserved at the Public Record Office. Some versions of regional returns also survive. One of them, from Ely Abbey,[3] copies out the Commissioners' brief. They were to ask

> The name of the place. Who held it, before 1066, and now?
> How many *hides*?[4] How many ploughs, both those in lordship and the men's?
> How many villagers, cottagers and slaves, how many free men and Freemen?[5]
> How much woodland, meadow and pasture? How many mills and fishponds?
> How much has been added or taken away? What the total value was and is?
> How much each free man or Freeman had or has? All threefold, before 1066,
> when King William gave it, and now; and if more can be had than at present?

The Ely volume also describes the procedure. The Commissioners took evidence on oath 'from the Sheriff; from all the barons and their Frenchmen; and from the whole Hundred, the priests, the reeves and six villagers from each village'. It also names four Frenchmen and four Englishmen from each Hundred, who were sworn to verify the detail.

The King wanted to know what he had, and who held it. The Commissioners therefore listed lands in dispute, for Domesday Book was not only a tax-assessment. To the King's grandson, Bishop Henry of Winchester, its purpose was that every 'man should know his right and not usurp another's'; and because it was the final authoritative register of rightful possession 'the natives called it Domesday Book, by analogy

---

[1] Before he left England for the last time, late in 1086.   [2] Robert Losinga, Bishop of Hereford 1079-1095 (see *E.H.R.* 22, 1907, 74).   [3] *Inquisitio Eliensis*, first paragraph.   [4] A land unit, reckoned as 120 acres.   [5] *Quot Sochemani*.

from the Day of Judgement'; that was why it was carefully arranged by Counties, and by landholders within Counties, 'numbered consecutively ... for easy reference'.[6]

Domesday Book describes Old English society under new management, in minute statistical detail. Foreign lords had taken over, but little else had yet changed. The chief landholders and those who held from them are named, and the rest of the population was counted. Most of them lived in villages, whose houses might be clustered together, or dispersed among their fields. Villages were grouped in administrative districts called Hundreds, which formed regions within Shires, or Counties, which survive today with minor boundary changes; the recent deformation of some ancient county identities is here disregarded, as are various short-lived modern changes. The local assemblies, though overshadowed by lords great and small, gave men a voice, which the Commissioners heeded. Very many holdings were described by the Norman term *manerium* (manor), greatly varied in size and structure, from tiny farmsteads to vast holdings; and many lords exercised their own jurisdiction and other rights, termed *soca*, whose meaning still eludes exact definition.

The Survey was unmatched in Europe for many centuries, the product of a sophisticated and experienced English administration, fully exploited by the Conqueror's commanding energy. But its unique assemblage of facts and figures has been hard to study, because the text has not been easily available, and abounds in technicalities. Investigation has therefore been chiefly confined to specialists; many questions cannot be tackled adequately without a cheap text and uniform translation available to a wider range of students, including local historians.

**Previous Editions**

The text has been printed once, in 1783, in an edition by Abraham Farley, probably of 1250 copies, at Government expense, said to have been £38,000; its preparation took 16 years. It was set in a specially designed type, here reproduced photographically, which was destroyed by fire in 1808. In 1811 and 1816 the Records Commissioners added an introduction, indices, and associated texts, edited by Sir Henry Ellis; and in 1861-1863 the Ordnance Survey issued zincograph facsimiles of the whole. Texts of individual counties have appeared since 1673, separate translations in the Victoria County Histories and elsewhere.

**This Edition**

Farley's text is used, because of its excellence, and because any worthy alternative would prove astronomically expensive. His text has been checked against the facsimile, and discrepancies observed have been verified against the manuscript, by the kindness of Miss Daphne Gifford of the Public Record Office. Farley's few errors are indicated in the notes.

[6] *Dialogus de Scaccario* 1,16.

The editor is responsible for the translation and lay-out. It aims at what the compiler would have written if his language had been modern English; though no translation can be exact, for even a simple word like 'free' nowadays means freedom from different restrictions. Bishop Henry emphasized that his grandfather preferred 'ordinary words'; the nearest ordinary modern English is therefore chosen whenever possible. Words that are now obsolete, or have changed their meaning, are avoided, but measurements have to be transliterated, since their extent is often unknown or arguable, and varied regionally. The terse inventory form of the original has been retained, as have the ambiguities of the Latin.

Modern English commands two main devices unknown to 11th century Latin, standardised punctuation and paragraphs; in the Latin, *ibi* ('there are') often does duty for a modern full stop, *et* ('and') for a comma or semi-colon. The entries normally answer the Commissioners' questions, arranged in five main groups, (i) the place and its holder, its hides, ploughs and lordship; (ii) people; (iii) resources; (iv) value; and (v) additional notes. The groups are usually given as separate paragraphs.

King William numbered chapters 'for easy reference', and sections within chapters are commonly marked, usually by initial capitals, often edged in red. They are here numbered. Maps, indices and an explanation of technical terms are also given. Later, it is hoped to publish analytical and explanatory volumes, and associated texts.

The editor is deeply indebted to the advice of many scholars, too numerous to name, and especially to the Public Record Office, and to the publisher's patience. The draft translations are the work of a team; they have been co-ordinated and corrected by the editor, and each has been checked by several people. It is therefore hoped that mistakes may be fewer than in versions published by single fallible individuals. But it would be Utopian to hope that the translation is altogether free from error; the editor would like to be informed of mistakes observed.

The maps are the work of Rosalind Brewer and Jim Hardy.

The preparation of this volume has been greatly assisted by a generous grant from the Leverhulme Trust Fund.

**Conventions**

| | | |
|---|---|---|
| * | refers to a note to the Latin text. | b. = bovate; c. = carucate. |
| [ ] | enclose words omitted in the MS. | ( ) enclose editorial explanations. |

262 c

*CIVITAS DE CESTRE* Tēpore regis . E . geldƀ ᵱ . L . hiđ.
Tres hidæ 7 dimiđ quæ fuꝶ exᵗ ciuitatē . Hoc . ē una
hida 7 dimiđ ulᵗ pontē . 7 II . hidæ . In Neutone 7 Rede
cliue 7 in burgo epῖ: hæ geldaƀ cū ciuitate.

T.R.E. eraꝶ in ipfa ciuitate . cccc . 7 xxxi . dom̉ gelđ.
7 p̄ter has habeƀ eps . lvi . dom̉ gelđ.

Tc̄ reddeƀ ħ ciuitas . x . marꝁ argenti 7 dimiđ . Duæ
partes eraꝶ regis . 7 ᵗcia comitis . 7 Hæ leges erant ibi.

Pax data manu regis uel fuo breui uel ᵱ fuū legatū.
Si ab aliꝗ fuiffet infraċta: inde rex . c . foliđ habebat.

Qđ fi | ipfa | pax regis juffu ej̉ á comite data fuiffet infraċta:
de . c . foliđ qui ᵱ hoc—dabant̉ tciū denar com̉ habeƀ.

Si ū a p̄pofito regis aut miniftro comitis eađ pax data
infringeret: ᵱ . xl . foliđ emdabat̉ . 7 comitis erat ᵗcius deñ.

Ꮆ Siđs liƀ hō regis——pacē datā infringe̷s in domo
hominē occidiffet: tra ej̉ 7 pecunia tota regis erat.

7 ipfe utlagh fiebat . Hoc idē habeƀ comes de fuo tanᵗ
homine hanc forisfaċturā faciente . Cuilibet autē utlagh
nullus poterat reddere pacē nifi ᵱ regē.

Ꮆ Qui fanguinē facieƀ a mane fcđæ feriæ ufꝗ ad nonā
fabƀi: x . foliđ emdaƀ.                    Ꮆ . xx . foliđ emdabat̉.

A nona ū fabƀi ufꝗ ad mane fcđæ feriæ fanguis effufus:
Similit̉ . xx . foliđ folueƀ qui hoc facieƀ in . xii . dieƀⱿ
natiuitatis . & in die purificat̉ Ꞩ MARIE . 7 p̄mo die pafchæ.
7 p̄mo die pentecost̉ . 7 die afcenfion̉ . 7 in afꝛuptione uel
natiuitate Ꞩ MARIÆ . 7 in die fefto om̄iū fcōⱿ.

# CHESHIRE

1    paid tax on 50 hides before 1066. 3½ hides which are outside
     the City, that is 1½ hides beyond the bridge and 2 hides in
     Newton and 'Redcliff' and in the Bishop's Borough, these paid tax
     with the City.

2     Before 1066 there were 431 houses in the City paying tax, and
     besides these the Bishop had 56 houses paying tax. This City then
     paid 10½ silver marks; two parts were the King's, the third the
     Earl's.


These were the laws there.

3    If the peace given by the King's hand, or by his writ or his
     commissioner, were broken by anyone, the King had 100s thereby.
     But if the King's peace, given by the Earl or on his orders, were
     broken, the Earl had the third penny of the 100s which were given
     for it; and if the peace given by the King's reeve or the Earl's
     officer were broken, the fine was 40s and the third penny was the
     Earl's.

4    If a free man, breaking the peace given by the King, killed a man in
     a house, his land and all his goods were the King's, and he became
     an outlaw himself. The Earl had the same (right), but only over
     his own man who paid this penalty. But no one could restore peace
     to any outlaw except through the King.

5    Whoever shed blood between Monday morning and Saturday noon
     was fined 10s; but from Saturday noon to Monday morning the
     fine for bloodshed was 20s. Similarly, whoever did so in the Twelve
     Days of Christmas, on Candlemas Day, on the first day of Easter,
     on the first day of Whitsun, on Ascension Day, on the day of the
     Assumption or of the Nativity of St. Mary, or on All Saints' Day,
     paid 20s.

¶Qui in iſtis ſcis diebȝ hominē intficieƀ. ıııı . liƀ emdaƀ.

In alijs auꞇ diebȝ. xl . ſolid . Similiꞇ Heinfarā uel

Foreſtel in his feſtis diebȝ|qui facieƀ. ıııı . liƀ exſoluebat. ^die dnico^

In alijs diebȝ. xl . ſolid.

¶Hangeuuithā facieȿ in ciuitate. x . ſoł daƀ . Ꝓpoſiꞇ auꞇ

regis uel comitis hanc forisfaꞇurā facieȿ. xx . ſolid emdaƀ.

¶Qui Reuelach faciebat. uel Latrociniū . uel uiolentiā

feminæ|inferabat. uñqdȝ hoȝ . xl . ſolid emdabatur. ^in domo^

¶Vidua ſi alicui ſe ñ legitime cōmiſceƀ. xx . ſolid emdabat.

Puella û . x . ſolid ꝓ ſimili cauſa.

¶Qui in ciuitate trā alteri ſaiſibat 7 ñ poterat diratioci

nare ſuā . ee. xl . ſoł emdaƀ. Similiꞇ 7 ille qui clamorē

inde facieƀ. ſi ſuā . ee . debere ñ poſſet diratiocinare.

★ ¶Qui trā ſuā uel ꝓpinq ſui releuare uoleƀ. x . ſolid daƀ. ^a^

◉ ¶Qui ad tminū qđ debeƀ gablū ñ reddeƀ. x . ſoł emdaƀ. ^c^

Qđ ſi ñ poterat uel nolebat . trā eȷ in manu regis ꝑpoſiꞇ ^b^

◉ ¶Si ignis ciuitatē cōbureƀ. de cuȷ domo exibat accipiebat. ^d^

emdaƀ ꝑ. ııı . oras denar. 7 ſuo ꝓpinqori uicino daƀ . ıı . ſolid.

Omiū Harū forisfaꞇurarū . ıı . partes eraȿ regis. 7 tcia comitis.

¶Si ſine Licentia regis ad portū ciuitatis naues uenireȿ

uel á portu recedereȿ. de unoꝗ̈ hōē qui nauibȝ eſſet

xl . ſoł habeƀ rex 7 comes.

Si ctra pacē regis 7 ſup eȷ ꝓhibitiōe nauis adueniret.

tā ipſā quā hōes cū omibȝ qui ibi eraȿ habeƀ rex 7 com.

¶Si û cū pace 7 licentia regis ueniſſet. qui in ea eraȿ

quiete uendeƀ quæ habeƀ . Sed cū diſcedet. ıııı . denar

de ûno ꝗ̈ Leſth habeƀ rex 7 comes. Si hūtes martrinas ^tibȝ^

pelles juberet ꝑpoſiꞇ regis ut nulli uenderent donec ſibi

pus oſtenſas cōpararet. qui hoc ñ obſeruaƀ . xl . ſoł emdaƀ. ^i^

6 Whoever killed a man on these holy days was fined £4; on other days, 40s. Similarly, whoever committed breaking and entering or highway robbery on these Holidays and on a Sunday paid out a fine of £4; on other days 40s.

7 Whoever committed collusion with a thief in the City gave up 10s; but if a reeve of the King or the Earl incurred this penalty, he paid 20s.

8 Whoever committed robbery or theft or did violence to a woman in a house was fined 40s for each of these (offences).

9 If a widow had intercourse with any one unlawfully, she was fined 20s, but a girl 10s for such an offence.

10 Whoever took possession of another's land in the City, and could not prove it to be his own, was fined 40s; likewise whoever made a claim thereto, if he could not prove that it should be his.

11 Whoever wished to enter possession of his own or his kinsman's land paid 10s. But if he could not or would not, the reeve received his land into the King's hand.

12 Whoever did not pay tribute at the due term was fined 10s.

13 If a fire burnt the City, the man from whose house it came was fined 3 ora of pence and gave 2s to his next door neighbour.

14 Two parts of all sums forfeit were the King's, the third part the Earl's.

15 If ships arrived at the City port or left port without the King's permission, the King and the Earl had 40s from each man in the ships.

16 If a ship arrived against the King's peace and despite his prohibition, the King and the Earl had both the ship itself and its crew, together with everything in it.

17 But if it came with the King's peace and permission, those in it sold what they had without interference. But when it left the King and the Earl had 4d from each cargo; if the King's reeve instructed those who had marten-skins not to sell to anyone until they were first shown to him and he had made his purchase, whoever did not observe this instruction was fined 40s.

ꝼVir fiue mulier falsā m̄furā in ciuitate facieɴ̃:́dep̄hen

fus . IIII . folid em̄dab̄ . Similit̃ malā ceruifiā facieɴ̃:́

aut in cathedra ponebat̃ ſtercoris . aut . IIII . ſoł dab̄ p̄p̄oſitis.

262 d

Hanc forisfaɔturā accipieb̄ miniſt̃ regis 7 comitis in ciuitate.

in cujcunq̃ tra fuiſſet:́ſiue ep̄i ſiue alteri hominis.

Similit̃ 7 theloneū . Siq̃s illud detineb̄ ultra tres noɔtes:́XL . ſoł

em̄dab̄.

ꝼT.R.E. erant in ciuitate hac . VII . monetarij . qui dab̄ . VII . lib̄ regi

7 comiti ext̃ firmā . q̃do moneta uertebatur.

ꝼTc̄ eraɴ̃ . XII . judices ciuitatis . 7 hi eraɴ̃ de hōibȝ regis 7 ep̄i 7 comit̃.́

Hoȝ ſiq̃s de hundret remaneb̄ die q̃ ſedeb̄ ſine excuſatione mani

feſta:́x . ſolid em̄dab̄ int̃ regē 7 comitē.

ꝼAd murū ciuitatis 7 pontē reædificand̃ . de una q̃q̃ȝ hida comitat̃

unū hōem uenire p̄p̄oſit̃ edicéb̄ . Cuj hō n̄ uenieb̄ . dn̄s ej . XL . ſoł

em̄dab̄ regi 7 comiti . H̃ forisfaɔtura . ext̃ firmā erat.

ꝼHæc Ciuitas tc̄ reddeb̄ de firma . XLV . lib̄ 7 III . timbres pelliū

martriniū . Tercia pars erat comitis . 7 ii . regis.

ꝼQdo Hugo receṕ:́non ualb̄ niſi . XXX . lib̄ . Valde en̄ erat uaſtata.

Ducentæ 7 v . dom min ibi erant . quā T.R.E. fuerant.

ꝼModo totid̃ funt ibi quod inuenit.          ꝼmarka auri.

ꝼHanc ciuitatē Mundret tenuit de comite ᵱ . LXX . lib̄ 7 una

Ipſe habuit ad firmā ᵱ . L . lib̄ 7 I . mark̃ auri . om̄a placita

comitis in comitatu 7 Hundretis . p̄ter Inglefeld.

ꝼTerra in qua . e̅ tēplū S PETRI quā Robt̃ de Rodelend

clamab̄ ad teinland:́ſic̄ diratiocinauit comitat̃ . nunq̃

ᵱtinuit ad Maneriū ext̃ ciuitatē . fed ad burgū ᵱtinet.

7 sēp̄ fuit in c̄ſutudine regis 7 comitis . ſic̃ alioȝ burgenſiū.

IN CE̠STRE SCIRE teñ ep̄s ejd̄e ciuitatis de rege . qd̃ ad

ſuum ᵱtinet epiſcopatum.          ꝗ cū ſuis hominibus.

Totā reliquā trā comitatus:́tenet Hugo comes de rege

TERRĀ INTER RIPE 7 MERSHĀ . tenuit Rogerius piɔtau.́

Modo tenet Rex.          262 c, d

18    Any man or woman who gave false measure in the City was
fined 4s when caught; similarly anyone who made bad beer was
either put in the dung-stool or paid 4s to the reeves. The officer    262 d
of the King or the Earl received this fine in the City, on whoever's
land it was, whether the Bishop's or any other man's. Similarly
with the toll; if anyone withheld it for more than three nights,
he was fined 40s.

19    Before 1066 there were 7 moneyers in the City, who paid £7 to
the King and the Earl, additional to the revenue, when the coinage
was changed.

20    There were then 12 judges in the City; they were from the King's,
the Bishop's and the Earl's men. If any of them stayed away from
the Hundred on a day when it sat without plain excuse, he was
fined 10s, (shared) between the King and the Earl.

21    For the repair of the city wall and the bridge, the reeve used to
call out one man to come from each hide in the County. The lord
of any man who did not come paid a fine of 40s to the King and
the Earl. The fine was additional to the revenue.

22    This City then paid in revenue £45 and 3 timbers of marten-
skins.    The third part was the Earl's and two parts the King's.

23    When Earl Hugh acquired it, its value was only £30, for it was
thoroughly devastated; there were 205 houses less than before
1066. Now there are as many as he found there.

24    Mundret held this City from the Earl for £70 and 1 gold mark.
He also had all the Earl's pleas in the County and the Hundreds,
except Englefield, at a revenue of £50 and 1 gold mark.

25    The land on which St. Peter's Temple stands, which Robert of
Rhuddlan claimed as thaneland, never belonged to a manor outside
the City, as the County proved, but belonged to the Borough, and
was always in the King's and the Earl's customary dues, like (the
lands) of the other burgesses.


In CHESHIRE the Bishop holds from the King what belongs to his
Bishopric. Earl Hugh, with his men, holds all the rest of the County
from the King. Roger of Poitou held the land between RIBBLE and
MERSEY. Now the King holds it.

In all counties, Domesday Book arranges its entries under the chief
landholders, each with a seperate chapter. As a general rule, the chapters
are numbered, normally with a heading, and a list of landholders giving
chapter numbers and headings is placed immediately before the first
chapter, normally the land of the King.

   Cheshire is arranged in the same way as other counties. But since
all land, except the Bishop's and the Abbey's, was held from the King by
Earl Hugh, the chapter numbers and headings and the list of landholders
were omitted. In the translation, they are here reconstructed from the
text. The names of each chief landholder, who held from Earl Hugh, is
printed in bold capitals at the beginning of his chapter, with its number;
the List of Landholders is given opposite.

EPS DE CESTRE hī in ipſa ciuitate has c̄ſuetūdines.
Siꝗs liber hō facit opᵃ in die feriato . inde eꝑs hē
VIII . ſolid . De ſeruo autē uel ancilla feriatū diē infrin
gente: hē eꝑs . IIII . ſolid.

Mercator ſuꝑueniens in ciuitatē 7 truſſellū deferens.
ſi abſꝗ licentia miniſtri eꝑi diſſoluerit eū á nona hora ſabbi
uſꝗ ad diē lunis: aut in alio feſto die: inde hē eꝑs . IIII . ſolid
de forisfaɔtura . Si hō eꝑi inuenenerit aliquē hominē
carricantē infra leuuā ciuitatis: inde hē eꝑs de foris
faɔtura . IIII . ſolid aut . II . boues.  IN DVDESTAN HVND.
Iꝑſe eꝑs ten FERENTONE . 7 tenuit T.R.E. Ibi . IIII . hidæ geld.
Tra . ē . v . car . In dn̄io ſunt . II . 7 VII . uilli cū . I . car.
Silua . ibi . I . leuua lḡ . 7 dimid lat.
De hac tra ten . II . pbri . I . hidā 7 dimid . de eꝑo . Ibi . I . car
In dn̄io . 7 II . franciḡ 7 II . uilli 7 un bord cū . I . car 7 dimid.
7 IIII . ſeruis . Prbr uillæ hē dimid car . 7 v . bord cū . I . car.
Toē T.R.E. ualb . XL . ſolid . Modo . LX . ſolid . Waſt fuit.

## LAND OF EARL HUGH AND HIS MEN

| | | | |
|---|---|---|---|
| 1 | Earl Hugh himself | 17 | Gilbert of Venables |
| 2 | Robert son of Hugh | 18 | Gilbert Hunter |
| 3 | Robert of Rhuddlan | 19 | Jocelyn |
| 4 | Robert Cook | 20 | Ranulf (Mainwaring) |
| 5 | Richard of Vernon | 21 | Ralph Hunter |
| 6 | Richard Butler | 22 | Reginald (Balliol) |
| 7 | Walter of Vernon | 23 | Ilbert |
| 8 | William Malbank | 24 | Osbern son of Tezzo |
| 9 | William son of Nigel | 25 | Nigel |
| 10 | Hugh of Delamere | 26 | The Earl's Men |
| 11 | Hugh son of Norman | 27 | Shared Lands |
| 12 | Hugh son of Osbern | S | The Saltworks |
| 13 | Hamo (of Mascy) | 1 | Nantwich |
| 14 | Bigot (of Loges) | 2 | Middlewich |
| 15 | Baldric | 3 | Northwich |
| 16 | Hugh son of Osbern | | |

**B**  **The Bishop of Chester** has these customary dues within the City.   263 a

1  If a free man works on a Holiday, the Bishop has 8s therefrom; from a male or female slave, however, who breaks a Holiday, the Bishop has 4s.

2  If a merchant reaches the City, bringing a bale of goods, and opens it between Saturday noon and Monday, or on any other Holiday, without permission from the Bishop's officer, the Bishop has 4s fine therefrom; if one of the Bishop's men finds any man loading within the City territory (on a Holiday) the Bishop has therefrom a fine of 4s or 2 oxen.

In BROXTON Hundred

3  The Bishop holds FARNDON himself and held it before 1066. 4 hides paying tax. Land for 5 ploughs. In lordship 2;
  7 villagers with 1 plough.
  Woodland 1 league long and ½ wide.
    2 priests hold 1½ hides of this land from the Bishop. 1 plough in lordship;
    2 Frenchmen, 2 villagers and 1 smallholder with 1½ ploughs and 4 slaves.
  The village priest has ½ plough, and 5 smallholders with 1 plough.
Total value before 1066, 40s; now 60s; it was waste.

Iſd epſ tenuit *TERVE*.7 tenet. IN *RISETONE HVND*.

Ibi. VI. hidæ gelđ. Tra. é. XXII. cař. In dñio ſunt. III. cař

7 VI. bouař. 7 III. radmans 7 VII. uitti 7 VII. borđ cũ. VI. cař.

Silua. I. leuua in lḡ. 7 dimiđ in lat̄.

De hac tra huj ᄊ ten Witts. II. hiđ de epo. 7 ibi ht̄ dimiđ

cař. 7 IIII. uitt 7 III. borđ cũ. III. cař 7 dimiđ.

Tot̄ T.R.E. ualb̄. VIII. lib̄. Modo. IIII. lib̄ 7 x. ſot. Waſtař fuit.

Ipſe epſ tenuit 7 ten *SVDTONE*. IN *WILAVESTON HĐ*.

Ibi. I. hida gelđ. Tra. é. III. cař. In dñio. é una. 7 v. uitti

7 II. borđ cũ. I. cař. Ibi. VI. ač pti.

T.R.E. ualb̄. XL. ſoliđ. Modo. xx. ſoliđ. IN *EXESTAN HVND*.

Sc̄s CEDDE tenuit *EITVNE* T.R.E. Ibi. I. hida.

★ R In *EITVNE* ht̄ iſd Sc̄s uñ uittm 7 dimiđ piſcariã. 7 dimiđ

acrã pti. 7 II. ač̄s filuæ. Valuit. v. ſoliđ.

Rex. E. deđ regi Grifino totā trā quæ jacebat trans aquā

quæ DE uocatur. Sed poſtq ipſe Grifin foriſfecit ei.

abſtulit ab eo hanc trā. 7 reddiđ epo de Ceſtre 7 om̄ib₂

ſuis hōib₂ qui antea ipſā tenebant. IN *WARMVNDESTROV HĐ*.

Ipſe epſ ten *WIMEBERIE* 7 tenuit T.R.E. 7 m̄ ten Witts de eo.

Ibi dimiđ hida gelđ. Tra. é. II. cař. Ibi. I. pb̄r 7 II. uitti 7 II. borđ

cũ. I. cař. Ibi Silua dimiđ leuua lḡ. 7 tntđ lat̄. 7 ibi. II. haiæ.

T.R.E. ualb̄. LX.IIII. den. modo. IIII. ſot. Waſt fuit. IN *RISETON*

Ipſe epſ ten *BVRTONE*. 7 tenuit T.R.E. Ibi. III. hidæ gelđ. *HVND*.

Tra. é. VII. cař. In dñio ſunt. II. cař. 7 VII. uitti 7 IIII. borđ. 7 pb̄r

7 uñ radman cũ. III. cař. Ibi. I. ač pti.

T.R.E. ualb̄. XL. ſot. Modo tntđ. Qdo recep̄. xv. ſoliđ.

Ipſe epſ tenuit 7 ten in *REDECLIVE*. duas partes uni hidæ gelđ.

T.R.E. ualb̄. XIII. ſot. Modo uat. II. denař plus. Ad æcctam S Johis ptinet.

263 a

In EDDISBURY (South) Hundred

4  The Bishop also held and holds TARVIN . 6 hides paying tax.
Land for 22 ploughs. In lordship 3 ploughs; 6 ploughmen;
3 riders, 7 villagers and 7 smallholders with 6 ploughs.
Woodland 1 league in length and ½ in width.
William holds 2 hides of this manor's land from the Bishop.
He has ½ plough;
4 villagers and 3 smallholders with 3½ ploughs.
Total value before 1066 £8; now £4 10s; it was laid waste.

In WIRRAL Hundred

5  The Bishop held and holds (Guilden) SUTTON himself. 1 hide
paying tax. Land for 3 ploughs. In lordship 1;
5 villagers and 2 smallholders with 1 plough.
Meadow, 6 acres.
Value before 1066, 40s; now 20s.

In MAELOR CYMRAEG Hundred

6  St Chad's held EYTON before 1066. 1 hide.
R  In Eyton St Chad's also has
1 villager.
½ fishery; meadow, ½ acre; woodland, 2 acres.
The value was 5s.

7  King Edward gave to King Gruffydd all the land that lies beyond
the river called Dee. But when King Gruffydd wronged him, he
took this land from him and gave it back to the Bishop of Chester
and to all his men, who had formerly held it.

In NANTWICH Hundred

8  The Bishop holds WYBUNBURY himself and held it before 1066.
William now holds from him. ½ hide paying tax. Land for 2 ploughs.
1 priest, 2 villagers and 2 smallholders with 1 plough.
Woodland, ½ league long and as wide; 2 enclosures.
Value before 1066, 64d; now 4s; it was waste.

In EDDISBURY (South) Hundred

9  The Bishop holds BURTON himself, and held it before 1066. 3 hides
paying tax. Land for 7 ploughs. In lordship 2 ploughs;
7 villagers, 4 smallholders, a priest and 1 rider with 3 ploughs.
Meadow, 1 acre.
Value before 1066, 40s; now as much; when acquired 15s.

10  The Bishop held and holds two parts of 1 hide paying tax in
'REDCLIFF' himself.
Value before 1066, 13s; now 2d more.
It belongs to St. John's Church.

In Monasterio S̄ MARIÆ quæ.ē juxta æcclam S̄ Jok̄is jacent
duæ bouatæ terræ.quæ uuastæ eraɴ 7 modo sunt uuastæ.
Eccła S̄ Jok̄is in ciuitate hт̄.VIII.dom q̄etas ab om̄i c̄suetud̄.
vna ex his.ē matricularij æcclæ. alie sunt canonico꜡.

In ꝏ Robti.F.Hugon caluniat eps de cestre. II.hid̄.q̄ de ep̄atu eraɴ
Tpr Cnut regis.7    comitat ei testificat.q̄a sc̄s Cedda injuste p̄dit

263 b

IN CIVITATE CESTRE hт̄ æccła S̄ WAREBVRG.XIII.domos
    q̄etas ab om̄i c̄suetudine.Vna.ē custodis æcclæ.aliæ|canonico꜡.

Ipsa æccła ten̄ SALTONE.7 tenuit T.R.E. IN DVDESTAN HD̄.
Ibi.II.hidæ geld̄.Tra.ē.VIII.car̄.In dn̄io.ē una car̄.7 un
seruus.7 IX.uilti cū.v.car̄.        Valuit 7 ual.XL.solid̄.

Ipsa æccła ten̄ CAVELEA.7 tenuit T.R.E Ibi.III.hidæ
geld̄.Tra.ē.v.car̄.In dn̄io sunt.II.7 III'.serui.7 III.uilti
7 un bord cū.II'.car̄. Ibi nauicula 7 rete.
T.R.E.ualb̄.xxx.solid̄.Modo.xx.solid̄.

Ipsa æccła ten̄ HVNDITONE.7 tenuit T.R.E.Ibi.III.hidæ
geld̄.Tra.ē.VI.car̄.In dn̄io sunt.II.7 IIII.serui.7 II.uilti
7 II.bord cū.I.car̄.Ibi.I.ac̄ p̄ti.7 nauicula 7 rete.
T.R.E.fuit wast.Modo ual.XVI.solid̄.

Ipsa æccła ten̄ BOCSTONE 7 tenuit T.R.E.Ibi.III.hidæ
geld̄.Tra.ē.v.car̄.In dn̄io sunt.II.7 IIII.serui.7 v.uilti
7 IIII.bord cū.III.car̄.
T.R.E.ualb̄.xx.solid̄.modo.XVI.sol. IN RISETON HD̄.

Ipsa æccła ten̄ ETINGEHALLE.7 tenuit T.R.E.Ibi.I.hida
geld̄.Tra.ē.I.car̄.In dn̄io.ē dimid̄ car̄.7 I.seruus.
Ibi Silua dimid̄ leuua lḡ.7 una ac̄ lat̄.
T.R.E.ualb̄.VIII.sol.Modo.v.solid̄. IN WILAVESTON HD̄.

Ipsa æccła ten̄ WIVEVRENE.7 tenuit T.R.E.Ibi.I.hida
7 II.partes.I.hidæ        Tra.ē.III.car̄.
Ibi.IIII.uilti 7 II.bord hn̄t.I.car̄ 7 dimid̄.Ibi dimid̄ ac̄ p̄ti.
T.R.E.ualb̄.xxx.solid̄.Modo.xx.solid̄.

263 a, b

11   In (the lands of) St.Mary's Monastery by St.John's Church lie 2
     bovates of land which were and now are waste.
12   St. John's Church has 8 houses in the city exempt from all
     customary dues; one of these is the Church Registrar's; the others
     are the Canon's.

[In BROXTON Hundred]
13   In BETTISFIELD, a manor of Robert son of Hugh, the Bishop of Chester
     claims 2 hides which were the Bishopric's in King Canute's time;
     the County testifies that St. Chad's lost them wrongfully.

A    St Werburgh's Church                                           263 b
1    has 13 houses in the City of Chester, exempt from all customary dues;
     one is the Church Warden's; the others are the Canon's.

The Church itself holds and held before 1066.

     in BROXTON Hundred
2    SAIGHTON. 2 hides paying tax. Land for 8 ploughs. In lordship 1
     plough; 1 slave;
         9 villagers with 5 ploughs.
     The value was and is 40s.
3    CHEAVELEY. 3 hides paying tax. Land for 5 ploughs.
     In lordship 2; 3 slaves;
         3 villagers and 1 smallholder with 2 ploughs.
         A small boat and a net.
     Value before 1066, 30s; now 20s.
4    HUNTINGTON. 3 hides paying tax. Land for 6 ploughs.
     In lordship 2; 4 slaves;
         2 villagers and 2 smallbolders with 1 plough.
         Meadow, 1 acre; a small boat and a net.
     Before 1066 it was waste; value now 16s.
5    BOUGHTON. 3 hides paying tax. Land for 5 ploughs.
     In lordship 2; 4 slaves;
         5 villagers and 4 smallholders with 3 ploughs.
     Value before 1066, 20s; now 16s.

     in EDDISBURY (South) Hundred
6    IDDINSHALL. 1 hide paying tax. Land for 1 plough.
     In lordship ½ plough; 1 slave.
         Woodland ½ league long and 1 acre wide.
     Value before 1066, 8s; now 5s.

     in WIRRAL Hundred
7    WERVIN. 1 hide and 2 parts of 1 hide. Land for 3 ploughs.
         4 villagers and 2 smallholders have 1½ ploughs.
         Meadow, ½ acre.
     Value before 1066, 30s; now 20s.

Ipſa æccła teñ CROSTONE.7 tenuit T.R.E.Ibi.1.hida
gelđ.Tra.e̅.1.caɼ.Ibi.1.radman 7 11.uitti 7 1.borđ.
hn̅t.1.caɼ.Ibi.1.ač p̃ti.  Valuit 7 uał.x.ſoliđ.

Ipſa æccła tenuit 7 teñ WISDELEA.Ibi.1.hida gelđ.Tra.e̅.111.
caɼ.In dn̅io.e̅ una.7 11.ſerui.7 11.uitti 7 11.borđ cu̅.1.caɼ.7 1.ač p̃ti.
T.R.E.ualɓ.x.ſoł.modo tn̅tđ.

Ipſa æccła teñ SVDTONE.7 tenuit T.R.E.Ibi.1.hida gelđ.
Tra.e̅.v.caɼ.In dn̅io.e̅ dimiđ caɼ.7 v.uitti 7 1x.borđ cu̅.11.
caɼ.T.R.E.ualɓ.xL.ſoliđ.Modo.xxx.ſoliđ.

Ipſa æccła tenuit 7 teñ SALHARE.Ibi.1.hida gelđ.Tra.e̅.1.
caɼ.Ibi.e̅ in dn̅io.7 11.ſerui.7 1.uitt 7 1.borđ.
T.R.E.ualɓ.xv1.ſoł.Modo tn̅tđ

Ipſa æccła tenuit 7 teñ SOTOWICHE.Ibi.1.hida gelđ.Tra
eſt.111.caɼ.Ibi.1111.uitti 7 11.borđ cu̅.1.caɼ.7 una ač p̃ti.
T.R.E.ualɓ.xv1.ſoliđ.Modo.x111.ſoliđ 7 111.den̅.

Ipſa æccła tenuit 7 teñ NESTONE.7 Witts de ea.
Ibi t̅cia pars duaɼ hiđ gelđ.Tra.e̅.1.caɼ.
Rediđ 7 redđ de firma.xv11.ſoliđ.7 1111.denaɼ.

Ipſa æccła tenuit 7 teñ RABIE.7 Witts de ea.Ibi dimiđ
hida gelđ.Tra.e̅.1.caɼ.
Reddiđ 7 redđ de firma.v1.ſoliđ 7 v111.denaɼ.

Ipſa æccła tenuit 7 teñ TROSFORD.Ibi.1. IN ROELAV HĐ.
hida gel.Tra.e̅.       In dn̅io.e̅.1.caɼ.7 1111.ſerui.7 1.an
cilla.7 1.borđ.7 1.ač p̃ti.7 un̅ h̅o redđ.xx.denaɼ.
T.R.E.ualɓ.v.ſoł.Modo.v111.ſoliđ.

Ipſa æccła tenuit 7 teñ INISE.Ibi.111.hidæ glđ.Tra.e̅.v.
caɼ.In dn̅io.e̅.1.caɼ.7 11.ſerui.7 v111.uitti 7 1.borđ cu̅.1.caɼ.
T.R.E.ualɓ xxx.ſoł.Modo.xv.ſoł.Ibi.11.ač p̃ti.

8   CROUGHTON. 1 hide paying tax. Land for 1 plough.
    1 rider, 2 villagers and 1 smallholder have 1 plough.
    Meadow, 1 acre.
The value was and is 10s.

9   The Church held and holds LEA itself. 1 hide paying tax.
Land for 3 ploughs. In lordship 1; 2 slaves;
    2 villagers and 2 smallholders with 1 plough.
    Meadow, 1 acre.
Value before 1066, 10s; now as much.

10   The Church holds SUTTON itself and held it before 1066.
1 hide paying tax. Land for 5 ploughs. In lordship ½ plough;
    5 villagers and 9 smallholders with 2 ploughs.
Value before 1066, 40s; now 30s.

The Church itself held and holds

11   SAUGHALL. 1 hide paying tax. Land for 1 plough. It is there, in
lordship; 2 slaves;
    1 villager and 1 smallholder.
Value before 1066, 16s; now as much.
12   SHOTWICK. 1 hide paying tax. Land for 3 ploughs.
    4 villagers and 2 smallholders with 1 plough.
    Meadow, 1 acre.
Value before 1066, 16s; now 13s 3d.
13   (Great) NESTON. William holds from the (Church).
A third part of 2 hides paying tax. Land for 1 plough.
It pays and paid 17s 4d in revenue.
14   RABY. William holds from the (Church). ½ hide paying tax.
Land for 1 plough.
It pays and paid   6s 8d in revenue.

   in EDDISBURY (North) Hundred
15   TRAFFORD. 1 hide paying tax. Land for ...... In lordship 1 plough;
  4 male slaves and 1 female;
    1 smallholder.
    Meadow, 1 acre.
    1 man who pays 20d.
Value before 1066, 5s; now 8s.
16   INCE. 3 hides paying tax. Land for 5 ploughs. In lordship 1 plough;
2 slaves;
    8 villagers and 1 smallholder with 1 plough.
Value before 1066, 30s; now 15s.
    Meadow, 2 acres.

Ipſa æccła tenuit 7 teñ *MIDESTVNE*. *IN TVNENDVNE HVND*. Ipſa æccła tenuit 7 teñ

7 Wiłłs de ea.Ibi.ı.hida gełd.Tra.ē.ııı.car.In dñio.ē dimid car. CLISTVNE 7 Wiłłs de ea.

7 ı.bouar.7.ııı.uiłł cū dimid car.7 ı.bord.Ibi.ıı.ãc ſiluæ. Ibi.ı.hida gełd.Tra.ē.ıı.car.In dñio.ē una.7 ıı.bou 7 un radman 7 ı.bord cū.ı.

T.R.E.reddeb xvı.ſoł.Modo uał.x.ſoł. *IN EXESTAN HD*. Vał.x.ſoł.Waſf ſuiţ

Ipſa æccła tenuit 7 teñ *ODESLEI*.Ibi dimid hida gełd.Tra.ē.ı.car.

Ibi.ē un uiłłs redd.vııı.denar.Vał.ııı.ſolid.Waſf ſuit.

263 c

Ipſa æccła teñ *PVLFORD* 7 tenuit T.R.E. *IN DVDESTAN HD*.

Ibi dimid hida gełd.Tra.ē.ı.car.Ibi.ē cū.ı.uiłło 7 ı.bord.

Vałb.ıııı.ſolid.modo.v.ſolid. *IN ATISCROS HD*.

Ipſa æccła tenuit 7 teñ *WEPRE*.Ibi.ıı.partes.uni hidæ gełd.

Tra.ē.ı.car.Ibi.ē cū.ıı.uiłłis 7 ıı.bord.Wiłłs teñ de æccła.

Ibi.ē Silua.ı.leuu łḡ.7 dimid leuu lata.

Ipſa æccła tenuit *LECHE*.Ibi.ı.virg gełd.Tra.ē dimid car.

Waſta fuit 7 eſt.

### *IN ROELAV HD*.

Hvgo Comes tenet in dñio *WIVREHAM*.Comes

Eduin tenuit.Ibi.xııı.hidæ gełd.Tra.ē xvııı.

car.In dñio ſunt.ıı.7 ıı.bouarij 7 ıı.ſerui.7 x.uiłłi

7 un bord.7 ı.radman cū.ı.uiłło.Int oms hñt.ııı.car.

Ibi eccła 7 pbr.7 moliñ ſeruieṣ aulæ.7 una ãc pti.

Silua.ıı.leuu łḡ.7 una leuua łaf.7 ibi.ıı.haiæ capreołoʒ.

Huic ꝏ ptiñ.x.burgſes in ciuitate.Ex his.vı.reddt

x.ſolid 7 vııı.den.7 ıııı.nil reddt.Franciḡ teñ de comite.

in BUCKLOW (West) Hundred

17 MIDDLE ASTON. William holds from the (Church). 1 hide paying tax.
Land for 3 ploughs. In lordship ½ plough; 1 ploughman;
3 villagers with ½ plough and 1 smallholder.
Woodland, 2 acres.
Before 1066 it paid 16s; value now 10s.

18 CLIFTON. William holds from the (Church). 1 hide paying tax.
Land for 2 ploughs. In lordship 1; 2 ploughmen;
1 rider and 1 smallholder with 1 [plough].
Value 10s; it was waste.

In MAELOR CYMRAEG Hundred

19 HOSELEY. ½ hide paying tax. Land for 1 plough.
1 villager who pays 8d.
Value 3s; it was waste.

In BROXTON Hundred                                        263 c

20 The Church holds PULFORD itself and held it before 1066.
½ hide paying tax. Land for 1 plough. It is there, with
1 villager and 1 smallholder.
The value was 4s; now 5s.

In ATI'S CROSS Hundred

21 The Church held and holds WEPRE itself. Two parts of 1 hide
paying tax. Land for 1 plough. It is there, with
2 villagers and 2 smallholders.
William holds from the Church
Woodland 1 league long and ½ league wide.
[Value....]

22 The Church held LACHE itself. 1 virgate paying tax.
Land for ½ plough. It was and is waste.

1                    **EARL HUGH holds**

in EDDISBURY (North) Hundred

1 WEAVERHAM in lordship. Earl Edwin held it. 13 hides paying tax.
Land for 18 ploughs. In lordship 2; 2 ploughmen; 2 slaves.
10 villagers, 1 smallholder; 1 rider with 1 villager;
between them they have 3 ploughs.
A church and a priest; a mill which serves the hall; meadow, 1
acre; woodland 2 leagues long and 1 league wide; 2 deer
enclosures.
10 burgesses in the City belong to this manor; 6 of them pay
10s 8d and 4 pay nothing. A Frenchman holds from the Earl.

In Wich fuer̄.vii.falinæ huic � ptinent̄.Vna ex his
m̊ redd̄ fal aulæ.aliæ funt waftæ.

De alio Hund̄.i.uirḡ træ Entrebus dicta huic � ptiñ.7 wafta.ē.

De hac tra huj � ten Gozelin.iiii.hid̄ de com̄.7 ibi h̄t
.i.car̄.7 iii.feruos.7 v.uilt 7 i.radman cū.ii.car̄.7 dimid̄
pifcar̄./De hac tra.iii.hid̄ mifit com in forefta.

Tot̄ � T.R.E.erat ad firmā ꝑ.x.lib̄.Com̄ waft̄ inuen̄.
Modo dñium ej.'ᴸ.folid̄.Gozelini.'x.folid̄.

Ipfe com̄ ten Kenardeslie.Vᴵfac.i.lib̄ hō tenuit.Ibi.i.
hida.Tra,ē.ii.car̄.Tota.ē in forefta.Silua.i.leuua lḡ.7 dim
leuua lat̄.T.R.E.ualb̄.vi.folid̄.Waft̄ fuit.

Ipfe com̄ ten Donehā.Eſſul tenuit in paragio ut lib̄ hō.
Ibi.iii.hidæ geld̄.Tra.ē.ix.car̄.In dñio.ē dim car̄.7 vii.
uilt 7 fab 7.iii.bord̄ cū.i.car̄ 7 dimid̄.Ibi.ii.ac̄ p̄ti.
Silua dimid̄ leuua lḡ.7 iiii.parte lat̄.

T.R.E.ualb̄.xʟ.folid̄.modo xvi.folid̄.Waft̄ fuit.

Ipfe com̄ ten Eltone.Tochi 7 Grim tenuer̄ ut libi hōes.
Ibi.ii.hidæ geld̄.Tra.ē.vii.car̄.In dñio.ē una.7 ii.bouar̄.
7 vi.uilti 7 un bord̄ cū.i.car̄.

T.R.E.ualb̄.xxxviii.fot.Modo.vi.fot.Waft̄ fuit.

Ipfe com̄ ten Troford.Leuric 7 Gotlac ꝑ.ii.� tenuer̄
ut libi hōes.Ibi.i.hida geld̄.Tra.ē.i.car̄.Ibi.c̄ cū.i.rad
man 7 ii.bord̄.

T.R.E.ualb̄.x.fot.Modo.ii.folid̄.Waft̄ inuen̄.

Ipfe com̄ ten Menlie.Tochi tenuit.ut lib̄ hō.Ibi dimid̄
hida gld̄.Tra.ē.i.car̄.Redd̄ de firma.mark argenti.

T.R.E.ualb̄.x.folid̄.

Ipfe com̄ ten Helesbe.Ernui tenuit ut lib̄ hō.Ibi.i.hida
gld̄.Tra.ē.iii.car̄.Ibi.iii.uilti cū.i.bord̄ hn̄t.i.car̄.
Ibi.i.ac̄ p̄ti.7 Silua dimid̄ leuua lḡ.7 tntd̄ lat̄.

T.R.E.ualb̄.xii.folid̄.modo.x.folid̄.

In *Wich* there were 7 salthouses which belonged to this manor; one of them now pays salt to the hall; the others are disused.

In another Hundred 1 virgate of land, called Antrobus, belongs to this manor; it is waste.

Jocelyn holds 4 hides of this manor's land from the Earl. He has 1 plough, 3 slaves;
    5 villagers and 1 rider with 2 ploughs.
    ½ fishery.
The Earl has put 3 hides of this land in the Forest.
Before 1066 the revenue from the whole was £10; the Earl found it waste; now, his lordship 50s, Jocelyn's 10s.

The Earl himself holds

2 'CONERSLEY'. Wulfheah, a free man, held it. 1 hide paying tax.
    Land for 2 ploughs. It is all in the Forest.
        Woodland 1 league long and ½ league wide.
    Value before 1066, 6s; it was waste.

3 DUNHAM. Aescwulf held it, jointly, as a free man. 3 hides paying tax. Land for 9 ploughs. In lordship ½ plough;
        7 villagers, a smith and 3 smallholders with 1½ ploughs.
        Meadow, 2 acres; woodland ½ league long and ¼ league wide.
    Value before 1066, 40s; now 16s; it was waste.

4 ELTON. Toki and Grim held it as 2 manors as free men. 2 hides paying tax. Land for 7 ploughs. In lordship 1; 2 ploughmen.
        6 villagers and 1 smallholder with 1 plough.
    Value before 1066, 38s; now 6s; it was waste.

5 TRAFFORD. Leofric and Guthlac held it as 2 manors as free men.
    1 hide paying tax. Land for 1 plough. It is there, with
        1 rider and 2 smallholders.
    Value before 1066, 10s; now 2s; found waste.

6 MANLEY. Toki held it as a free man. ½ hide paying tax.
    Land for 1 plough. It pays 1 silver mark in revenue.
    Value before 1066, 10s.

7 HELSBY. Ernwy Foot held it as a free man. 1 hide paying tax.
    Land for 3 ploughs.
        3 villagers with 1 smallholder have 1 plough.
        Meadow, 1 acre; woodland ½ league long and as wide.
    Value before 1066, 12s; now 10s.

Ipſe com̃ ten̄ *FROTESHAM*. Eduin tenuit. Ibi. iii . hidæ gld̄.

Tra. ē. ix . car̄. In dn̄io ſunt. ii.7 un̄ ſeru.7 viii.uilti 7 iii.bord

*In Bvchlavhd.* Ipſe com̃ ten̄ *ALRETVNE*. Godric tenuit.Ibi.i.virg̃ træ geld̄.⌠cũ.ii.car̄.

Tra. ē dimid̄ car̄. Waſta fuit 7 eſt.

263 d

Ibi pb̃r 7 æccła hn̄t.i.virg̃ træ.7 molin̄ ibi hiemale.7 ii.piſ

cariæ 7 dimid̄.7 iii.ac̃ pti.7 Silua.i.leuua lḡ.7 dimid̄ leuua

lat̄.7 ibi.ii.haiæ.7 in Wich dimid̄ ſalina.ſeruie,ſ aulæ.

Terci denari de placitis iſti hund̄.ptineb̃ T.R.E.huic M̃.

Tc̄ ualb̄.viii.lib̄;modo.iiii.lib̄.Waſt fuit.

Ipſe com̃ ten̄ *ALDREDELIE*.Carle tenuit.

Ibi.iii.hidæ geld̄.Tra.ē.vi.car̄.Waſta fuit 7 ē m̃ in foreſta com̃

T.R.E.ualb̄.xxx.ſolid̄.

Ipſe com̃ ten̄ *DONE*.Vuiet tenuit ut lib̄ hō.Ibi.ii.hidæ geld̄.

Tra.ē.ii.car̄.Waſta fuit.7 eſt m̃ in foreſta comitis.

T.R.E.ualb̄.x.ſolid̄.

Ipſe com̃ *EDESBERIE*.Gōduin tenuit ut lib̄ hō.Ibi.ii.hidæ

geld̄.Tra.ē.vi.car̄.Waſta fuit 7 eſt.

H̄ tra.i.leuua lḡ.ē.7 tn̄td lat̄       *IN DVDESTAN HVND.*

Ipſe com̃ ten̄ *ETONE*.Eduin tenuit.Ibi.i.hida 7 dim geld̄.Tra

ē.ii.car̄.In dn̄io.ē una 7 ii;bouar.7 ii;uilti cũ.i.car̄.Ibi piſca

ria redd̄ mille ſalmones.7 vi;piſcatores.7 una ac̃ pti.

T.R.E.ualb̄.x.lib̄.7 poſt.viii.lib̄.modo;x.lib̄.

Ipſe com̃ ten̄ *LAI*.Goduin lib̄ hō tenuit.Ibi.i.hida 7 dimid̄

geld̄.Tra.ē.iiii.car̄.In dn̄io.ē una.7 ii.bouar.7 viii.uilti cũ

una car̄.Ibi.i.ac̃ filuæ.

T.R.E.ualb̄.xxx.ſolid̄.7 poſt.v.ſol.Modo.x.ſolid̄.

Ipſe com̃ ten̄ *COTINTONE*.Ernui 7 Anſgot 7 Dot tenuer̄ p.iii.

M̃.Ibi.ii.hidæ geld̄.Tra.ē.iiii.car̄.In dn̄io.ē una.7 ii.bouar.

7 v.uilti 7 un̄ bord.7 un̄ radman 7 i.francig cũ.ii.car̄

Ibi molin̄ 7 xii;ac̃ pti;

T.R.E.ualb̄.ix.ſolid̄ 7 vi.den;modo.xii;ſol.Waſt inuen̄.

8   FRODSHAM. Earl Edwin held it. 3 hides paying tax.
Land for 9 ploughs. In lordship 2; 1 slave;
  8 villagers and 3 smallholders with 2 ploughs.
  A priest and a church have 1 virgate of land.      263 d
  A winter mill; 2½ fisheries; meadow, 3 acres; woodland
    1 league long and ½ league wide; 2 enclosures; ½ salthouse
    in *Wich* that serves the hall.
The Third Penny from the pleas of this Hundred belonged to
this manor before 1066.
Value then £8; now £4; it was waste.

in BUCKLOW (East) Hundred                   263 c
9   OLLERTON. Godric held it. 1 virgate of land paying tax.
Land for ½ plough. It was and is waste.

[in EDDISBURY (North) Hundred]            263 d
10  *ALDREDELIE.* Karl held it. 3 hides paying tax. Land for 6 ploughs.
It was waste and is now in the Earl's forest.
Value before 1066, 30s.
11  *DONE.* Wulfgeat held it as a free man. 2 hides paying tax.   held it.
Land for 2 ploughs. It was waste and is now in the Earl's forest.
Value before 1066, 10s.
12  EDDISBURY. Godwin held it as a free man. 2 hides paying tax.
Land for 6 ploughs. It was and is waste.
This land is 1 league long and as wide.

in BROXTON Hundred
13  EATON. Earl Edwin held it. 1½ hides paying tax.
Land for 2 ploughs. In lordship 1; 2 ploughmen;
  2 villagers with 1 plough.
  A fishery paying 1000 salmon; 6 fishermen; meadow 1 acre.
Value before 1066 £10; later £8; now £10.
14  LEA. Godwin, a free man, held it. 1½ hides paying tax.
Land for 4 ploughs. In lordship 1; 2 ploughmen;
  8 villagers with 1 plough.
  Woodland, 1 acre.
Value before 1066, 30s; later 5s; now 10s.
15  CODDINGTON. Ernwy, Ansgot and Dot held it as 3 manors.
2 hides paying tax. Land for 4 ploughs. In lordship 1; 2 ploughmen;
  5 villagers, 1 smallholder, 1 rider and 1 Frenchman
    with 2 ploughs.
  A mill; meadow, 12 acres.
Value before 1066, 9s 6d; now 12s; found waste.

Ipſe com̄ ten̄ _LAI_. Stein tenuit ut lib̄ hō.
Ibi dimid̄ hida geld̄. Tra . ē . I . car̄ . Waſta . ē.

Ipſe com̄ ten̄ _RVSITONE_ . Chepin tenuit ut lib̄ hō . Ibi dim̄ hida
geld̄ . Tra . ē . II . car̄ . Waſta . ē.

Ipſe com̄ ten̄ _OPETONE_ . Erni lib̄ hō tenuit . Ibi . I . hida geld̄ .
Tra . ē . II . car̄ . Waſta . ē . Silua ibi . I . leuua lḡ . 7 II . ac̄s lat̄.

Ipſe com̄ ten̄ _BODEVRDE_ . Dedol lib̄ hō tenuit . Ibi dimid̄
hida geld̄ . Tra . ē . II . car̄ . Waſta . ē . Silua . I . leuua lḡ . 7 dim̄ lat̄.

Ipſe com̄ ten̄ _ALRETONE_ . Stein tenuit . lib̄·hō fuit . Ibi . I . hida
geld̄ . Tra . ē . II . car̄ . Waſta . ē.

Ipſe com̄ ten̄ _OVRE_ . Quattuor lib̄i hōes tenuer̄ p . IIII . m̄.
Ibi . I . hida geld̄ . Tra . ē . v . car̄ . Ibi . I . radman cū . I . car̄ . Silua
ibi dimid̄ leuua lḡ . 7 tntd̄ lat̄ . Valb̄ . VI . ſolid̄ . m̄ . v . ſolid̄.

Ipſe com̄ ten̄ _ESTHA_ . Eduin tenuit . _IN WILAVESTON HD̄._
Ibi . XXII . hidæ geld̄ . Tra|totid̄ car̄ . In dn̄io ſunt . II . car̄ . 7 IIII .
ſerui . 7 XIIII . uilli . 7 x . bord̄ . cū . VI . car̄ . Ibi molin̄ 7 II . radman .
7 un pb̄r.

De tra huj m̄ ten Mundret . II . hid̄ . 7 Hugo . II . hid̄ . 7 Will̄s
una hid̄ . Hamo . VII . hid̄ . Rob̄t . I . hid̄ . Rob̄t dimid̄ hidā .

7 Walt
dim̄ hid̄

In dn̄io ſunt . IIII . car̄ . 7 VIII . bouar̄ . 7 XXII . uilli 7 XI . bord̄ .
7 v . radmans 7 II . francig cū . IX . car̄.

Tot m̄ T.R.E . ualb̄ . XXIIII . lib̄ . 7 poſt . IIII . lib̄ . Modo dn̄ium
comitis . ual̄ . IIII . lib̄ . Hōum .̷ c . XII . ſot.

Ipſe com̄ ten̄ _TRAFORD_ . Ordm tenuit . lib̄ hō fuit . Ibi . II . hidæ
geld̄ . Tra . ē . VI . car̄ . In dn̄io ſunt . II . 7 II . ſerui . 7 IIII . uilli 7 II .
bord̄ cū . I . car̄.

T.R.E . ualb̄ . c . ſolid̄ . Modo . XL . ſol . Waſt inuen̄.

Ipſe com̄ ten̄ _EDELAVE_ . Eduin tenuit . Ibi . I . hida geld̄ . Tra . ē
. I . car̄ . Waſta fuit . Modo arat ibi q̄dā hō 7 redd̄ . II . ſolid̄.

Ipſe com̄ ten̄ _MACLESFELD_ . Eduin tenuit _IN HAMESTAN HD̄._
Ibi . II . hidæ geld̄ . Tra . ē . x . car̄ . In dn̄io . ē una car̄ . 7 IIII . ſerui.

16     LEA. Stein held it as a free man. ½ hide paying tax.
Land for 1 plough. Waste.

17     RUSHTON. Chipping held it as a free man. ½ hide paying tax.
Land for 2 ploughs. Waste.

18     *OPETONE*. Arni, a free man, held it. 1 hide paying tax.
Land for 2 ploughs. Waste.
     Woodland 1 league long and 2 acres wide.

19     BUDWORTH. Dedol, a free man, held it. ½ hide paying tax.
Land for 2 ploughs. Waste.
     Woodland 1 league long and ½ wide.

20     'ALRETONE'. Stein held it; he was a free man. 1 hide paying tax.
Land for 2 ploughs. Waste.

21     OVER. 4 free men held as 4 manors. 1 hide paying tax.
Land for 5 ploughs.
     1 rider with 1 plough.
     Woodland ½ league long and as wide.
The value was 6s; now 5s.

   in WIRRAL Hundred

22     EASTHAM. Earl Edwin held it. 22 hides paying tax.
Land for as many ploughs. In lordship 2 ploughs; 4 slaves;
     14 villagers and 10 smallholders with 6 ploughs.
     A mill, 2 riders and a priest.
     Mundret holds 2 hides of this manor's land, Hugh 2 hides,
William 1 hide, Walter ½ hide, Hamo 7 hides, Robert 1 hide and
Robert ½ hide.
     In lordship 4 ploughs; 8 ploughmen;
     22 villagers, 11 smallholders, 5 riders and 2 Frenchmen with 9 ploughs.
Total value of the manor before 1066 £24; later £4; now the
value of the Earl's lordship £4, of his men's 112s.

23     TRAFFORD. Ording held it; he was a free man. 2 hides paying
tax. Land for 6 ploughs. In lordship 2; 2 slaves;
     4 villagers and 2 smallholders with 1 plough.
Value before 1066, 100s; now 40s; found waste.

24     HADLOW. Earl Edwin held it. 1 hide paying tax. Land for 1 plough.
It was waste; now a man ploughs it and pays 2s.

   in MACCLESFIELD Hundred

25     MACCLESFIELD. Earl Edwin held it. 2 hides paying tax.
Land for 10 ploughs. In lordship 1 plough; 4 slaves.

Ibi molin̄ seruie͡ꝰ curiæ. Silua. vi. leuū lḡ. 7 iiii. lat̄.
7 ibi. vii. haiæ erant. P̃tum bobꝫ. T̉cius denari de hundret
ptinet huic M. T.R.E. ualb̄. viii. lib̄. Modo. xx. sol̄. Wast̄ fuit.
264 a
Isd̄ com̄ ten̉ *Edvlvintvne*. Eduin com tenuit. Ibi. iiii. hidæ 7 dim'. geld̉.
T̉ra. ē. x. car̉. Ibi. ii. radmans. 7 vi. uitti 7 iii. bord̄ cū. iii. car̉.
Ibi. xxi. ac̄ p̃ti. Silua. xi. leuủ lḡ. 7 ii. lat̉. 7 ibi. vii. haiæ.
7 iiii. airæ accipitrū.
T.R.E. ualb̄. viii. lib̄. Modo. xx. sol̄. Wast̉ inuenit.
Ipse com̄ ten̉ *Govesvrde*. Bernulf lib̄ hō tenuit. Ibi. i. hida.
geld̄. T̉ra. ē. vi. car̄. Wasta. ē. T.R.E. ualb̄ xx. sol̄. Ibi Silua
ii. leuū lḡ. 7 ii. leuủ lat̄. 7 ii. haiæ.
Ipse com̄ ten̉ *Mervtvne*. Godric tenuit lib̄ hō fuit. Ibi. i. virḡ
t̉ræ geld̄. T̉ra. ē. i. car̄. Wasta fuit 7 est. Ibi. xx. ptcæ siluæ.
Ipse com̄ ten̄ *Hvngrewenitvne*. Goduin tenuit. Ibi dim̉ hida
geld̄. Wasta fuit 7 est.
Ipse com̄ ten̉ *Celeford*. Brun tenuit. Ibi dimid̄ hida geld̄. T̉ra
ē. ii. car̄. Wasta fuit 7 est.
Ipse com̄ ten̉ *Hameteberie* de dimid̄ hida.
7 *Copestor* de dimid̄ hida. 7 *Hamedeberie* de. i. hida geld̄.
7 *Hofinchel* de. i. hida. 7 *Tengestvisie*. de. i. virḡ t̉ræ.
7 *Holisvrde* de. i. virḡ. 7 *Warnet* de. i. virḡ. 7 *Rvmelie*
de. i. virḡ. 7 *Laitone* de. i. virḡ t̉ræ. Om̄s geldabant.
Has t̉ras tenuer̄. viii. libi hoēs p Maner̉. T̉ra. ē. xvi. car̉ int̉ tot̄.
Wasta fuit 7 est tota.
In Hofinghel. ē silua. ii. leuủ lḡ. 7 ii. lat̉. In *Tengestvisie* Silua. ē
iiii. leuū lḡ. 7 ii. lat̉. In *Warnet* Silua. ē. iii. leuủ lḡ. 7 ii. lat̄.
T.R.E. ualb̄ istud hund̄ xl. solid̄. Modo. x. solid̄. *In Mildestvic hd̄*.
Ipse com̄ ten̉ *Eleacier*. Vluric lib̄ hō tenuit. Ibi dimid̄ hida
geld̄. T̉ra. ē. i. car̄. Wasta. ē. T.R.E. ualb̄. iii. solid̄.

A mill which serves the Hall; woodland 6 leagues long
and 4 wide; 7 enclosures; meadow for the oxen.
The Third Penny of the Hundred belongs to this manor.
Value before 1066, £8; now 20s; it was waste.

26  ADLINGTON. Earl Edwin held it. 4½ hides paying tax.          264 a
Land for 10 ploughs.
  2 riders, 6 villagers and 3 smallholders with 3 ploughs.
  Meadow, 21 acres; woodland 11 leagues long and 2 wide;
    7 enclosures; 4 hawks' eyries.
Value before 1066, £8; now 20s; found waste.

27  GAWSWORTH. Bernwulf, a free man, held it. 1 hide paying tax.
Land for 6 ploughs.
Waste. Value before 1066, 20s.
  Woodland 2 leagues long and 2 leagues wide; 2 enclosures.

28  MARTON. Godric held it; he was a free man. 1 virgate of land
paying tax. Land for 1 plough. It was and is waste.
  Woodland, 20 perches.

29  (Lower) WITHINGTON. Godwin held it. ½ hide paying tax.
It was and is waste.

30  CHELFORD. Brown held it. ½ hide paying tax. Land for 2 ploughs.
It was and is waste.

31  HENBURY, at ½ hide; CAPESTHORNE, at ½ hide; HENBURY, at 1 hide
paying tax; HOFINCHEL, at 1 hide; TINTWISTLE, at 1 virgate of
land; HOLLINGWORTH, at 1 virgate; WERNETH, at 1 virgate; ROMILEY,
at 1 virgate; LAITONE, at 1 virgate of land.
All paid tax. 8 free men held these lands as a manor.
Land for 16 ploughs in all. It was and is all waste.
  In Hofinchel, woodland 2 leagues long and 2 wide; in
    Tintwhistle, woodland 4 leagues long and 2 wide; in
    Werneth, woodland 3 leagues long and 2 wide.
Value of this Hundred before 1066, 40s; now 10s.

in NORTHWICH Hundred
32  ALSAGER. Wulfric, a free man, held it. ½ hide paying tax.
Land for 1 plough.
Waste. Value before 1066, 3s.

Ipſe com̄ ten̄ *SANBEC* de . ii . virg̉ 7 dimid . geld̄

7 *CLIVE* de . i . virg̉ geld̄ . 7 *SVTONE* de . iiii . bouatis træ geld̄.

7 *WIBALDELAI* de . i . virg̉ geld̄ . 7 *WEVRE* . de . i . virg̉ træ geld̄.

7 *ACVLVESTVNE* de . i . hida geld̄.

Has tras tenuer̄ . vi . libi hoēs p̄ . vi . Man . Tra . ē vii car̄ int̉ tot̄.

Waſta fuit 7 ē tota . In Wibaldelai . ē una ac̄ p̄ti . 7 iiii . pars

ſiluæ quæ ht̄ . i . leuu̇ l̄g 7 iiii . p̄tic̄ lat̄ . In Weure . dimid ac̄ p̄ti.

7 iiii . pars ſiluæ q̇ ht̄ . i . leuu l̄g . 7 tntd lat̄ . *IN WILAVESTON HD̄.*

Ipſe com̄ ten̄ *OPTONE* . Eduin tenuit . Ibi . iiii . hidæ 7 dim̄ geld̄ . Tra . ē

xii . car̄ . In dn̄io . ē una . 7 ii . bouar̄ . 7 xii . uilli 7 ii . radmans cū . v . car̄.

De hac tra huj c̄o ten̄ Hamo . ii . partes . i . hidæ 7 Herbert dim̄ hidā.

7 Mundret . i . hid̄ . Ibi ſunt in dn̄io . iiii . car̄ . 7 viii . bouarij.

7 ii . uilli 7 ii . bord̄ cū . i . car̄ . Ibi . i . ac̄ p̄ti.

Tot̄ c̄o T.R.E. ualb̄ . lx . ſol . Modo dn̄iu comitis . xlv . ſolid . uat̄.

Hōum ej̉ . xl . ſol.

Ipſe com̄ ten̄ *STANEI* . 7 Reſtald̉ de eo . Ragenal tenuit ſic̄

lib̄ hō . Ibi . i . hida geld̄ . Tra . c̄ . ii . car̄ . In dn̄io . ē una . 7 ii . bouar̄.

7 ii . uilli 7 ii . bord̄ . 7 una piſcaria . T.R.E. ualb̄ . xii . ſol . M̊ . xiiii . ſol.

De hac tra q̇nta acra fuit 7 ee debet in æccła S̄ *WAREBVRG*.

teſte comitatu . Canonici calūniant̉ q̇a injuſte p̄dunt.

Ipſe com̄ ten̄ *ENTREBVS* . Leuenot tenuit *IN TVNENDVNE HD̄.*

7 lib̄ hō fuit . Ibi . i . uirg̉ træ 7 dimid geld̄ . Tra . ē . i . car̄ . Waſta

fuit 7 eſt . Silua ibi . i . leuua l̄g 7 dimid lat̄ . T.R.E. ualb̄ . iiii . ſol.

*IN DVDESTAN HD̄.*

264 b

Rotbert . F . Hugonis ten̄ de Hugone *BEDDESFELD*.

Eduin tenuit . Ibi . vii . hidæ geld̄ . Tra . ē . viii . car̄.

In dn̄io . ē una 7 ii . ſerui . 7 iii . uilli cū . i . car̄ . Ibi dimid̄

ac̄ p̄ti . Silua . iii . leuu l̄g . 7 ii . lat̄.

33 SANDBACH, at 2½ virgates paying tax; CLIVE, at 1 virgate paying
tax; SUTTON, at 4 bovates of land paying tax; \WIMBOLDSLEY, at
1 virgate paying tax; WEAVER, at 1 virgate of land paying tax;
OCCLESTON, at 1 hide paying tax.
6 free men held these lands as 6 manors. Land for 7 ploughs in all.
It was and is all waste.
    In Wimboldsley is 1 acre of meadow; a fourth part of a wood which
    is 1 league long and 4 perches wide; in Weaver is ½ acre of meadow;
    a fourth part of a wood which is 1 league long and as wide.

in WIRRAL Hundred

34 UPTON. Earl Edwin held it. 4½ hides paying tax. Land for 12 ploughs.
In lordship 1; 2 ploughmen;
    12 villagers and 2 riders with 5 ploughs.
Of this land, Hamo holds 2 parts of 1 hide of this manor;
Herbert ½ hide; Mundret 1 hide. In lordship 4 ploughs; 8 ploughmen.
    2 villagers and 2 smallholders· with 1 plough.
    Meadow, 1 acre.
Value of the whole manor before 1066, 60s; now the Earl's lordship
45s, his men's 40s.

35 STANNEY. Restald holds from him. Ragenald held it like a free man.
1 hide paying tax. Land for 2 ploughs. In lordship 1; 2 ploughmen;
    2 villagers and 2 smallholders.
    A fishery.
Value before 1066, 12s; now 14s.
    The fifth acre of this land was and ought to be St. Werburgh's
church's, as the county witnesses; the Canons claim it, because
they lost it wrongfully.

in BUCKLOW (West) Hundred

36 ANTROBUS. Leofnoth held it; he was a free man. 1½ virgates of
land paying tax. Land for 1 plough. It was and is waste.
    Woodland 1 league long and ½ wide.
Value before 1066, 4s.

# 2           [FROM EARL HUGH]          264 b

**Robert son of Hugh** holds
In BROXTON Hundred

1 BETTISFIELD. Earl Edwin held it. 7 hides paying tax.
Land for 8 ploughs. In lordship 1; 2 slaves;
    3 villagers with 1 plough.
    Meadow, ½ acre; woodland 3 leagues long and 2 wide.

In hac ťra hñt.III.milites.III.cař in dñio.7 IX.uiłłos

7 v.borđ.7 II.ſeruos.7 III.hões alios.Inť oms hñt.III.caŕ.

Prƀr hť.I.caŕ.

Toť T.R.E.ualƀ xvIII.liƀ.7 xvII.ſoliđ.7 IIII.den̄.Wasť fuit.
Modo inť toť ual.III.liƀ.Hoc ᴔ p̄ť Siluā hť.II.leuū

lg̃.7 tntđ lať.

De hoc ᴔ calūniať ep̄s de Ceſtre.II.hiđ.q̃s teneƀ S̃ CEDD

tp̄r cnuti regis.ſed ex tc̄ uſq̨ m̃ ſe plangit amiſiſſe.

Iſđ Roƀť ten̄ *BVRWARDESTONE*.Eduin tenuit.Ibi.v.

hidæ gelđ.Tra.ē.xIIII.caŕ.In dñio.ē una.7 xII.uiłłi 7 II.

borđ cū.III.caŕ.7 un miles hť.I.caŕ ibi.7 alt miles ten̄

dimiđ hiđ quæ redđ ei.xII.ſoliđ.Ibi ſalina de.xxIIII.ſoł.

T.R.E.ualƀ.vI.liƀ 7 IIII.ſoł.Modo.LIIII.ſoł.Wasť inuen̄.

Hoc ᴔ hť.II.leuū lg̃.7 unā lať.

De hoc ᴔ calūniať ep̄s de Ceſtre.I.hiđ 7 dim̃.7 unā ſalinā.

Iſđ Ro.ten̄ *HVRDINGBERIE*.Eduin tenuit.Ibi.v.hidæ gelđ.

Tra.ē.x.caŕ.In dñio.ē una.7 un ſeruus.7 III.uiłłi.7 III.francig̃

7 un radman cū.IIII.caŕ.Ibi moliñ nouū.7 una ac̃ p̃ti.

De hoc ᴔ ten̄ un miles.I.hiđ 7 dimiđ.7 ibi hť.I.caŕ.cū hōib̃ ſuis.

T.R.E.ualƀ.xII.oras q̃s uiłłi redđeƀ.Modo ual.xxx.ſoł.

Wasť inuen̄.hť in lg̃.II.leuū.7 I.in laŕ.

Iſđ Ro.ten̄ *DEPENBECH*.Eduin tenuit.Ibi.vIII.hidæ gelđ.

Tra.ē.xIIII.caŕ.In dñio ſunt.III.7 I.borđ.7 dimiđ ac̃ p̃ti.

De hac ťra ten̄.v.milites de Roƀto.v.hiđ 7 dimiđ.

7 ibi hñt.III.caŕ.7 vII uiłłos cū.II.caŕ 7 dimiđ.Ibi.II.ac̃ p̃ti.

Toť T.R.E.ualƀ.xI.liƀ.7 IIII.ſoł.Wasť poſtea fuit.Modo

inť toť ual.LII.ſoł.Hť.II.leuū lg̃.7 unā lat.

Iſđ.Ro.ten̄ *TILLESTONE*.Eduin tenuit.Ibi.IIII.hidæ gelđ.

Tra.ē.vIII.caŕ.In dñio.ē una.7 II.ſerui.7 IIII.uiłłi 7 II.

borđ.7 IIII.radmans 7 p̄poſit 7 faƀ 7 molinari cū.IIII.caŕ.

inť oms.Ibi moliñ de.vIII.ſoliđ.

On this land 3 men-at-arms have 3 ploughs in lordship.
9 villagers, 5 smallholders, 2 slaves and 3 other men have
3 ploughs between them; a priest has 1 plough.
Total value before 1066 £18 17s 4d; it was waste; total value now £3.
This manor also has woodland 2 leagues long and as wide.
The Bishop of Chester claims 2 hides of this manor which St. Chad's
held in King Canute's time which, he complains, have been lost
ever since.

Robert also holds

2    ISCOYD. Earl Edwin held it. 5 hides paying tax. Land for 14 ploughs.
In lordship 1;
12 villagers and 2 smallholders with 3 ploughs. 1 man-at-arms
has 1 plough; another man-at-arms holds ½ hide which pays
him 12s.
A salthouse at 24s.
Value before 1066 £6 4s; now 54s; found waste.
This manor was 2 leagues long and 1 wide. The Bishop
of Chester claims 1½ hides and a salthouse from this manor.

3    WORTHENBURY. Earl Edwin held it. 5 hides paying tax. Land
for 10 ploughs. In lordship 1; 1 slave;
3 villagers, 3 Frenchmen and 1 rider with 4 ploughs.
A new mill; meadow, 1 acre.
1 man-at-arms holds 1½ hides of this manor and has 1 plough
with his men.
Value before 1066, 12 ora which the villagers paid; now 30s;
found waste. It is 2 leagues long and 1 wide.

4    MALPAS. Earl Edwin held it. 8 hides paying tax. Land for 14
ploughs. In lordship 3;
1 smallholder.
Meadow, ½ acre.
5 men-at-arms hold 5½ hides of this land from Robert and
have 3 ploughs there.
7 villagers with 2½ ploughs.
Meadow, 2 acres.
Value of the whole before 1066 £11 4s; later on it was waste;
total value now 52s.
It is 2 leagues long and 1 wide.

5    TILSTON. Earl Edwin held it. 4 hides paying tax. Land for 8
ploughs. In lordship 1; 2 slaves;
4 villagers, 2 smallholders, 4 riders, a reeve, a smith and a
miller with 4 ploughs between them.
A mill at 8s.

De hac t̃ra ten̅ Rannulf dimid hiđ de Robto.redđ.vi.ſol 7 viii.den̅.

Tot̃ T.R.E.ualb.vi.lib.Modo.xxx.ſol.Waſt inuen̅.

ht̃.i.leuua lg̅.7 alia lat̃.            ꞇ teſtificat̃ eā de ep̅atu ſuo.

De huj m̅ t̃ra calūniat̃ ep̅s de ceſtre dimid hiđ.ſed comitat̃ non

Iſđ Ro.ten̅ CRISTETONE.com̅ Eduin tenuit.Ibi.vii.hidæ gelđ.

Tra.ē.xiiii.car̃.In dn̅io.ē.i.car̃.7 ii.ancillæ.7 xii.uil̅li 7 v.

borđ.7 ii.p̅poſiti çū.viii.car̃.Ibi moliñ de.xii.ſol.7 ii.radmans

ibi.De hoc m̅ ten̅ Rannulf de Robto.ii.hiđ.redđt ei.xii.den̅.

Tot̃ T.R.E.ualb.vi.lib.Modo ual̃.iii.lib.Waſt inuen̅.

ht̃.ii.leuu lg̅.7 una lat̃.

Iſđ Ro.ten̅ CALMVNDELEI.Eduin 7 Dot tenuer̃ libi h̅oes Ibi.ii.hidæ  p̅.ii.ʒ.

gelđ.Tra.ē.iiii.car̃.Eduin 7 Drogo ten̅ de Robto.In dn̅io

eſt.i.car̃.7 v.ſerui.7 un uil̅ls 7 iii.borđ 7 un p̅poſit 7 fab

cū.i.car̃.7 Silua ibi.i.leuu 7 dimid lg̅.7 una lat̃.Ibi.iii.haiæ.

T.R.E.ualb.xiii.ſolid.Modo.vi.ſolid 7 iii.denar̃.

Ht̃ dimiđ leuua de plano.

Iſđ Ro.ten̅ EGHE.Eduin tenuit 7 adhuc ten̅ de Robto.

lib h̅o fuit.Ibi.ii.hidæ 7 dimid gelđ.Tra.ē.i.car̃.Moræ

ſunt ibi.In dn̅io.ē una car̃.7 iii.ſerui.Siluæ.ii.ac̃s lg̅.

7 una lat̃.Waſt fuit 7 inuen̅.Modo.iiii.ſolid.

Iſđ.Ro.ten̅ HANTONE.7 Eduin 7 Drogo de eo.Ipſe Eduin

★ tenuit 7 lib h̅o fuit.Ibi.ii.hidæ 7       gelđ.Tra.ē.iiii.car̃.  p̅.ii.ʒ.

Ibi ſunt.iii.hoſpites nil h̅ntes.Ibi Silua.v.ac̃s lg̅.7 ii.lat̃.

Tot̃ T.R.E.ualb.v.ſol.Modo.ii.ſol 7 uñ ſp̅reuariū redđ.

Ranulf holds ½ hide of this land from Robert and pays 6s 8d.
Value of the whole before 1066 £6; now 30s; found waste.
    It is 1 league long and another wide. The Bishop of
Chester claims ½ hide of this manor's land, but the County
do not testify that it is his Bishopric's.


6    CHRISTLETON. Earl Edwin held it. 7 hides paying tax.
Land for 14 ploughs. In lordship 1 plough; 2 female slaves;
    12 villagers, 5 smallholders and 2 reeves with 8 ploughs.
    A mill at 12s; 2 riders.
    Ranulf holds 2 hides of this manor from Robert; it pays him 12d.
Value of the whole before 1066 £6; value now £3; found waste.
    It has 2 leagues length and 1 width.


7    CHOLMONDELEY. Edwin and Dot, free men, held it as 2 manors. 2
hides paying tax. Land for 4 ploughs. Edwin and Drogo hold
from Robert. In lordship 1 plough; 5 slaves;
    1 villager, 3 smallholders, a reeve and a smith with 1 plough.
    Woodland 1½ leagues long and 1 wide; 3 enclosures.
Value in 1066, 13s; now 6s 3d.
    It has ½ league of open country.


8    EDGE. Edwin held it and still holds from Robert; he was a free
man. 2½ hides paying tax. Land for 1 plough.
Moors there. In lordship 1 plough; 3 slaves.
    Woodland 2 acres long and 1 wide.
It was and was found waste; [value] now 4s.


9    HAMPTON. Edwin and Drogo hold from him. Edwin held it
himself as 2 manors; he was a free man. 2[½?] hides paying
tax. Land for 4 ploughs.
    3 settlers who have nothing.
    Woodland 5 acres long and 2 wide.
Value of the whole before 1066, 5s; now 2s, and 1 sparrow-hawk.

Iſd Roƀt ten *LAVORCHEDONE*.7 Eduin 7 Drogo de eo.Iſd Eduin
tenuit.liƀ hō fuit.Ibi.ı.hida gelđ.Tra.ē.ııı.caɼ.

Ibi.ē un hō 7 redđ.xıı.denaɼ.7 un borđ redđ.ıı.ſoliđ.

T.R.E.ualƀ.vııı.ſoliđ.Hꞇ.ıııı.leuū lḡ.7 ıııı.laꞇ.

Iſd Ro.ten *DOCHINTONE*.7 Eduin de eo.Ipſemeꞇ tenuit
ut liƀ hō.Ibi.ı.hiđ gelđ.Tra.ē.ıı.caɼ.Waſta.ē.

Iſd Ro.7 Eduin de eo ten *EGHE*.7 tenuit ut liƀ hō.Ibi dimiđ
hida gelđ.Tra.ē.ı.caɼ.Waſta.ē.Silua ibi.ıı.aĉs lḡ.

7 una laꞇ.Val xıı.den.

Iſd Ro.ten *CELELEA*.7 Mundret de eo.Vlueue tenuit
7 liƀa fuit.Ibi.ı.hida gelđ.Tra.ē.ı.caɼ.Ibi.ē cū.ıı.rad
mans.Silua dimiđ leuū lḡ.7 una aĉ laꞇ.7 ıı.haiæ.

T.R.E.ualƀ.x.ſoliđ.modo.v.ſoliđ.Waſꞇ inueñ.

Iſd Roƀt ten *BROSSE*.7 Roger|de eo.Briſmer 7 Rauen
ıı.liƀi hōes tenueɼ ₽.ıı.Ṁ.Ibi.v.hidæ gelđ.Tra.ē.vı.
caɼ.In dñio.ē.ı.caɼ.7 ııı.uiꞇi cū.ı.caɼ.Siluæ.ı.leuua.

T.R.E.ualƀ.x.ſol 7 vııı.den.Modo.xvııı.ſol 7 vııı.den.

Iſd Ro.ten *OVRETONE*.Vluoi tenuit.liƀ hō fuit.

Ibi.ı.hida 7 dimiđ gelđ.Tra.ē.ıı.caɼ.In dñio.ē una.

Silua.ıı.aĉs lḡ.7 una laꞇ.Valƀ.v.ſol.Modo.vı.ſol.

Iſd Ro.ten *CVNTITONE*.Vluoi tenuit.Ibi dimiđ hida
gelđ.Tra.ē.ı.caɼ.Ibi ſunt.ıı.borđ cū.ıı.bobʒ arantes.

Valƀ.xvı.den.Waſꞇ fuit.

Iſd Ro.ten *SOCHELIÇHE*.7 Drogo de eo.Dot liƀ hō tenuit.

Ibi.ııı.hidæ gelđ.Tra.ē.ıııı.caɼ.In dñio ſunt.ıı.7 ıı.bouaɼ.
7 ıı.uiꞇi cū.ı. Ibi dimiđ aĉ p̄ti.

T.R.E.ualƀ.vııı.ſol.Modo.xıı.ſoliđ.

Iſd Ro.ten *TVSIGEHA*.7 Hunfrid de eo.Ernuin tenuit.

Ibi.ı.hida gelđ.Tra.ē.ıı.caɼ.In dñio.ē una.cū.ı.borđ.

Siluæ dimiđ leuua.T.R.E.ualƀ.x.ſol.Modo.ıııı.ſol.Waſꞇ fuit.

10 LARKTON. Edwin and Drogo hold from him. Edwin also held 264 c
it; he was a free man. 1 hide paying tax. Land for 3 ploughs.
1 man; he pays 12d; 1 smallholder pays 2s.
Value before 1066, 8s. It has 4 leagues length and 4 width.

11 DUCKINGTON Edwin holds from him. He held it himself as
a free man. 1 hide paying tax. Land for 2 ploughs. Waste.

12 EDGE. Edwin holds from him and held it as a free man. ½
hide paying tax. Land for 1 plough. Waste.
Woodland, 2 acres long and 1 wide.
Value 12d.

13 CHOWLEY. Mundret holds from him. Wulfeva held it; she was a
free woman. 1 hide paying tax. Land for 1 plough. It is there, with
2 riders
Woodland ½ league long and 1 acre wide; 2 enclosures.
Value before 1066, 10s; now 5s; found waste.

14 BROXTON. Roger and Picot hold from him. Brictmer and Raven,
two free men, held it as 2 manors. 5 hides paying tax.
Land for 6 ploughs. In lordship 1 plough;
3 villagers with 1 plough.
Woodland, 1 league.
Value before 1066, 10s 8d; now 18s 8d.

15 OVERTON. Wulfwy held it; he was a free man. 1½ hides paying
tax. Land for 2 ploughs. In lordship 1.
Woodland 2 acres long and 1 wide.
The value was 5s; now 6s.

16 CUDDINGTON. The above Wulfwy held it. ½ hide paying tax.
Land for 1 plough.
2 smallholders who plough with 2 oxen.
The value was 16d; it was waste.

17 SHOCKLACH. Drogo holds from him. Dot, a free man, held it. 3 hides
paying tax. Land for 4 ploughs. In lordship 2; 2 ploughmen;
2 villagers with 1 plough.
Meadow, ½ acre.
Value before 1066, 8s; now 12s.

18 TUSHINGHAM. Humphrey holds from him. Ernwin, a free man,
held it. 1 hide paying tax. Land for 2 ploughs. In lordship 1;
1 smallholder.
Woodland, ½ league.
Value before 1066, 10s; now 4s; it was waste.

Iſd Ro.ten̄ *Bicheleí*.7 Fulco de eo.Vdeman tenuit.

★ 7 liƀ hō fuit.Ibi.ɪ.hida gelđ.Tra.ē.ɪɪ.car̄.In dn̄io.ē
una car̄.7 p̄poſit 7 ɪɪ.borđ cū.ɪ.car̄.

T.R.E.ualƀ.v.ſoliđ.Modo.vɪɪɪ.ſoliđ.Waſt inuen̄.

Iſd Ro.ten̄ *Bicretone*.7 Drogo de eo.Dot.7 Eduin.7 Ernuin̄.
Tres taini liƀi hōes tenuer̄.Ibi.ɪɪɪ.hidæ gelđ.Tra.ē.ɪɪɪɪ.car̄.
Ibi ſunt.ɪɪ.uiłłi cū.ɪ.car̄.Siluæ dimiđ leuua.

T.R.E.ualƀ.xvɪɪɪ.ſoliđ.Modo.xɪ.ſoliđ.Waſta fuit 7 eſt
ex maxima parte.

Iſd Ro.ten̄ *Bvrwardeslei*.7 Hunfrid de eo.Aluric
p.ɪɪɪ.☉.7 Colƀt 7 Rauenchel tenuer̄.7 liƀi hōes fuer̄.Ibi.ɪɪɪ.hidæ
gelđ.Tra.ē.ɪɪɪ.car̄.Ibi.ɪɪɪ.borđ cū.ɪ.car̄.7 Silua.ɪ.leuu
lḡ.7 dimiđ lat̄.T.R.E.ualƀ.ɪɪ.ſol.Modo.v.ſol.Waſt fuit.
De hac tra.ɪ.hidà fuit ablata ab æccła S̄ Warbvrgæ.
Hanc uendider̄ p̄poſiti comit̄ Eduini 7 Morcar cuidà Rauechil.

Iſd Ro.ten̄ *Crevhalle*.7 Eli de eo.Ipſemet tenuit 7 liƀ hō
fuit.Ibi.ɪ.hida gelđ.Tra.ē.ɪ.car̄.Ibi.ē in dn̄io.cū.ɪɪ.borđ.
7 dimiđ piſcaria.Val.x.ſoliđ.Waſta fuit 7 ſic inuen̄.

Iſd Ro.ten̄ *Tidvlstane*.7 Wiłłs de eo.IN RISEDON HD̄.
Stenulf tenuit.7 liƀ hō fuit.Ibi.ɪɪ.hidæ gelđ.Tra.ē.ɪɪ.car̄.
In dn̄io.ē una.cū.ɪ.borđ.Ibi modic̄ ſiluæ.

T.R.E.ualƀ.vɪ.ſol.7 vɪɪɪ.den̄.Modo.ɪɪɪɪ.ſol.Waſt inuen̄.

Iſd Ro.ten̄ *Bvistane*.Vluoi tenuit 7 liƀ hō fuit.Ibi.una
hida gelđ.Tra.ē.ɪɪ.car̄ 7 dimiđ.In dn̄io.ē una cū.ɪɪ.bou.

T.R.E.ualƀ.x.ſoliđ.modo.v.ſoliđ.Waſt inuenit.

Iſd Ro.ten̄ *Boleberie*.Dedol tenuit 7 liƀ hō fuit.Ibi.ɪ.hida
gelđ.Tra.ē.ɪɪ.car̄.In dn̄io.ē una.7 pƀr cū.ɪɪ.uiłłis hn̄t.ɪ.car̄.
Silua.ɪ.leuu lḡ.7 una ac̄ lat̄.Valƀ.ɪɪɪɪ.ſol.Modo.xɪɪɪ.ſol.

Iſd Ro.ten̄ *Tevretone*.Dedol 7 Hundulf tenuer̄ p.ɪɪ.℧.7 liƀi
hōes fuer̄.Ibi.ɪɪ.hidæ gelđ.Tra.ē.ɪɪ.car̄.Ibi.ɪɪɪ.uiłłi 7 ɪɪ.borđ hn̄t
unā car̄.Silua.ɪ.leuu lḡ.7 alia lat̄.Valƀ.x.ſol.Modo.xxv.ſol.

19 BICKLEY. Fulk holds from him. Woodman held it; he was a free
man. 1 hide paying tax. Land for 3 ploughs. In lordship 1 plough;
   a reeve and 2 smallholders with 1 plough.
Value before 1066, 5s; now 8s; found waste.

20 BICKERTON. Drogo holds from him. Dot, Edwin and Ernwin, three
thanes, free men, held it as 3 manors. 3 hides paying tax.
Land for 4 ploughs.
   2 villagers with 1 plough.
   Woodland ½ league.
Value before 1066, 18s; now 11s; it was and is mostly waste.

21 BURWARDSLEY. Humphrey holds from him. Aelfric, Colbert and
Ravenkel held it as 3 manors; they were free men. 3 hides
paying tax. Land for 3 ploughs.
   3 smallholders with 1 plough.
   Woodland 1 league long and ½ wide.
Value before 1066, 2s; now 5s; it was waste.
   1 hide of this land was taken from St. Werbergh's Church;
the reeves of Earls Edwin and Morcar sold it to one Ravenkel.

22 CREWE HALL. Eli holds from him. He held it himself; he was a
free man. 1 hide paying tax. Land for 1 plough. It is there
in lordship, with
   2 smallholders.
   ½ fishery.
Value 10s; it was waste; so found.

  In EDDISBURY (South) Hundred
23 TILSTONE. William holds from him. Stenulf held it; he was a free
man. 2 hides paying tax. Land for 2 ploughs. In lordship 1, with
   1 smallholder.
   A small wood.
Value before 1066, 6s 8d; now 4s; found waste.

24 BEESTON. Wulfwy held it; he was a free man. 1 hide paying tax.
Land for 2½ ploughs. In lordship 1;
   2 ploughmen.
Value before 1066, 10s; now 5s; found waste.

25 BUNBURY. Dedol held it; he was a free man. 1 hide paying tax.
Land for 2 ploughs. In lordship 1.
   A priest with 2 villagers have 1 plough.
   Woodland 1 league long and 1 acre wide.
The value was 4s; now 13s.

26 TIVERTON. Dedol and Hundulf held it as 2 manors; they were
free men. 2 hides paying tax. Land for 2 ploughs.
   3 villagers and 2 smallholders have 1 plough.
   Woodland 1 league long and another wide.
The value was 10s; now 25s.

Iſd Ro.ten SPVRETONE.Vluric tenuit.7 liƀ hõ fuit.Ibi hida

7 dimiđ gelđ.Tra.ē.III.car.Ibi.II.radmans 7 III.borđ hñt.I.car.

Silua ibi.I.leuu 7 dim lg.7 dim leuu lat.7 una ac̃ p̃ti.

T.R.E.ualƀ.XVI.ſoliđ.modo.VI.ſoliđ.Waſt inueñ.

Ipſe Ro.ten PEVRETONE.Vluric tenuit.Ibi.I.hida gelđ.Tra.ē

II.car.Ibi.ē un uilłs cũ.I.car.Valƀ.VIII.ſol.Modo.XX.ſoł redđ.

Iſd Ro.ten SVDTONE.Tochi tenuit. IN WILAVESTON HVNĐ.

7 liƀ hõ fuit.Ibi.I.hida gelđ.Tra.ē.III.car.In dñio.ē una.7 III.

★ borđ cũ.I.uiłło.Ibi.VI.ac̃ p̃ti.

T.R.E.ualƀ.XL.ſoł.7 poſt.VI.ſoliđ.Modo redđ.LXIIII.deñ de firma.

Roƀt ten de com̃ BVTELEGE.Hundin tenuit IN HAMESTAN HVNĐ.

7 liƀ hõ fuit.Ibi.I.hida glđ.Tra.ē.V.car.Waſta.ē.p̃t.XII.as ſatas.

T.R.E.ualƀ.XXX.ſoliđ.Modo.II.ſoliđ.Ibi.II.ac̃ p̃ti 7 dimiđ.Silua ibi

.III.leuu lg.7 una lat.7 una haia ibi.

Roƀt ten de com̃ CROENECHE.Godric tenuit 7 liƀ hõ fuit.Ibi.I.hida

gelđ.Tra.ē.I.car 7 dimid.Ibi.I.radman 7 un uilłs hñt dim car.

Ibi Silua dimiđ leuu lg.7 XL.p̃tic lat.7 ibi.I.haia.

Waſt fuit.modo ual.III.ſoliđ.     IN WILAVESTON HVNĐ.

ROBERT de Rodelent ten de Hugone comite MOLINTONE.Goduin tenuit.

7 liƀ hõ fuit.Ibi hida.7 dim gelđ.Tra.ē.III.car.In dñio.ē una.7 III.

ſerui.7 III.uilłi 7 III.borđ.7 II.ac̃ p̃ti.7 II.ac̃ ſiluæ.

T.R.E.fuit waſt. Qdo recep̃.ualƀ.XX.ſoł.Modo.XV.ſoliđ.

Iſd Roƀt ten MOLINTONE.7 Lanƀt de eo.Gunner tenuer̃ 7 liƀi hões

fueř.Ibi una hida gelđ.Tra.ē.II.car.Ibi.ē una in dñio cũ.II.ſeruis.

7 Ibi.II.ac̃ p̃ti. Val.XIIII.ſoł.Waſt fuit 7 waſt inueñ.

27   SPURSTOW. Wulfric held it; he was a free man. 1½ hides paying tax.  264 d
Land for 3 ploughs.
    2 riders and 3 smallholders have 1 plough.
    Woodland 1½ leagues long and ½ league wide; meadow, 1 acre.
Value before 1066, 16s; now 6s; found waste.

28   PECKFORTON. Wulfric, a free man, held it. 1 hide paying tax.
Land for 2 ploughs.
    1 villager with 1 plough.
The value was 8s; now it pays 20s.

  In WIRRAL Hundred
29   SUTTON. Toki held it; he was a free man. 1 hide paying tax.
Land for 3 ploughs. In lordship 1;
    3 smallholders with 1 [plough? ].
    Meadow, 6 acres.
Value before 1066, 40s; later 6s; now it pays 64d in revenue.

  In MACCLESFIELD Hundred
30   Robert holds BUTLEY from the Earl. Hunding held it; he was
a free man. 1 hide paying tax. Land for 5 ploughs.
Waste, apart from 12 sown acres; value before 1066, 30s; now 2s.
    Meadow, 2½ acres; woodland 3 leagues long and 1 wide;  1
enclosure.

31   Robert holds CRANAGE from the Earl. Godric held it; he was a
free man. 1 hide paying tax. Land for 1½ ploughs.
    1 rider and 1 villager have ½ plough.
    Woodland ½ league long and 40 perches wide; 1 enclosure.
It was waste; value now 3s.

3    **Robert of Rhuddlan** holds

  In WIRRAL Hundred
1   MOLLINGTON from Earl Hugh. Godwin held it; he was a free man. 1½
hides paying tax. Land for 3 ploughs. In lordship 1; 3 slaves;
    3 villagers and 3 smallholders.
    Meadow, 2 acres; woodland, 2 acres.
Before 1066 it was waste; value when acquired 20s; now 15s.
Robert also holds
2   MOLLINGTON. Lambert holds from him. Gunner and Ulf held
it as 2 manors; they were free men. 1 hide paying tax.
Land for 2 ploughs. In lordship 1, with 2 slaves.
    Meadow, 2 acres.
Value 14s; it was waste; found waste.

Iſd Ro.ten *LESTONE*.7 Wiłłs de eo.Leuenot tenuit 7 liƀ hō fuit.

Ibi.i.hida gelđ.Tra.ē.ii.caŕ.In dñio.ē una caŕ.cū uno ſeruo.

7 un francig 7 ii.borđ.7 ii.piſcariæ.Valuit 7 uał.xv.ſoliđ.

Iſd Ro.ten *TORINTONE*.7 Wiłłs de eo.Vlchetel tenuit 7 liƀ

hō fuit.Ibi dimiđ hida gelđ.Tra.ē.ii.caŕ.Ibi.i.radman 7 i.uiłł

7 un borđ hn̄t dimiđ caŕ.Valuit.x.ſoł.7 poſt 7 modo.v.ſoliđ.

Iſd Roƀt ten *GAITONE* 7 Wiłłs de eo.Leuenot liƀ hō tenuit.

Ibi.i.hida gelđ.Tra.ē.ii.caŕ.Ibi.ii.uiłłi 7 iii.borđ hn̄t.i.caŕ.

7 ibi.ii.piſcariæ.Valuit.xv.ſoł.7 poſt.ii.ſoł.Modo.iii.ſoliđ.

Iſd Ro.ten *ESWELLE*.7 Herƀt de eo.Vlchel tenuit.7 liƀ hō fuit.

Ibi.ii.hidæ gelđ.Tra.ē.iiii.caŕ.In dñio.ē una caŕ.7 ii.bouarij.

7 iii.uiłłi 7 i.borđ cū.i.caŕ.

T.R.E.ualƀ.xvi.ſoł.7 poſt.xx.ſoł.Modo.xxii.ſoliđ.

Iſd.Ro.ten *TVRSTANETONE* 7 Wiłłs de eo.Leuenot tenuit.liƀ hō.fuit.

Ibi.ii.hidæ gelđ.Tra.ē.iiii.caŕ.In dñio.ē una.7 ii.bouaŕ.7 iiii.

uiłłi 7 iiii.borđ cū.i.caŕ 7 dimiđ.

T.R.E.ualƀ.xxx.ſoliđ.7 poſt.viii.ſoł.Modo.xvi.ſoliđ.

Iſd Ro.ten *CALDERS*.Leuenot tenuit.liƀ hō fuit.Ibi.iii.hidæ

gelđ.Tra.ē.x.caŕ.Ibi.v.uiłłi 7 v.borđ hn̄t.ii.caŕ.7 un fran

cig cū.i.ſeruiente hŕ.ii.caŕ.  In dñio.ii.boues.7 ii.ac ṕti.

T.R.E.ualƀ.L.ſoliđ.7 poſt.x.ſoł.modo.xxiiii.ſoliđ.

Iſd Ro.ten *MELAS*.Leuenot tenuit.Ibi.i.hida gelđ.Tra.ē

.i.caŕ 7 dimiđ.Ibi.i.radman 7 ii.uiłłi 7 ii.borđ hn̄t.i.caŕ.

T.R.E.ualƀ.xv.ſoł.Modo.x.ſoł.Waſt inuen̄.

Iſd Ro.ten *MELAS*.Leuenot tenuit.Ibi.i.hida gelđ.Tra.ē.iii.

caŕ.Ibi.i.radman 7 iii.uiłł 7 iii.borđ hn̄t.i.caŕ.

T.R.E.ualƀ.x.ſoł.7 poſt.viii.ſoł.Modo.xii.ſoliđ.

Iſd Ro.ten *WALEA*.Vêtred tenuit.7 liƀ hō fuit.Ibi.i.hida

7 dimiđ gelđ.Tra.ē.iiii.caŕ.Ibi.i.uiłł 7 i.borđ cū dim caŕ.

7 un francig hŕ.i.caŕ cū.ii.bouaŕ.7 i.radman.7 i.borđ.

3  LEIGHTON. William holds from him. Leofnoth held it;
he was a free man. 1 hide paying tax. Land for 2 ploughs.
In lordship 1 plough, with 1 slave;
   1 Frenchman and 2 smallholders.
   2 fisheries.
The value was and is 15s.

4  THORNTON. William holds from him. Ulfketel held it;
he was a free man. ½ hide paying tax. Land for 2 ploughs.
   1 rider, 1 villager and 1 smallholder have ½ plough.
The value was 10s; later and now 5s.

5  GAYTON. William holds from him. Leofnoth, a free man, held it.
1 hide paying tax. Land for 2 ploughs.
   2 villagers and 3 smallholders have 1 plough.
   2 fisheries.
The value was 15s; later 2s; now 3s.

6  HESWALL. Herbert holds from him. Ulfkel held it;
he was a free man. 2 hides paying tax. Land for 4 ploughs.
In lordship 1 plough; 2 ploughmen;
   3 villagers and 1 smallholder with 1 plough.
Value before 1066, 16s; later 20s; now 22s.

7  THURSTASTON. William holds from him. Leofnoth held it;
he was a free man. 2 hides paying tax. Land for 4 ploughs.
In lordship 1; 2 ploughmen;
   4 villagers and 4 smallholders with 1½ ploughs.
Value before 1066, 30s; later 8s; now 16s.

8  CALDY. Leofnoth held it; he was a free man.
3 hides paying tax. Land for 10 ploughs.
   5 villagers and 5 smallholders have 2 ploughs;
   1 Frenchman with 1 servant has 2 ploughs.
   In lordship 2 oxen.
      Meadow, 2 acres.
   Value before 1066, 50s; later 10s; now 24s.

9  MEOLS. Leofnoth held it. 1 hide paying tax. Land for 1½ ploughs.
   1 rider, 2 villagers and 2 smallholders have 1 plough.
Value before 1066, 15s; now 10s; found waste.

10  MEOLS. Leofnoth held it. 1 hide paying tax. Land for 3 ploughs.
   1 rider, 3 villagers and 3 smallholders have 1 plough.
Value before 1066, 10s; later 8s; now 12s.

11  WALLASEY. Uhtred held it; he was a free man. 1½ hides paying tax.
Land for 4 ploughs.
   1 villager and 1 smallholder with ½ plough; 1 Frenchman
      has 1 plough with 2 ploughmen; 1 rider and 1 smallholder.
   [Value . . .]

Robt⁹ cocus ten̄ de comite NESTONE. Ofgot tenuit 7 lib̄ hō fuit.

Ibi.i.hida geld̄.Tra.ē.iii.car̄.In dn̄io funt.ii.7 i.feruus.7 ii.uill̄
7 iiii.bord̄.cū.i.car̄.7 un̄ francig ibi.

T.R.E.ualb̄.xiii.fol 7 iiii.den̄.Modo xvi.fol.Wast inuenit.

Iſd Ro.ten̄ HAREGRAVE.Ofgot tenuit.Ibi.i.hida geld̄.Tra.ē
.ii.car̄.Ibi.iii.uilti 7 ii.bord̄ hn̄t.i.car̄.

T.R.E.ualb̄.vi.fol 7 viii.den̄.Modo.x.folid̄.Valuit. cū receṕ iiii.fol

*IN RISETON HD̄.*

RICARD⁹ de Vernon ten̄ ESTONE.Toret tenuit 7 lib̄ hō fuit.

Ibi.iiii.hidæ geld̄.Tra.ē.v.car̄.In dn̄io.ē una.7 ii.ferui.
7 v.uilti 7 ii.radmans.7 iii.bord̄ cū.ii.car̄.Ibi Silua
dim leuu lḡ.7 una ac̄ lat̄.

T.R.E.ualb̄.xvi.fol.Modo.xx.folid̄.Wast inuen̄.

Iſd Ri.ten̄ PICHETONE.Tochi tenuit. *IN WILAVESTON HD̄.*
7 lib̄ hō fuit.Ibi.i.hida geld̄.Tra.ē.iii.car̄.In dn̄io.ē una.
7 ii.bouar.7 i.radman 7 iii.bord̄ cū.i.car̄.Ibi dimid̄ ac̄ p̄ti.
T.R.E.ualb̄.xl.fol.7 poft.v.fol.Modo.xx.folid̄.

Iſd.Ri.ten̄ HOTONE.Tochi tenuit.Ibi.i.hida.7 ii.part.i.hidæ
geld̄.Tra.ē.iii.car̄.Ibi.iiii.radmans 7 un̄ uilts 7 iiii.bord̄
cū.ii.car̄.T.R.E.ualb̄.xxx.fol.7 poft.v.fol.Modo.xvi.folid̄.

Iſd.R.ten̄ COCHESHALLE.7 Pagen de eo. *IN TVNENDVN HD̄.*
Leuenot 7 Dedou.tenuer̄ p̄.ii.Ṁ.7 libi hōes fuer̄.Ibi dimid̄
hida geld̄.Tra.ē.i.car̄.Ibi.ē cū.i.radman 7 i.bord̄.Silua
una leuu lḡ.7 dimid̄ lat̄.T.R.E.ualb̄.ii.fol.Modo.v.folid̄.

Iſd.Ri.ten̄ SIBROC.Ofmer tenuit.lib̄ hō fuit. *IN MILDESTVICH HD̄.*
Ibi.ii.hidæ geld̄.Tra.ē.v.car̄.In dn̄io.ē una.7 ii.ferui.7 ii.uilti
cū.ii.car̄.Ibi.iii.ac̄ p̄ti.7 ii.ac̄ filuæ

T.R.E.ualb̄.xx.fol.Modo.x.fol.Wast inuen̄.

# 4
## Robert Cook holds

1    NESTON from the Earl. Osgot held it; he was a free man. 1 hide
     paying tax. Land for 3 ploughs. In lordship 2; 1 slave;
        2 villagers and 4 smallholders with 1 plough; 1 Frenchman.
     Value before 1066, 13s 4d; now 16s; found waste.

2    Robert also holds HARGRAVE. Osgot held it. 1 hide paying tax.
     Land for 2 ploughs.
        3 villagers and 2 smallholders have 1 plough.
     Value before 1066, 6s 8d; now 10s; value when acquired 4s.

# 5
## Richard of Vernon holds

### In EDDISBURY (South) Hundred

1    ASHTON. Thored held it; he was a free man. 4 hides paying tax.
     Land for 5 ploughs. In lordship 1; 2 slaves;
        5 villagers, 2 riders and 3 smallholders with 2 ploughs.
        Woodland ½ league long and 1 acre wide.
     Value before 1066, 16s; now 20s; found waste.

## Richard also holds

### In WIRRAL Hundred

2    PICTON. Toki held it; he was a free man. 1 hide paying tax.
     Land for 3 ploughs. In lordship 1; 2 ploughmen;
        1 rider and 3 smallholders with 1 plough.
        Meadow, ½ acre.
     Value before 1066, 40s; later 5s; now 20s.

3    HOOTON. Toki held it. 1 hide and two parts of 1 hide paying tax.
     Land for 3 ploughs.
        4 riders, 1 villager and 4 smallholders with 2 ploughs.
     Value before 1066, 30s; later 5s; now 16s.

### In BUCKLOW (West) Hundred

4    COGSHALL. Payne holds from him. Leofnoth and Dedol held it
     as 2 manors; they were free men. ½ hide paying tax.
     Land for 1 plough. It is there, with
        1 rider and 1 smallholder.
        Woodland 1 league long and ½ wide.
     Value before 1066, 2s; now 5s.

### In NORTHWICH Hundred

5    SHIPBROOK. Osmer held it; he was a free man. 2 hides paying tax.
     Land for 5 ploughs. In lordship 1; 2 slaves;
        2 villagers with 2 ploughs.
        Meadow, 3 acres; woodland, 2 acres.
     Value before 1066, 20s; now 10s; found waste.

Iſd.Ri.ten SVRVELEC.Eluuard 7 Bers tenueſ ꝓ.ii.ꝳ.7 liɓi fꝛt.

Ibi.i.hida gelđ.Tra.ē.ii.caꝛ.In dñio.ē una caꝛ.7 ii.ſerui.

7 ii.uilti cū dimiđ caꝛ.7 i.borđ.7 i.piſcaria.7 iii.aꝯ ꝓti.

T.R.E.ualɓ.viii.ſol.Modo.vii.ſol.Waſt inueñ.

Iſd.Ri.ten WICE.Oſmer 7 Alſi tenueſ ꝓ.ii.ꝳ.7 liɓi fueꝛ.

Ibi.i.hida gelđ.Tra.ē.iii.caꝛ.In dñio.ē una.7 ii.ſerui.7 iii.

uilti cū.i.caꝛ.7 iiii.aꝯ ꝓti.T.R.E.ualɓ.xii.ſol.modo.vi.ſol.

Iſd Ri.ten MOLETVNE.Leuenot tenuit.7 liɓ hō fuit.Ibi.i.hida

gelđ.Tra.ē.ii.caꝛ.Ibi.i.uiltſ 7 i.borđ hñt dimiđ caꝛ.

Ibi.i.aꝯ ꝓti.Silua.i.leuu lḡ.7 una lat.Ibi.i.haia.

Valuit 7 ual.v.ſol.

Iſd.Ri.ten WANETVNE.Haregrim 7 Alſi tenueſ ꝓ.ii.ꝳ
liɓi hōes fueꝛ.

Ibi dimiđ hida gelđ.Tra.ē.i.caꝛ.Ibi.ē in dñio.7 ii.ſerui.7 ii.

borđ.T.R.E.ualɓ.iiii.ſolid.Modo.vi.ſol.Waſt inueñ.

Iſd Ri.ten DEVENEHA.Oſmer tenuit.liɓ hō fuit.Ibi dimiđ hida

gelđ.Tra.ē.ii.caꝛ.In dñio.ē una caꝛ.7 ii.ſerui.7 pɓr cū æccła.

7 un uilt 7 un borđ cū dim caꝛ.Valɓ.viii.ſol.Modo.v.ſol.

Iſd Ri.ten BOTESTOCH.Oſmer tenuit.Ibi.i.hida gelđ.Tra.ē

.ii.caꝛ.Ibi ſunt cū.iii.radman 7 ii.ſeruis.7 ii.aꝯ ꝓti.7 ii.aꝯ

filuæ.T.R.E.ualɓ.iii.ſol.modo.x.ſol.Waſt inueñ.

Iſd.Ri.ten ALDELIME.Oſmer tenuit. IN WARMVNDESTROV HD.

Ibi.ii.hidæ gelđ.Tra.ē.v.caꝛ.In dñio.ē una.7 i.ſeruus.

7 i.uilt 7 i.radman 7 i.borđ cū.i.caꝛ.Ibi.ii.aꝯ ꝓti.Silua

.ii.leuu lḡ.7 i.leuu lat.7.ii.haiæ.7 aira accipitris.

T.R.E.ualɓ.xx.ſol.modo.viii.ſolid.Waſt inuenit.

Iſd.Ri.ten CREV.Oſmer tenuit.Ibi.i.hida gelđ.Tra.ē.ii.caꝛ.

Ibi.i.radman 7 un uilt 7 ii.borđ.cū.i.caꝛ.Ibi.i.aꝯ 7 dim

ꝓti.Silua.i.leuu lḡ.7 dimiđ lat.

T.R.E.ualɓ.x.ſol.modo.v.ſol.Waſt inueñ.

5

6   SHURLACH. Alfward and Bersi held it as 2 manors; they were
    free. 1 hide paying tax. Land for 2 ploughs.
    In lordship 1 plough; 2 slaves;
        2 villagers with ½ plough; 1 smallholder.
        1 fishery; meadow, 3 acres.
    Value before 1066, 8s; now 7s; found waste.

7   LEFTWICH. Osmer and Alfsi held it as 2 manors; they were free.
    1 hide paying tax. Land for 3 ploughs. In lordship 1; 2 slaves;
        3 villagers with 1 plough.
        Meadow, 4 acres.
    Value before 1066, 12s; now 6s.

8   MOULTON. Leofnoth held it; he was a free man. 1 hide paying tax.
    Land for 2 ploughs.
        1 villager and 1 smallholder have ½ plough.
        Meadow, 1 acre; woodland 1 league long and 1 wide; 1 enclosure.
    The value was and is 5s.

9   WHARTON. Arngrim and Alfsi held it as 2 manors; they were free
    men. ½ hide paying tax. Land for 1 plough.
    It is there, in lordship; 2 slaves;
        2 smallholders.
    Value before 1066, 4s; now 6s; found waste.

10  DAVENHAM. Osmer held it; he was a free man. ½ hide paying tax.
    Land for 2 ploughs. In lordship 1 plough; 2 slaves;
        a priest with a church; 1 villager and 1 smallholder with ½ plough.
    The value was 8s; now 5s.

11  BOSTOCK. Osmer held it. 1 hide paying tax. Land for 2 ploughs.
    They are there, with
        3 riders and 2 slaves.
        Meadow, 2 acres; woodland, 2 acres.
    Value before 1066, 3s; now 10s; found waste.

    In NANTWICH Hundred

12  AUDLEM. Osmer held it. 2 hides paying tax. Land for 5 ploughs.
    In lordship 1; 1 slave;
        1 villager, 1 rider and 1 smallholder with 1 plough.
        Meadow, 2 acres; woodland, 2 leagues long and 1 league wide;
            2 enclosures; a hawk's eyrie.
    Value before 1066, 20s; now 8s; found waste.

13  CREWE. Osmer held it. 1 hide paying tax. Land for 2 ploughs.
        1 rider, 1 villager and 2 smallholders with 1 plough.
        Meadow, 1½ acres; woodland 1 league long and ½ wide.
    Value before 1066, 10s; now 5s; found waste.

†   *(14 is added at the foot of the column, after 6,2, directed to its proper place by transposition
    signs)*

R<sup>pincerna</sup>ICARDVS ten de cõm PONTONE . Eduin tenuit.7 lib hõ fuit.

Ibi . 1 . hida geld.Tra̅ . ē . v . car̅.In dñio funt.111.car̅.7 v1.

bouar̅.7 p̅pofit 7 111.bord.cū.11.car̅.Ibi.v1н.ac̅ p̅ti.

T.R.E.ualb.xL.fol.7 poft tn̅td.Modo.1111.lib.

Ifd Ric̅.ten CALVINTONE . Dot tenuit.7 lib hõ fuit.Ibi.1r.

hidæ geld . Tra̅.ē.11.car̅.Wafta fuit 7 Waft̅a inueñ.

Modo.ē ad firmā ⫲ Lx.folid.   IN HAMESTAN HVND.

☞ Ifd Ric̅ de Vernon ten BRETBERIE 7 Vluric de eo.qui 7 tenuit ut lib hõ.

Ibi . 1 . hida geld.Tra̅.ē.111.car̅.Ibi.1.radman 7 v1.uilti 7 11.bord

hn̅t.1.car̅.Silua ibi.1.leuū lḡ.7 dimid leuu lat̅.7 111.haie 7 una

aire Accipitris.T.R.E.ualb.x.fol.Modo fimilit.

265 b                          IN RISETON HVND.

W<sup>comite</sup>ALTERIVS De Vernon ten de Hugone WINFLETONE.

Erniet tenuit 7 lib hõ fuit.Ibi . 1 . hida geld . Tra̅ . ē . 11.car̅.

Ibi . 11 . uilti hn̅t.1.car̅ . Silua ibi dimid leuu lḡ.7 una ac̅ lat̅.

T.R.E.ualb.v111.fol.Modo.x.fol.Waf̅t inuenit.

Ifd Walt̅ ten NESSE .Erniet tenuit. IN WILAVESTON HD

Ibi.1.hida 7 dimid geld.Tra̅.ē.11.car̅.In dñio.ē.1.7 11.bouar̅.

7 v.uilti 7 111 bord cū.11.car̅.Ibi dimid ac̅ p̅ti.

T.R.E.ualb.xx.fol.Modo.xv1.folid.

Ifd.W.ten LEVETESHA.Erniet tenuit.Ibi.1.hida geld.

Tra̅.ē.11.car̅.In dñio.ē dimid car̅.7 un feru.7 1.radman

7 un bord cū dimid car̅ int oms.

T.R.E.ualb.v.fol.7 poft.v111.fol.Modo.x.fol

Ifd.W.ten PRESTVNE . Vluiet Edric 7 Luuede tenuer̅

⫲.111.ꟽ.7 libi fuer̅.Ibi.1.hida 7 dim geld.Tra̅.ē.111.car̅.

In dñio.ē una.7 11.bouar̅.7 11.bord.Ibi moliñ feruieȿ curiæ:

Silua.1.leuu lḡ.7 una lat̅.Valb v11.fol.modo.v.folid.

**6** [In BROXTON Hundred]

1  **Richard Butler** holds POULTON from the Earl. Edwin held it; he was
a free man. 1 hide paying tax. Land for 5 ploughs.
In lordship 3 ploughs; 6 ploughmen;
   A reeve and 3 smallholders with 2 ploughs.
   Meadow, 8 acres.
Value before 1066, 40s; later the same; now £4.

2  Richard also holds *CALVINTONE*. Dot held it; he was a free man.
2 hides paying tax. Land for 2 ploughs.
It was, and was found, waste. It is now at a revenue for 60s.

†  *(directed to its proper place by transposition signs)*

In MACCLESFIELD Hundred

5,14  Richard of Vernon also holds BREDBURY. Wulfric, who also held it
as a free man, holds from him. 1 hide paying tax. Land for 3 ploughs.
   1 rider, 6 villagers and 2 smallholders have 1 plough.
   Woodland 1 league long and ½ league wide; 3 enclosures;
      1 hawk's eyrie.
Value before 1066, 10s; now the same.

**7**                                                        265 b

## Walter of Vernon holds

In EDDISBURY (South) Hundred

1  WILLINGTON from Earl Hugh. Erngeat held it; he was a free
man. 1 hide paying tax. Land for 2 ploughs.
   2 villagers have 1 plough.
   Woodland ½ league long and 1 acre wide.
Value before 1066, 8s; now 10s; found waste.

Walter also holds

in WIRRAL Hundred

2  NESS. Erngeat held it. 1½ hides paying tax. Land for 2 ploughs.
In lordship 1; 2 ploughmen;
   5 villagers and 3 smallholders with 2 ploughs.
   Meadow, ½ acre.
Value before 1066, 20s; now 16s.

3  LEDSHAM. Erngeat held it. 1 hide paying tax. Land for 2 ploughs.
In lordship ½ plough; 1 slave;
   1 rider and 1 smallholder with ½ plough between them.
Value before 1066, 5s; later 8s; now 10s.

4  PRENTON. Wulfgeat, Edric and Luvede held it as 3 manors· they
were free. 1½ hides paying tax. Land for 3 ploughs.
In lordship 1; 2 ploughmen;
   2 smallholders.
   A mill which serves the court; woodland 1 league long and 1 wide.
The value was 7s; now 5s.        265 a, b

WILLELM Malbedeng ten de Hugone comite TATENALE. Ernuin
tenuit 7 lib hõ fuit. Ibi. v. hidæ geld. Tra. ē. vi. car.
In dñio. ē una. 7 ii. uilli 7 ii. bord hñt aliã. 7 un francig tcia.
Ibi. i. leuu filue. T.R.E. ualb. xx. fol. modo. xxvi. Wast fuit.

Iſd Witts ten COLEVRNE. Loten tenuit. Ibi dimid hida geld.
Tra. ē. i. car. quæ ibi. ē in dñio. 7 ii. bouar cu. i. uilto. 7 iii. bord.
Ibi molin hiemale. Valb. v. fol. modo. vi. fol. Wast inuen.

Iſd. W. ten VLVRE. Vlfac tenuit        IN RISETON HVND.
7 lib hõ fuit. Ibi. ii. hidæ geld. Tra. ē. iiii. car. Ibi. i. radman
7 ii. uilli 7 iii. bord hñt. ii. car. Ibi. ii. ac pti. Silua. i. leuu lg.
7 dimid lat. T.R.E. ualb xl. fol. Modo. x. fol. Wast inuen.

Iſd. W. ten WIVREVENE. Colbt tenuit  IN WILAVESTON HD.
7 lib hõ fuit. Ibi. iii. pars uni hidæ geld. Tra. ē. i. car. Ibi funt
.ii. uilli cu dimid car. Valb. viii. fol. Modo. iiii. folid.

★ Iſd. W. ten POL. Ernuin tenuit p M. Ibi tra. iiii. bou geld.
Ibi. i. uill 7 i. bord hñt dimid car. Valuit 7 ual. iiii. folid.

Iſd. W. ten SALHALE. Leuing tenuit. 7 lib hõ fuit. Ibi vi.
hidæ geld. Tra. ē. vi. car. In dñio. ē una 7 dimid. 7 un feruus.
7 vii. uilli. 7 i. radman 7 iiii. bord cu. iii. car. 7 dim. Ibi pifcaria.
T.R.E. ualb. xx. fol. 7 poft. xxii. fol. Modo. xlv. folid.

Iſd. W. ten LANDECHENE. Efful tenuit. 7 lib hõ fuit. Ibi
vii. hidæ geld. Tra. ē. viii. car. In dñio. ē una. 7 pbr 7 ix.
uilli 7 vii. bord. 7 iiii. francig cu. v. car int oms.
T.R.E. ualb. l. fol. Modo. xl. fol. Wast inuen.

Iſd. W. ten OPTONE. 7 Colbt de eo. qui 7 tenuit ut lib hõ.
Ibi. iii. hidæ geld. Tra. ē. v. car. In dñio. ē una 7 iiii. ferui.
7 ii. uilli 7 un radman 7 iiii. bord cu. i. car. Ibi. ii. ac pti.
T.R.E. ualb. xxv. fol. Modo. xx. folid.

**William Malbank holds**

In BROXTON Hundred

1　TATTENHALL from Earl Hugh. Ernwin held it; he was a free man. 5 hides paying tax. Land for 6 ploughs. In lordship 1.
2 villagers and 2 smallholders have another, and 1 Frenchman a third.
Woodland, 1 league.
Value before 1066, 20s; now 26s; it was waste.

William also holds

2　GOLBORNE. Lothen held it. ½ hide paying tax. Land for 1 plough which is there, in lordship; 2 ploughmen, with
1 villager and 3 smallholders.
A winter mill.
The value was 5s; now 6s; found waste.

in EDDISBURY (South) Hundred

3　ULURE. Wulfheah held it; he was a free man. 2 hides paying tax. Land for 4 ploughs.
1 rider, 2 villagers and 3 smallholders have 2 ploughs.
Meadow, 2 acres; woodland 1 league long and ½ wide.
Value before 1066, 40s; now 10s; found waste.

in WIRRAL Hundred

4　WERVIN. Colbert held it; he was a free man. A third part of 1 hide paying tax. Land for 1 plough.
2 villagers with ½ plough.
The value was 8s; now 4s.

5　POOL. Ernwin held it as a manor. Land for 4 bovates paying tax.
1 villager and 1 smallholder have ½ plough.
The value was and is 4s.

6　SAUGHALL. Leofing held it; he was a free man. 6 hides paying tax. Land for 6 ploughs. In lordship 1½; 1 slave;
7 villagers, 1 rider and 4 smallholders with 3½ ploughs.
A fishery.
Value before 1066, 20s; later 22s; now 45s.

7　LANDICAN. Aescwulf held it; he was a free man. 7 hides paying tax. Land for 8 ploughs. In lordship 1;
a priest, 9 villagers, 7 smallholders and 4 Frenchmen with 5 ploughs between them.
Value before 1066, 50s; now 40s; found waste.

8　UPTON. Colbert, who also held it as a free man, holds from him. 3 hides paying tax. Land for 5 ploughs. In lordship 1; 4 slaves;
2 villagers, 1 rider and 4 smallholders with 1 plough.
Meadow, 2 acres.
Value before 1066, 25s; now 20s.

Iſd.W.ten̄ *TVIGVELLE*.7 Durand̄ de eo.Wintrelet tenuit
7 lib̄ hō fuit.Ibi.ɪ.hida geld̄.Tra.ē.ɪɪ.car̄.In dn̄io.ē una.
7 ɪɪ.ſerui.7 ɪ.uiłłs 7 ɪ.bord̄ hn̄t aliā.

T.R.E.ualb̄.vɪɪɪ.ſoł.modo.v.ſolid̄.

Iſd.W.ten̄ *CHENOTERIE*.7 Ricard̄ de eo.Colb̄t tenuit 7 lib̄
hō fuit.Ibi dimid̄ hida geld̄.Tra.ē.ɪ.car̄.quæ ibi.ē in dn̄io
cū.ɪɪ.bouar̄.7 ɪɪ.uiłłis.Valuit.xv.ſoł.Modo.x.ſoł.Waſt fuit.

Iſd.W.ten̄ *ETESHALE*.Outi tenuit. *IN MILDESTVIC HD̄.*
7 lib̄ hō fuit.Ibi dimid̄ hida geld̄.Tra.ē.ɪɪ.car̄.Ibi.ɪ.radman
cū dimid̄ car̄.7 ɪ.ſeruo.7 ɪ.radman 7 ɪɪ.uiłłi 7 ɪɪɪ.bord̄ cū.ɪ.car̄.
Silua.ɪ.lcuū lḡ.7 haia ibi 7 aira accipitris.

T.R.E.ualb̄.ɪɪɪɪ.ſoł.Modo.v.ſoł.

Iſd.W.ten̄ *ETESHALE*.Godric tenuit 7 lib̄ hō fuit.Ibi dimid̄
hida geld̄.Tra.ē.ɪɪ.car̄.Ibi.ɪ.radman cū.ɪ.bord̄ h̄t dim car̄.
T.R.E.ualb̄.v.ſoł.Modo.v.ſoł.Waſt fuit.

265 c

Iſd Wiłłs ten̄ *MANESSELE*.Leuenot tenuit 7 lib̄.hō fuit.Ibi
una hida geld̄.Tra.ē.ɪ.car̄.Ibi.ɪ.radman 7 ɪɪ.ſerui.7 ɪɪ.bord̄
hn̄t.ɪ.car̄.Ibi.ɪ.ac̄ p̄ti.Silua.ɪ.leuū lḡ.7 una lat̄.7 ɪɪɪɪ.haiæ.
7 aira accipitris.Valb̄ 7 uał.ɪɪɪɪ.ſoł.Waſt ſuit.

Iſd.W.ten̄ *MANESHALE*.Derch 7 Aregrim tenuer̄ p.ɪɪ.m̄
7 libi hōes fuer̄.Ibi.ɪ.hida geld̄.Tra.ē.ɪɪ.car̄.Ibi ſunt cū
.ɪɪɪ.radmans 7 ɪɪ.bord̄.Ibi.ɪ.ac̄ p̄ti.7 Silua dimid̄ leuū lḡ
7 dim lat̄.7 haia.7 aira accipitris.Valb̄.ɪɪɪɪ.ſoł.m̄.vɪɪɪ.ſoł.

Iſd.W.ten̄ *SPROSTVNE*.Elmær tenuit 7 lib̄ fuit.Ibi
dimid̄ hida geld̄.Tra.ē.ɪ.car̄.Ibi.ē cū.ɪ.radman 7 ɪ.ſeruo.
7 ɪɪ.uiłł 7 ɪɪ.bord̄.Ibi dimid̄ ac̄ p̄ti.Silua.ɪɪ.q̄ʒ lḡ.

T.R.E.ualb̄.v.ſoł.Modo.ɪɪɪɪ.ſoł.Waſt inuen̄. *HVND.*

Iſd.W.ten̄ *ACTVNE*.Morcar tenuit. *IN WARMVNDESTROV*
Ibi.vɪɪɪ.hidæ geld̄.Tra.ē.xxx.car̄.In dn̄io ſunt.ɪɪɪ.7 ɪɪ.ſerui.

9   THINGWALL. Durand holds from him. Winterlet held it; he was
a free man. 1 hide paying tax. Land for 2 ploughs.
In lordship 1; 2 slaves .
    1 villager and 1 smallholder have another (plough).
Value before 1066, 8s; now 5s.

10   NOCTORUM. Richard holds from him. Colbertheld it; he was a free
man. ½ hide paying tax. Land for 1 plough, which is there, in
lordship, with 2 ploughmen;
    2 villagers.
The value was 15s; now 10s; it was waste.

in NORTHWICH Hundred

11   HASSALL. Auti held it; he was a free man. ½ hide paying tax.
Land for 2 ploughs.
    1 rider with ½ plough and 1 slave; 1 rider, 2 villagers and
        3 smallholders with 1 plough.
    Woodland 1 league long; an enclosure; a hawk's eyrie.
Value before 1066, 4s; now 5s.

12   HASSALL. Godric held it; he was a free man. ½ hide paying tax.
Land for 2 ploughs.
    1 rider with 1 smallholder has ½ plough.
Value before 1066, 5s; now 5s; it was waste.

13   MINSHULL. Leofnoth held it; he was a free man. 1 hide paying tax.   265 c
Land for 1 plough.
    1 rider, 2 slaves and 2 smallholders have 1 plough.
    Meadow, 1 acre; woodland 1 league long and 1 wide; 4 enclosures;
      a hawk's eyrie.
The value was and is 4s; it was waste.

14   MINSHULL. Derch and Arngrim held it as 2 manors; they were free
men. 1 hide paying tax. Land for 2 ploughs. They are there, with
    3 riders and 2 smallholders.
    Meadow, 1 acre; woodland ½ league long and ½ wide;
      an enclosure; a hawk's eyrie.
The value was 4s; now 8s.

15   SPROSTON. Aelmer held it; he was free. ½ hide paying tax. Land
for 1 plough. It is there, with
    1 rider and 1 slave;
    2 villagers and 2 smallholders.
    Meadow, ½ acre; woodland 2 furlongs long.
Value before 1066, 5s; now 4s; found waste.

in NANTWICH Hundred

16   ACTON. Earl Morcar held it. 8 hides paying tax. Land for 30 ploughs.
In lordship 3; 2 slaves;

7 XIII.uilł 7 xv.borđ cū.vII.cař.Ibi molin̄ ſeruieɟs curiæ

7 x.ãc p̄ti.Silua.vI.leuū lḡ.7 una lař.7 una Aira accipitris.

Ibi.II.p̄bri cū.I.cař.7 II.francig hn̄tes.I.cař 7 dim̄.7 I.ſeruū.

7 vI.uilłos 7 vII.borđ cū.IIII.cař.

Hoc c͠ø hŧ ſuū placiŧ in aula dn̄i ſui.7 in.Wich.I.domū đetã

ad ſal faciendū.Toŧ T.R.E.ualb̄.x.lib̄.Modo.vI.lib̄.

Iſđ.W.ten̄ ESTVNE.Dot tenuit.7 lib̄ hō fuit.Ibi.I.hida gelđ.

Ťra.ē.II.cař.In dn̄io.ē.I.7 II.bouař.7 II.uilłi 7 III.borđ hn̄t

aliã cař.Ibi Silua.I.leuu lḡ.7 tntđ lař.

T.R.E.ualb̄.x.ſoł.Modo.v.ſolđ.Waſŧ inuen̄.

Iſđ.W.ten WILAVESTVNE.Vluiet tenuit. lib̄ hō Ibi.I.v geld.

Ťra.ē dimiđ cař.Ibi.ē.I.borđ.Valb̄.v.ſoł.Modo.II.ſolđ.

Iſđ.W.ten WARENEBERIE.Carłe tenuit.7 lib̄ hō fuit.

Ibi.I.hida 7 dim̄ gelđ.Ťra.ē.II.cař.In dn̄io.ē una.7 II.bouař.

7.I.borđ.Ibi Silua.II.leuu lḡ.7 una lař.7 II.haiæ.7 aira

accipitris.Valuit 7 uał.v.ſoł.Waſŧ inuen̄.

Iſđ.W.ten CERLETVNE.Fran̄ tenuit.7 lib̄ hō fuit.Ibi dim̄

hida gelđ.Ťra.ē.dim̄ cař.Ibi.ē un̄ uilłs cū.II.bob.

valuit 7 uał.II.ſoł.Waſŧ inuen̄.

Iſđ.W.ten MERBERIE de.I.hida 7 dimiđ.7 NORBERIE

de.I.hida 7 dim̄.7 WIRESWELLE.de.I.hida.Hæ træ gelđ.

Bereuuicħ fuer̄.In WESTONE iacuer̄.Herald com̄ tenuit.

Ťra.ē.v.cař.In dn̄io.ē una.7 II.bouař.7 II.uilłi 7 III.borđ

cū.I.cař.Silua.II.leuu lḡ.7 I.leuu lŧ.7 XL.ptic.

Toŧ T.R.E.ualb̄.xxI.ſoł.Modo.x.ſoł.Wireſuelle.ē waſta.

Iſđ.W.ten WALCRETVNE.Gunninc 7 Alden tenuer̄. ⊕

7 libi hōes fuer̄.⊕p.II.c͠ø.Ibi.I.hida 7 una v gelđ.Ťra.ē

II.cař.Ibi.ē una cū.I.bouař.7 I.radman.7 II.borđ.

T.R.E.ualb̄.Ix.ſolđ.Modo.v.ſoł.Waſŧ inuen̄.

13 villagers and 15 smallholders with 7 ploughs.
A mill which serves the Court; meadow, 10 acres; woodland
   6 leagues long and 1 wide; a hawk's eyrie.
2 priests with 1 plough; 2 Frenchmen who have 1½ ploughs and
   1 slave; 6 villagers and 7 smallholders with 4 ploughs.
This manor has its assembly in its lord's hall, and has 1 exempt
   house for salt-making in Nantwich.
Total value before 1066 £10; now £6.

17  ASTON. Dot held it; he a free man. 1 hide paying tax. Land for
    2 ploughs. In lordship 1; 2 ploughmen.
       2 villagers and 3 smallholders have the other plough.
    Woodland 1 league long and as wide.
    Value before 1066, 10s; now 5s; found waste.

18  WILLASTON. Wulfgeat, a free man, held it. 1 virgate paying tax.
    Land for ½ plough.
       1 smallholder.
    The value was 5s; now 2s.

19  WRENBURY. Karl held it; he was a free man. 1½ hides paying tax.
    Land for 2 ploughs. In lordship 1; 2 ploughmen;
       1 smallholder.
    Woodland 2 leagues long and 1 wide; 2 enclosures; a hawk's eyrie.
    The value was and is 5s; found waste.

20  CHORLTON. Fran held it; he was a free man. ½ hide paying tax.
    Land for ½ plough.
       1 villager with 2 oxen.
    The value was and is 2s; found waste.

21  MARBURY at 1½ hides; NORBURY at 1½ hides; WIRSWALL at 1 hide.
    These lands pay tax. They were outliers, and lay in (the lands of)
    Whitchurch; Earl Harold held them. Land for 5 ploughs.
    In lordship 1; 2 ploughmen;
       2 villagers and 3 smallholders with 1 plough.
    Woodland 2 leagues long and 1 league and 40 perches wide.
    Total value before 1066, 21s; now 10s; Wirswall is waste.

22  WALGHERTON. Gunning and Haldane held it as 2 manors; they were
    free men. 1 hide and 1 virgate paying tax. Land for 2 ploughs.
    1 there, with 1 ploughman;
       1 rider and 2 smallholders.
    Value before 1066, 9s; now 5s; found waste.

Iſđ.W.teñ SANTVNE.Goduin 7 Dot tenueř.7 liƀi fueř.

Ibi.III.uirg̃ gelđ. p.II.Ⅽⅿ.Tra.ē.I.cař.Ibi.I.rad|ᵐᵃⁿ hẽ dimiđ cař.7 II.borđ.T.R.E.ualƀ.IIII.ſoł.Modo.III.ſoł.Waſt inuen.

ħ.II.ᷱ
T.R.E.ualƀ
XL.ſoł.
Modo x.ſoł

Iſđ.W.teñ BVRTVNE.Seuuarđ tenuit.7 liƀ hõ fuit.Ibi.I.hida gelđ.Tra.ē.III.cař.In dñio ſunt.II.7 uñ bouař.Ibi Silua dimiđ leuu lg̃.7 tñtđ laŧ.7 III.haiæ.7 aira Accipitris.Vł.x.ſoł.

Iſđ.W.teñ HARETONE.Vlchetel tenuit.7 liƀ hõ fuit.Ibi.I. hida gelđ.Tra.ē.v.cař.In dñio.ē una.7 II.bouař.7 II.uiłłi 7 uñ borđ cũ.I.cař.Silua ibi dimiđ leuu lg̃.7 tñtđ laŧ.Ibi.I.haia.

Iſđ.W.teñ WISTANESTVNE Vluric tenuit 7 liƀ hõ fuit. Ibi.I.hida gelđ.Tra.ē.v.cař.In dñio.ē una.7 II.bouař. 7 II.uiłłi 7 uñ radman 7 II.borđ cũ.I.cař.Ibi dimiđ aꝯ p̃ti. Silua.I.leuu lg̃.7 dimiđ laŧ.7 II.haiæ.

T.R.E.ualƀ.xxx.ſoł.Modo.x.ſoliđ.

Iſđ.W.teñ BERCHESFORD.Ouuin Erlechin 7 Leuric tenueř p.III.Maneř.7 liƀi hõēs fueř.Ibi.I.hida gelđ.Tra.ē.II.cař. Ibi.III.radmans 7 II.uiłłi 7 III.borđ.hñt.I.cař.Ibi.I.virg̃ p̃ti. Silua.IIII.q̃z lg̃.7 una laŧ.Valƀ.v.ſoł.Modo ſimiliŧ.

Waſta fueř.

265 d

Iſđ.W.teñ BERDELTVNE.Halđen 7 Derch tenueř p.II.Ⅽⅿ.7 liƀi hõēs fueř.Ibi dimiđ hida gelđ.Tra.ē.II.cař.In dñio.ē uña. 7 II.boŧiar.7 I.uiłłs 7 II.borđ.Ibi.XL.p̃tic ſiluæ.

T.R.E.ualƀ.vI.ſoliđ.Modo.III.ſoł.Waſŧ inuenit.

Iſđ.W.teñ WERBLESTVNE.Ꜧacon Eluuarđ 7 Elric tenueř p.III.Ⅽⅿ.7 liƀi fueř.Ibi dimiđ hida gelđ.Tra.ē.II.cař.In dñio eſt una.7 II.bouař.7 I.uiłł 7 I.radman 7 II.borđ cũ.I.cař. Ibi ſilua dimiđ leuu lg̃.7 dimiđ laŧ.7 una haia.

T.R.E.ualƀ.vII.ſoł 7 IIII.deñ.Modo.vIII.ſoliđ.Waſŧ fuit.

23 SHAVINGTON. Godwin and Dot held it as 2 manors; they were free.
3 virgates paying tax. Land for 1 plough.
    1 rider has ½ plough and 2 smallholders.
Value before 1066, 4s; now 3s; found waste.

24 BUERTON. Siward held it; he was a free man. 1 hide paying tax.
Land for 3 ploughs. In lordship 2; 1 ploughman.
    Woodland ½ league long and as wide; 3 enclosures; a hawk's eyrie.
Value 10s.

25 HATHERTON. Ulfketel held it; he was a free man. 1 hide paying tax.
Land for 5 ploughs. In lordship 1; 2 ploughman;
    2 villagers and 1 smallholder with 1 plough.
    Woodland ½ league long and as wide; 1 enclosure.
Value of these 2 manors before 1066, 40s; now 10s.

26 WISTASTON. Wulfric held it; he was a free man. 1 hide paying tax.
Land for 5 ploughs. In lordship 1; 2 ploughmen;
    2 villagers, 1 rider and 2 smallholders with 1 plough.
    Meadow, ½ acre; woodland 1 league long and ½ wide; 2 enclosures.
Value before 1066, 30s; now 10s.

27 BASFORD. Owen, Erlechin and Leofric held it as 3 manors; they were
free men. 1 hide paying tax. Land for 2 ploughs.
    3 riders, 2 villagers and 3 smallholders have 1 plough.
    Meadow, 1 virgate; woodland 4 furlongs long and 1 wide.
The value was 5s; now the same; they were waste.

28 BATHERTON. Haldane and Derch held it as 2 manors; they were free   265 d
men. ½ hide paying tax. Land for 2 ploughs. In lordship 1;
2 ploughmen;
    1 villager and 2 smallholders.
    Woodland, 40 perches.
Value before 1066, 6s; now 3s; found waste.

29 WORLESTON. Hakon, Alfward and Aelfric held it as 3 manors; they
were free. ½ hide paying tax. Land for 2 ploughs. In lordship 1;
2 ploughmen;
    1 villager, 1 rider and 2 smallholders with 1 plough.
    Woodland ½ league long and ½ wide; 1 enclosure.
Value before 1066, 7s 4d; now 8s; it was waste.

Iſd.W.ten̄ BERTEMELEV.Seuuard tenuit 7 lib̄ hō fuit.Ibi

una hida geld̄.Tra.ē.iii.car̄.In dn̄io.ē una.7.ii.bouar̄.Pb̄r

7 un̄ radman 7 i.uiłł 7 ii.bord cū.ii.car̄.Ibi.i.ac̄ p̄ti.Silua

una leuu lḡ.7 dimid̄ lat̄.7 una haia.7 aira accipitris.

Valuit 7 uał.xx.solid̄.Waſt inuen̄.

Iſd.W.ten̄ ESSETVNE.Oſmer 7 Ouuin̄ tenuer̄ p.ii.ꞯ.7 libi

hōēs fuer̄.Ibi.iii.virḡ geld̄.Tra.ē.v.car̄.In dn̄io.ē una.

7 ii.bouar̄.7 iii.bord cū.i.car̄.Ibi.i.ac̄ p̄ti.Silua.i.leuū lḡ.

7 dimid̄ lat̄.Ibi.iii.haiæ.7 una aira accipitris.

T.R.E.ualb̄.xx.solid̄.Modo.x.solid̄.Waſt inuen̄.

Iſd.W.ten̄ WIVELESDE.Dot 7 Godric tenuer̄ p.ii.ꞯ

7 libi hōēs fuer̄.Ibi.i.hida 7 una virḡ geld̄.Tra.ē.iii.car̄.

Ibi.i.radman 7 i.uiłł 7 vi.bord hn̄t.i.car̄.Ibi.i.ac̄ p̄ti.

Silua.i.leuu lḡ.7 tn̄td̄ lat̄.7 v.haiæ.7 una aira accipit̄.

T.R.E.ualb̄.xviii.solid̄.Modo.v.solid̄.

Iſd.W.ten̄ TITESLE.Edric tenuit 7 lib̄ hō fuit.Ibi.iii.virḡ

geld̄.Tra.ē.i.car̄.Ibi.ē cū.ii.uiłłis 7 ii.bord.Silua ibi

dimid̄ leuu lḡ.7 tn̄td̄ lat̄.Valb̄.iiii.soł.modo.v.solid̄.

Iſd.W.ten̄ STEPLE.Eluric 7 Dot p.ii.ꞯ tenuer̄.7 libi hōēs fuer̄.

Ibi dimid̄ hida geld̄.Tra.ē.ii.car̄.Ibi.ē una cū.ii.bouar̄.

7 uno uiłło 7 i.bord.Ibi.i.ac̄ p̄ti.Silua dim̄ leuu lḡ.7 tn̄td̄

lat̄.T.R.E.ualb̄.x.soł.Modo.vi.soł.Waſt inuen̄.

Iſd.W.ten̄ WISTETESTVNE.Leuuin̄ 7 Oſmer p.ii.ꞯ tenuer̄.

7 libi fuer̄.Ibi.iii.virḡ geld̄.Tra.ē.ii.car̄.In dn̄io.ē una

7 dimid̄.7 iii.bouar̄.7 i.uiłłs cū dimid̄ car̄.7 i.bord.Ibi.i.p̄tica

p̄ti.Silua dimid̄ leuu lḡ.7 tn̄td̄ lat̄.Valb̄.viii.soł.m̄.x.soł.

Iſd.W.ten̄ BRVNHALA.Edric 7 Edric p.ii.ꞯ tenuer̄.7 libi

fuer̄.Ibi dimid̄ hida geld̄.Tra.ē.i.car̄.In dn̄io.ē dimid̄.cū

uno bouar̄.Silua.ē.i.leuu lḡ.7 dimid̄ lat̄ 7 haia ibi.

30 BARTHOMLEY. Siward held it; he was a free man. 1 hide paying
tax. Land for 3 ploughs. In lordship 1; 2 ploughmen;
    a priest, 1 rider, 1 villager and 2 smallholders with 2 ploughs.
    Meadow, 1 acre; woodland 1 league long and ½ wide;
        1 enclosure; a hawk's eyrie.
The value was and is 20s; found waste.

31 AUSTERSON. Osmer and Owen held it as 2 manors; they were
free men. 3 virgates paying tax. Land for 5 ploughs. In lordship 1;
2 ploughmen;
    3 smallholders with 1 plough.
    Meadow, 1 acre; woodland 1 league long and ½ wide;
        3 enclosures; a hawks eyrie.
Value before 1066, 20s; now 10s; found waste.

32 WILKESLEY. Dot and Godric held it as 2 manors; they were
free men. 1 hide and 1 virgate paying tax. Land for 3 ploughs.
    1 rider, 1 villager and 6 smallholders have 1 plough.
    Meadow, 1 acre; woodland 1 league long and as wide;
        5 enclosures; a hawk's eyrie.
Value before 1066, 18s; now 5s.

33 TITTENLEY. Edric held it; he was a free man. 3 virgates paying tax.
Land for 1 plough. It is there, with
    2 villagers and 2 smallholders.
    Woodland ½ league long and as wide.
The value was 4s; now 5s.

34 STAPELEY. Aelfric and Dot held it as 2 manors; they were free men.
½ hide paying tax. Land for 2 ploughs. 1 there with 2 ploughmen;
    1 villager and 1 smallholder.
    Meadow, 1½ acres; woodland ½ league long and as wide.
Value before 1066, 10s; now 6s; found waste.

35 'WISTERSON'. Leofwin and Osmer held it as 2 manors; they were free.
3 virgates paying tax. Land for 2 ploughs. In lordship
1½; 3 ploughmen;
    1 villager with ½ plough and 1 smallholder.
    Meadow, 1 perch; woodland ½ league long and as wide.
The value was 8s; now 10s.

36 BROOMHALL. Edric and Edric held it as 2 manors; they were free.
½ hide paying tax. Land for 1 plough. In lordship ½, with
1 ploughman.
    Woodland 1 league long and ½ wide; an enclosure.

T.R.E.ualb.IIII.fot.Modo.II.fot.Wast inuen.Vna v́ iaceƀ in

Iſđ.W.ten̑ POL.Hacon tenuit 7 liƀ hō fuit.　⌐pol �common̄aner.

Ibi dimiđ hida gelđ.Tra.e̅.I.caȓ.Ipſa.e̅ in dn̅io.cū.II.bouaȓ
7 III.borđ.Ibi dimiđ ac̑ p̑ti.Valƀ.v.fot.Modo.vIII.ſoliđ.

Iſđ.W.ten̑ TERETH.Leuuin̑ 7 Oſmer ꝑ.II.cōm̄ tenueȓ.7 liƀi
hōes fueȓ.Ibi.I.uirg̅ gelđ.Tra.e̅.II.caȓ.Ibi.III.uiłłi
hn̅t.I.7 ibi.IIII.ac̑ p̑ti.7 Silua dimiđ leuū łg̅.7 III.q̅ʒ lat̑.
T.R.E.ualƀ.vII.ſoliđ.Modo.v.ſoliđ.

Iſđ.W.ten̑ CERLERE.Aluric liƀ hō tenuit.Ibi.III.virg̅
gelđ.Tra.e̅.I.caȓ 7 dim.Ibi ſunt.II.uiłłi 7 I.borđ.cū dim caȓ.
Silua dimiđ leuū łg̅.7 II.q̅ʒ lat̑.Ibi haia.Vat.III.ſoliđ.

Iſđ.W.ten̑ BEDELEI.Aluric liƀ hō tenuit.Ibi dimiđ virg̅
gelđ.Tra.e̅.I.caȓ.quæ ibi.e̅ in dn̅io.Silua dim̑ leuū łg̅.
7 tn̅tđ lat̑.Ibi haia.　Valƀ.x.ſoliđ.Modo.v.fot.

Iſđ.W.ten̑.I.bereuuick̑ STANLEV.H̄ iaceƀ in WESTONE.
Herald com̄ tenuit.Ibi dimiđ uirg̅ gelđ.Tra.e̅.II.boƀʒ.Ibi.e̅
un̑ radman.Silua.dimiđ leuū łg̅.7 dimiđ lat̑.Ibi haia.

Valuit 7 uat.II.ſoliđ.

Iſđ.W.ten̑ COPEHALE.Halden 7 Vlfac ꝑ.II.cōm̄ tenueȓ.7 liƀi
fueȓ.Ibi.I.hida gelđ.Tra.e̅.IIII.caȓ.In dn̅io.e̅ una.7 II.bouaȓ.
7 I.radman 7 I.uiłł 7 I.borđ.cū.I.caȓ.Ibi.III.acræ p̑ti.
Silua.I.leuū łg̅.7 una lat̑.Ibi.II.haiæ.

T.R.E.ualƀ.xxIIII.ſoliđ.Modo.xII.ſoliđ.

266 a

Iſđ.W.ten̑ POL.Vlueua tenuit.7 liƀa fuit.Ibi.I.virg̅ gelđ.
Tra.e̅.I.caȓ.Ibi.e̅ un̑ uiłłs 7 III.borđ cū dimiđ caȓ.Ibi.II.ac̑
p̑ti.7 una ac̑ filuæ modicæ.Valuit 7 uat.III.ſoliđ.

Iſđ.W.ten̑ ESTONE.Rauecate tenuit 7 liƀ fuit.Ibi.I.virg̅
gelđ.Tra.e̅.I.caȓ.Ibi.I.radman h̄t dimiđ caȓ cū.II.borđ.
Ibi.I.ac̑ p̑ti 7 dim.Silua.I.leuū łg̅.7 dimiđ lat̑.

Valƀ.v.ſoliđ.Modo.III.ſoliđ.Wast fuit.

Value before 1066, 4s; now 2s; found waste.
 1 virgate lay in Poole manor.

37   POOLE. Hakon held it. he was a free man. ½ hide paying tax.
Land for 1 plough. It is there in lordship, with 2 ploughmen;
 3 smallholders.
 Meadow, ½ acre.
The value was 5s; now 8s.

38   FRITH. Leofwin and Osmer held it as 2 manors; they were free men.
1 virgate paying tax. Land for 2 ploughs.
 3 villagers have 1 [plough].
 Meadow, 4 acres; woodland ½ league long and 3 furlongs wide.
Value before 1066, 7s; now 5s.

39   CHORLEY. Aelfric, a free man, held it. 3 virgates paying tax.
Land for 1½ ploughs.
 2 villagers and 1 smallholder with ½ plough.
 Woodland ½ league long and 2 furlongs wide; an enclosure.
Value 3s.

40   BADDILEY. Aelfric, a free man, held it. ½ virgate paying tax.
Land for 1 plough, which is there, in lordship.
 Woodland ½ league long and as wide; an enclosure.
The value was 10s; now 5s.

41   One outlier, STONELEY. It lay in (the lands of) Whitchurch. Earl
Harold held it. ½ virgate paying tax. Land for 2 oxen.
 1 rider.
 Woodland ½ league long and ½ wide; an enclosure.
The value was and is 2s.

42   COPPENHALL. Haldane and Wulfheah held it as 2 manors; they were
free. 1 hide paying tax. Land for 4 ploughs. In lordship 1;
2 ploughmen;
 1 rider, 1 villager and 1 smallholder with 1 plough.
 Meadow, 3 acres; woodland 1 league long and 1 wide; 2 enclosures.
Value before 1066, 24s; now 12s.

43   POOLE. Wulfeva held it; she was free. 1 virgate paying tax. Land for   266 a
1 plough.
 1 villager and 3 smallholders with ½ plough.
 Meadow, 2acres; a small wood, 1 acre.
The value was and is 3s.

44   ASTON. Ravenkel held it; he was free. 1 virgate paying tax. Land
for 1 plough.
 1 rider has ½ plough with 2 smallholders.
 Meadow, 1½ acres; woodland 1 league long and ½ wide.
The value was 5s; now 3s; it was waste.

Iſd . W . teñ *CHELMVNDESTONE* ; Vlueua tenuit 7 liƀa fuit.
Ibi . I . hida gelđ . Tra . ē . II . car . Ibi . ē uñ radman hñs . I . car.
7 III . uiłłi cū . I . car . T.R.E . ualƀ . x . ſoł . Modo . VI . ſoliđ.

## IN CESTRE HVNDR.

Wiłłs filius Nigelli teñ de Hugone comite *NEWENTONE*
Erne tenuit . Ibi . I . hida gelđ . Tra . ē . III . car . In dñio
ſunt . II . 7 IIII . bouar . 7 VI . uiłłi cū . I . car.

T.R.E . ualƀ . xx . ſoł . 7 poſt . x . ſoł . Modo . xx . ſoliđ.
Iſd . W . teñ *LEE* . Erne tenuit . Ibi . I . virg gelđ . Tra . ē
dimiđ car . Ibi . ē cū . III . uiłłis . Valƀ . v . ſoł . modo . VIII . ſoł.
Iſd . W . teñ unā car træ in *BRVGE* . gelđ . Erne tenuit
ꝑ M̄ . Ibi ſunt . III . borđ hñtes dimiđ cař.

Valƀ . x . ſoliđ . modo . IIII . ſoliđ.     IN *DVDESTAN* HD̄
Iſd . W . teñ *CLVTONE* . Eduuarđ 7 Vluuinchit ꝑ . II . M̄ tenueř:
7 liƀi hōes fueř . Ibi . I . hida gelđ . Tra . ē . II . cař . In dñio . ē
dimiđ cař . 7 uñ franciģ cū . III . uiłłis hƚ dimiđ cař . Ibi di
midia aĉ ꝑti . Siluæ dimiđ leuua.

T.R.E . ualƀ . xx . ſoł . modo . VIII . ſoliđ . IN *RISETON* HVND.
Iſd . W . teñ *BERO* . Toreth tenuit . 7 liƀ hō fuit . Ibi . III . hidæ
gelđ . Tra . ē . VIII . cař . Ibi . ē . I . in dñio . 7 II . bouar . 7 II . uiłłi
7 IIII . borđ 7 II . franciģ . Int eos . ē . I . cař . Ibi . II . molini de . x .
ſoliđ . 7 I . aĉ ꝑti . Silua . I . leuu łg . 7 dimiđ lat.        ꟼ HD̄.
T.R.E . ualƀ . xxx . ſoł . modo tñtđ . Waſt inueñ . IN *WILAVESTON*
Iſd . W . teñ *NESTONE* . Erne tenuit 7 liƀ hō fuit . Ibi . II . part
duař hidař gelđ . Tra . ē . IIII . cař . In dñio ſunt . II . cař . 7 I . ſeruus .
Pƀr 7 IIII . uiłłi 7 II . borđ hñt ibi . III . cař.

T.R.E . ualƀ . xx . ſoł . 7 poſt tñtđ . Modo . xxv . ſoliđ.
Iſd . W . teñ *RABIE* . 7 Harduiñ de eo . Erni tenuit . Ibi dimiđ
hida gelđ . Tra . ē . I . cař . In dñio . ē ibi . 7 uñ ſeruus . 7 II . uiłłi
7 II . borđ cū . I . cař.

T.R.E . ualƀ . x . ſoliđ . 7 poſt . XIIII . ſoł . Modo . xx . ſoliđ.

45    CHOLMONDESTON. Wulfeva held it; she was free. 1 hide paying tax.
Land for 2 ploughs.
     1 rider who has 1 plough; 3 villagers with 1 plough.
Value before 1066, 10s; now 6s.

# 9

**William son of Nigel** holds
In CHESTER Hundred
1    NEWTON from Earl Hugh. Arni held it. 1 hide paying tax. Land
for 3 ploughs. In lordship 2; 4 ploughmen;
     6 villagers with 1 plough.
Value before 1066, 20s; later 10s; now 20s.

William also holds
2    NETHERLEIGH. Arni held it. 1 virgate paying tax. Land for ½ plough.
It is there, with
     3 villagers.
The value was 5s; now 8s.

3    In HANDBRIDGE 1 carucate of land paying tax. Arni held it as a manor.
     3 smallholders who have ½ plough.
The value was 10s; now 4s.

  in BROXTON Hundred
4    CLUTTON. Edward and Young Wulfwin held it as 2 manors; they were
free men. 1 hide paying tax. Land for 2 ploughs. In lordship ½ plough.
     1 Frenchman with 3 villagers has ½ plough.
     Meadow, ½ acre; woodland ½ league.
Value before 1066, 20s; now 8s.

  in EDDISBURY (South) Hundred
5    BARROW. Thored held it; he was a free man. 3 hides paying tax. Land
for 8 ploughs. In lordship 1; 2 ploughmen;
     2 villagers, 4 smallholders and 2 Frenchmen; 1 plough between
       them.
     2 mills at 10s; meadow, 1 acre; woodland 1 league long and ½ wide.
Value before 1066, 30s; now as much; found waste.

  in WIRRAL Hundred
6    NESTON. Arni held it; he was a free man. 2 parts of 2 hides paying
tax. Land for 4 ploughs. In lordship 2 ploughs; 1 slave.
     A priest, 4 villagers and 2 smallholders have 3 ploughs.
Value before 1066, 20s; later as much; now 25s.

7    RABY. Hardwin holds from him. Arni held it. ½ hide paying tax.
Land for 1 plough. It is there, in lordship; 1 slave;
     2 villagers and 2 smallholders with 1 plough.
Value before 1066, 10s; later 14s; now 20s.

Iſd.W.ten CAPELES.7 Dauid de eo.Ibi dimiđ hida gelđ.

Erne tenuit.Tra.ē.ı.car.Ibi.ē cū.ı.uiłło 7 ıı.borđ.

T.R.E.7 poſt.ualb.v.ſoł.Modo.vııı.ſoliđ.

Iſd.W.ten BERNESTONE.7 Radulf de eo.Rauefuar 7 Leuiet
p.ıı.ᴍ̃.tenueꝛ.7 libi hões fueꝛ.Ibi.ı.hida gelđ.Tra.ē.ıı.car.
In dñio.ē una.7 ıı.bouaꝛ.7 ııı.borđ.Vał.x.ſoł.Waſt inuen.

Iſd.W.ten WAREBVRGETVNE.Ernui tenuit. IN BOCHELAV HĐ.
7 lib fuit.Ibi dimiđ hida gelđ.Tra.ē.ı.caꝛ.Ibi.ē un radman
☞cū.ıı.bobȝ.Valb.v.ſoł.modo.ıı.ſoł.

Iſd.W.ten MVLINTVNE.Dot un lib hō fuit.Ibi dimiđ hida gelđ.
Tra.ē.ı.caꝛ.Waſt fuit 7 eſt.

Iſd.W.ten CVNETESFORD.7 Erchebrand de eo.qui 7 tenuit
ut lib hō.Ibi dimiđ hida gelđ.Tra.ē.ıı.caꝛ.Waſta fuit 7 eſt.
Silua dimiđ leuū lg̃.7 ıı.aćs lat.Valuit.x.ſoliđ.

Iſd.W.ten STABELEI.Leuuin tenuit.7 lib fuit.Ibi.ııı.pars
uni hidæ gelđ.Tra.ē.ı.caꝛ.Waſta fuit 7 eſt.Silua ibi dimiđ
Leuua lg̃.7 xL.ptic lat.Valuit.x.ſoliđ.

Iſd.W.ten in ipſa uilla.ı.bouata træ.7 ııı.parte.ı.hidæ.
gelđ.Segrid 7 Vlſi tenueꝛ p.ıı.ᴍ̃.7 libi fueꝛ.Tra.ē.ı.caꝛ.
Waſta fuit 7 eſt.T.R.E.ualb.vıı.ſoliđ.

Iſd.W.ten PEVRE.Eduuard tenuit.Ibi.ıı.part uni hidæ gelđ.
7 lib hō fuit.Tra.ē.ı.caꝛ.Waſta fuit 7 eſt.Silua ibi.ı.leuū lg̃.7 una
ać lat.                    Valb.v.ſoliđ.Modo.xıı.den.

☞Iđ.W.ten TATVNE.Echebrant lib hō tenuit.Ibi.ı.hida glđ.
Tra.ııı.caꝛ 7 dimiđ.Ibi.ııı.uiłłi 7 ıııı.borđ    Vał.ıııı.ſoł.

8   CAPENHURST. David holds from him. ½ hide paying tax. Arni
held it. Land for 1 plough. It is there, with
     1 villager and 2 smallholders.
Value before 1066 and later 5s; now 8s.

9   BARNSTON. Ralph holds from him. Ravenswart and Leofgeat held
it as 2 manors; they were free men. 1 hide paying tax. Land for
2 ploughs. In lordship 1; 2 ploughmen;
     3 smallholders.
Value 10s; found waste.

   in BUCKLOW (East) Hundred
10   WARBURTON. Ernwy held it; he was free. ½ hide paying tax.
Land for 1 plough.
     1 rider with 2 oxen.
The value was 5s; now 2s.

†   *(11 is added at the foot of the column, after 9,16, directed to its proper place by
transposition signs)*

12   MILLINGTON. Dot (held it); he was a free man. ½ hide paying tax.
Land for 1 plough.
It was and is waste.

13   KNUTSFORD. Egbrand, who also held as a free man, holds from him.
½ hide paying tax. Land for 2 ploughs. It was and is waste.
     Woodland ½ league long and 2 acres wide.
The value was 10s.

14   TABLEY. Leofwin held it; he was free. A third part of 1 hide paying
tax. Land for 1 plough. It was and is waste.
     Woodland ½ league long and 40 perches wide
The value was 10s.

15   In the village itself, 1 bovate of land and a third part of 1 hide
paying tax. Sigerid and Wulfsi held it as 2 manors; they were
free. Land for 1 plough. It was and is waste.
Value before 1066, 7s.

16   PEOVER. Edward held it. 2 parts of 1 hide paying tax. He was a
free man. Land for 1 plough. It was and is waste.
     Woodland 1 league long and 1 acre wide.
The value was 5s; now 12d.

†   *(Directed to its proper place by transposition signs)*
11   TATTON. Egbrand, a free man, held it. 1 hide paying tax.
Land for 3½ ploughs.
     3 villagers and 4 smallholders.
Value 4s.

Iſd.W.ten' *HELETVNE* Orme tenuit. *IN TVNENDINE HD.*

7 lib hō fuit.Ibi.x.hidæ.Harū.v.gelđ.7 aliæ non gelđ.

Tra.ē.xx.caɼ.In dñio ſunt.ii.caɼ.7 iiii.bouaɼ.7 iiii.uilłi

7 ii.borđ 7 ii.pɓri cū.v.caɼ int oɱs.Ibi.ii.piſcatores redđt

.v.ſoł.7 una aĉ p̄ti.Silua.i.leuū łg.7 dimiđ laɼ.Ibi.ii.haiæ.

In Wich.i.dom waſta.

De hac tra huj m̄ ten' Odard dimiđ hidā.Goisfriđ.ii.hiđ.

Aitard.i.hiđ.7 dimiđ.Hunfrid.i.hiđ 7 dimiđ.Odard dimiđ

hidā.Harduin dimiđ hidā.

Ibi ſunt in dñio.iii.caɼ.7 xii.uilł 7 i.radman 7 v.borđ

cū.v.caɼ int oɱs.7 vi.bouaɼ.7 dimiđ aĉ p̄ti.7 xviii.

aĉs ſiluæ.

Toɼ m̄ T.R.E.ualɓ.xl.ſoł.7 poſt fuit waſt.Modo qđ Wiłłs

ten'.uał.l.ſoł.Qđ milites:uał.liiii.ſoł.

Iſd.W.ten' *WESTONE*.Griſin tenuit ut lib hō.Ibi.ii.hidæ

gelđ.Tra.ē.v.caɼ.Odard 7 Brieĉtric ten' de Wiłło.7 ibi hn̄t

.ii.caɼ in dñio.7 iii.bouaɼ.7 v.uilłos 7 iii.borđ.cū.iii.caɼ.

7 ii.piſcatores.7 ii.aĉs p̄ti.7 Siluæ.i.leuū łg 7 dimiđ laɼ.7 haiā.

T.R.E.ualɓ.viii.ſoł.Modo:xxx.v.ſoliđ.Waſt inuen.

Iſd.W.ten' *ESTONE* 7 Odard de eo.Leuric tenuit.Ibi.i.hida

gelđ.Tra.ē.ii.caɼ 7 dim.In dñio.ē.i.caɼ 7 dimiđ.7 iii.bouaɼ.

7 i.uilł 7 i.borđ cū.i.caɼ.Ibi moliñ ſeruieɲs curiæ.7 piſcator.

7 i.aĉ ſiluæ.        T.R.E.ualɓ.v.ſoł.Modo.xx.ſoliđ.

Iſd.W.ten' *NORTVNE* 7 Ansfred de eo.Vĉtred 7 Tochi p.ii.m̄

tenueɼ.7 liɓi hōes fueɼ.Ibi.ii.hidæ gelđ.Tra.ē.vi.caɼ.

In dñio.ē una.7 ii.ſerui.7 iii.uilłi cū.i.caɼ.Ibi.i.piſcator.

7 iii.aĉ p̄ti.7 iiii.aĉ ſiluæ.7 ii.haiæ

T.R.E.ualɓ.xvi.ſoł.Modo.ix.ſoł 7 iiii.denaɼ.Waſt inuen.

Iſd.W.ten' *ENELELEI*.Wighe tenuit.Ibi dimiđ hida gelđ.

Tra.ē dimiđ caɼ.        Waſta fuit 7 eſt.

17   HALTON. Orm held it; he was a free man. 10 hides, of which 5 pay
tax and the others do not. Land for 20 ploughs. In lordship 2
ploughs; 4 ploughmen;
> 4 villagers, 2 smallholders and 2 priests with 5 ploughs between
> them. 2 fishermen pay 5s.

Meadow, 1 acre; woodland 1 league long and ½ wide;
> 2 enclosures; 1 unoccupied house in *Wich*.

Of the land of this manor Odard holds ½ hide; Geoffrey 2 hides;
Aethelhard 1½ hides; Humphrey 1½ hides; Odard ½ hide;
Hardwin ½ hide. In lordship 3 ploughs;
> 12 villagers, 1 rider and 5 smallholders with 5 ploughs between
> them; 6 ploughmen.

Meadow, ½ acre; woodland 18 acres.
Total value of the manor before 1066, 40s; later waste; now, what
William holds 50s, what the men-at-arms hold 54s.

18   WESTON. Gruffydd held it as a free man. 2 hides paying tax. Land
for 5 ploughs. Odard and Brictric hold it from William; they
have 2 ploughs in lordship; 3 ploughmen;
> 5 villagers and 3 smallholders with 3 ploughs; 2 fishermen.

Meadow, 2 acres; woodland 1 league long and ½ wide;
> an enclosure.

Value before 1066, 8s; now 35s; found waste.

19   ASTON. Odard holds from him. Leofric, a free man, held it. 1 hide
paying tax. Land for 2½ ploughs. In lordship 1½ ploughs;
3 ploughmen;
> 1 villager and 1 smallholder with 1 plough.

A mill which serves the Court; a fisherman; woodland, 1 acre.
Value before 1066, 5s; now 20s.

20   NORTON. Ansfrid holds from him. Uhtred and Toki held it as 2
manors; they were free men. 2 hides paying tax. Land for 6
ploughs. In lordship 1; 2 slaves;
> 3 villagers with 1 plough; 1 fisherman.

Meadow, 3 acres; woodland, 4 acres; 2 enclosures.
Value before 1066, 16s; now 9s 4d; found waste.

21   EANLEY. Wicga held it. ½ hide paying tax. Land for ½ plough.
It was and is waste.

Iſd.W.ten *DVNTVNE*.Eduuard tenuit ut liħ hō ꝓ uno ꝏ.

Ibi dimiđ virg̅ gelđ.Tra.ē.ıı.boū.Ibi.ē un̅ radman 7 ı.uiłłs.

vał.vı.denar.Waſt fuit.

Iſd.W.ten *LEGE*.Eduuard̅ tenuit ut liħ hō.Ibi.ı.hida

gelđ.Tra.ē.ı.caŕ.Ibi.ē cū.ı.radman 7 ı.ſeruo.7 ıı.uiłłis 7 ı.borđ.

Vał.ıııı.ſoł.Valuit.v.ſoł.

Hugo com̅ ħt de hac tra.ı.uirg̅.quæ redđ.ııı.ſoł.

Iſd.W.ten *ESTONE*.7 Pagen de eo.Leuenot tenuit ut

liħ hō.Ibi.ıı.virg̅ 7 dimiđ gelđ.Tra.ē.ı.caŕ.quæ ibi.ē in

dn̅io.7 ıı.bouaŕ.7 ı.radman 7 ı.borđ.7 ı.ſeruus.Ibi Silua

lg̅.ı.leuua.7 xl.ptic̅ lat̅.7 ibi.ıı.haiæ.

Iſd.W.ten *BVDEWRDE*.7 Pagen de eo.Eduuard̅ tenuit ut hō liħ.

Ibi.ı.hida gelđ.Tra.ē.ıı.caŕ.In dn̅io.ē dimiđ caŕ.7 ı.ſeruus.

7 pħr 7 ıı.uiłłi 7 ı.borđ cū.ı.caŕ.7 molin̅ ſeruieẜ aulæ.

Ibi.ı.ač p̅ti 7 dimiđ.        T.R.E.uałħ.vı.ſoł.Modo.vııı.ſoł.

Iſd.W.ten *WITELEI*.7 Pagen 7 Odard de eo.Leuenot tenuit

ut liħ hō.Ibi.ıı.hidæ gelđ.Tra.ē.ıı.caŕ.In dn̅io.ē una cū.ı.

ſeruo.Ibi.ı.ač p̅ti.Silua.ı.leuu lg̅.7 dimiđ lat̅.Vał.vı.ſoł.

Iſd.W.ten *GOSTREL*.7 Radulf de eo.Colben tenuit ut liħ hō.

Ibi.ı.uirg̅ gelđ.Tra.ē.ıı.boū.Waſta fuit 7 eſt.*IN HAMSTAN HĐ.*

Wiłłs ten de comite *ALDREDELIC*.Brun tenuit 7 liħ hō fuit.

Ibi.ı.hida gelđ.Tra.ē.ıııı.caŕ.Waſta fuit 7 eſt.Silua.ıı.leuu lg̅.

7 ıı.lat̅.     *IN MILDESTVIC HVND.* ⌠T.R.E.uałħ.xx.ſoł.

Wiłłs ten de com̅ *LEGE*.Haſten tenuit 7 liħ hō fuit.

Ibi dimiđ hida gelđ.Tra.ē.ı.caŕ.Waſta fuit 7 eſt.

22 DUTTON. Edward held it as a free man as 1 manor. ½ virgate paying
tax. Land for 2 oxen.
1 rider and 1 villager.
Value 6d; it was waste.

23 LEIGH. Edward held it as a free man. 1 hide paying tax. Land
for 1 plough. It is there, with
1 rider and 1 slave; 2 villagers and 1 smallholder.
The value is 4s; it was 5s.
Earl Hugh has 1 virgate of this land which pays 3s.

24 ASTON. Payne holds from him. Leofnoth held it as a free man.
2½ virgates paying tax. Land for 1 plough which is there, in
lordship; 2 ploughmen;
1 rider, 1 smallholder and 1 slave.
Woodland 1 league long and 40 perches wide; 2 enclosures.
[Value ...]

25 BUDWORTH. Payne holds from him. Edward held it as a free man.
1 hide paying tax. Land for 2 ploughs. In lordship ½ plough; 1 slave;
a priest, 2 villagers and 1 smallholder with 1 plough.
A mill which serves the hall; meadow, 1½ acres.
Value before 1066, 6s; now 8s.

26 WHITLEY. Payne and Orde hold from him. Leofnoth held it as a
free man. 2 hides paying tax. Land for 2 ploughs. In lordship
1, with 1 slave.
Meadow, 1 acre; woodland 1 league long and ½ wide.
Value 6s.

in NORTHWICH Hundred
27 GOOSTREY. Ralph holds from him. Colben held it as a free man.
1 virgate paying tax. Land for 2 oxen.
It was and is waste.

In MACCLESFIELD Hundred
28 William holds ALDERLEY from the Earl. Brown held it; he was a
free man. 1 hide paying tax. Land for 4 ploughs. It was and is waste.
Woodland 2 leagues long and 2 wide.
Value before 1066, 20s.

In NORTHWICH Hundred
29 William holds LACH (Dennis) from the Earl. Hasten held it; he was a
free man. ½ hide paying tax. Land for 1 plough. It was and is waste.

Hvgo de Mara teñ de Hugone comite LEE. IN CESTRE HVND
ʹLeuuin tenuit. Ibi. ɪ. virg træ geld. Ibi ſunt. ɪɪ. uilli 7 ɪ. borđ
cū dimiđ caɍ. Valƀ T.R.E. x .ſoł. modo. vɪɪɪ . ſoł. Waſꞇ inueñ.

Iſđ Hugo teñ BRVGE. Leuuin tenuit. Ibi. ɪ. carucata træ
geld. Ibi. ɪɪ. borđ hūt dimiđ caɍ. Valƀ 7 uał. ɪɪɪ. ſoł.

Iſđ. H. teñ RADECLIFE. Gunnor tenuit. Ibi. ɪɪɪ. pars. ɪ. hidæ cia
geld. Ibi.c̄. ɪ. caɍ in dñio. cū. ɪɪ. bouar. Waſta fuit cū recep.
T.R.E. ualƀ. x. ſoł. Modo. vɪ. ſoł. 7 vɪɪɪ. denaɍ. IN WILAVEST HD.

Iſđ. H. teñ CALDERS. Erniet tenuit 7 liƀ hō fuit. Ibi. ɪ. hida glđ.
Tra.c̄. ɪɪɪ. caɍ. In dñio.c̄ una. cū. ɪ. borđ.

Valƀ. v. ſoł. Modo. x. ſoliđ.        IN MILDESTVIC HD.

Hugo teñ de cõ LAVTVNE. Godric tenuit 7 liƀ hō fuit.
Ibi. ɪ. hida geld. Tra.c̄. ɪɪɪ. caɍ. Waſta.c̄. Silua ibi. ɪ. leuū lḡ.
7 una laꞇ. 7 una ac̄ pꞇi. T.R.E. ualƀ. xvɪ. ſoł.

Hugo teñ de cõ LAVTVNE. Godric tenuit. Ibi dim̄ hida
geld. Tra.c̄. ɪɪɪ. caɍ. Waſta.c̄. Silūa ibi. ɪɪ. leuū lḡ. 7 ɪ. lat.
T.R.E. ualƀ. xx. ſoł.

Hugo teñ de cõ BEVELEI. Godric 7 Goduin 7 Archil
ᵱ. ɪɪɪ. Ꟁ tenueɍ. 7 liƀi fueɍ. Ibi. ɪ. hida geld. Tra.c̄. ɪɪ. caɍ.
Ibi. ɪɪ. radmans 7 ɪɪ. borđ hūt. ɪ. caɍ. Ibi. ɪɪ. ac̄ pꞇi. 7 ɪɪ.
ac̄ filuæ. T.R.E. ualƀ. x. ſoł. modo tñtđ.

Hugo teñ de cõ GOSTREL. Godric tenuit 7 liƀ hō
fuit. Ibi. ɪɪɪ. uirg tre    geld. Tra.c̄. ɪ. caɍ 7 dimiđ.
Waſta fuit ſēp 7 eſt.

## 10   Hugh of Delamere holds

In CHESTER Hundred
1     OVERLEIGH. from Earl Hugh. Leofwin held it. 1 virgate of land
      paying tax.
          2 villagers and 1 smallholder with ½ plough.
      Value before 1066, 10s; now 8s; found waste.

Hugh also holds

2     HANDBRIDGE. Leofwin held it. 1 carucate of land paying tax.
          2 smallholders have ½ plough.
      The value was and is 3s.

3     'REDCLIFF'. Gunner held it. A third part of 1 hide paying tax. In
      lordship 1 plough, with 2 ploughmen. Waste when acquired.
      Value before 1066, 10s; now 6s 8d.

      in WIRRAL Hundred
4     CALDY. Erngeat held it; he was a free man. 1 hide paying tax.
      Land for 3 ploughs. In lordship 1, with
          1 smallholder.
      The value was 5s; now 10s.

## 11   Hugh (son of Norman) holds from the Earl

In NORTHWICH Hundred
1     LAWTON . Godric held it; he was a free man. 1 hide paying tax.
      Land for 3 ploughs. Waste.
          Woodland 1 league long and 1 wide; meadow, 1 acre.
      Value before 1066, 16s.

2     LAWTON. Godric held it. ½ hide paying tax. Land for 3 ploughs. Waste.
          Woodland 2 leagues long and 1 wide.
      Value before 1066, 20s.

3     BYLEY. Godric, Godwin and Arkell held it as 3 manors; they were
      free. 1 hide paying tax. Land for 2 ploughs.
          2 riders and 2 smallholders have 1 plough.
          Meadow, 2 acres; woodland, 2 acres.
      Value before 1066, 10s; now as much.

4     GOOSTREY. Godric held it; he was a free man. 3 virgates of land
      paying tax. Land for 1½ ploughs. It is and always was waste.

†     *(Insert 11,5 - 11,8, entered below after 12,4)*

Hugo.F.Osbni ten de com BRVGE.unã carucatã tre

gelđ.Vlnod tenuit.Ibi funt.II.borđ cũ.III.bobʒ.

Val.III.folid.                    IN DVDESTAN HVND.

Iſđ Hugo ten CALDECOTE.Vlgar 7 alij.III.teini tenuer

p.III.Ⓜ.7 libi erant.Ibi.I.hida gelđ.Tra.ẽ.II.cař.

★ jpfe ibi funt cũ.I.radman 7 II.uiłłis.7 III.bouar.Ibi dimiđ

piſcaria.T.R.E.fuit waſta tam redđb.II.fol.m̃.xv.fol.

Iſđ.H.ten PVLFORD.Vluric tenuit ſic lib hõ.Ibi.I.

hida geld dimiđ.Tra.ẽ.I.cař.7 ibi.ẽ cũ.II.radmans 7.I.uiłło.

7 II.borđ.Waſta fuit h̃ tra.modo ual.v.fol.

Iſđ.H.ten WARHELLE.Aluuold IN RISETON HVND.

tenuit ut lib hõ.Ibi dimiđ hida gelđ.Tra.ẽ.I.cař.Ibi

un uiłłs h̃ dimiđ cař.Silua ibi dimiđ leuu lg̃.7 una

ać lat.Valuit 7 ual.III.folid. IN HAMSTANE HĐ.

Hugo ten de com BOSELEGA.Godric tenuit 7 lib hõ fuit.

Ibi dimiđ hida gelđ.Tra.ẽ.IIII.cař.Waſta.ẽ.Ibi Silua.II.leuu

lg̃.7 dimiđ leuu lat.T.R.E.ualb xx.fol.

Hugo ten de com MERETONE.Godric tenuit 7 lib hõ fuit.

| Tra.ẽ di mid car. | Ibi.I.uirg træ gelđ.Waſta fuit sẽp.Ibi Silua xx.ptic lg̃.7 tntđ lat

Hugo ten de com.I.bereuuich CERDINGHA.Godric tenuit.

Ibi dimiđ hida gelđ.Tra.ẽ.II.cař.Waſta fuit 7 eſt.Valuit.v.fol.

IN MILDES TVIC HVNĐ Hugo ten de com SVMREFORD.Godric tenuit ut lib hõ.Ibi

dimiđ hida gelđ.Tra.ẽ.I.cař.Waſta fuit 7 eſt adhuc.

## 12  **Hugh son of Osbern** holds

[In CHESTER Hundred]
1   In HANDBRIDGE  from the Earl 1 carucate of land paying tax.
     Wulfnoth held it.
        2 smallholders with 3 oxen.
     Value 3s.

Hugh also holds

in BROXTON Hundred
2   CALDECOTT. Wulfgar the priest and 3 other thanes held it as 3
     manors; they were free. 1 hide paying tax. Land for 2 ploughs.
     These are there, with
        1 rider, 2 villagers and 3 ploughmen.
        ½ fishery.
     Before 1066 it was waste; however, it paid 2s; now 15s.

3   PULFORD. Wulfric held it as a free man. 1½ hides paying tax.
     Land for 1 plough. It is there, with
        2 riders, 1 villager and 2 smallholders.
     This land was waste; value now 5s.

in EDDISBURY (South) Hundred
4   WARDLE. Alfwold held it as a free man. ½ hide paying tax. Land
     for 1 plough.
        1 villager has ½ plough.
        Woodland ½ league long and 1 acre wide.
     The value was and is 3s.

†   *(11,5 - 11,8 here misplaced should follow 11,4 above)*

Hugh (son of Norman) holds  from the Earl
in MACCLESFIELD Hundred
5   BOSLEY. Godric held it; he was a free man. ½ hide paying tax. Land
     for 4 ploughs. It is waste.
        Woodland 2 leagues long and ½ league wide.
     Value before 1066, 20s.

6   MARTON. Godric held it; he was a free man. 1 virgate of land paying
     tax. Land for ½ plough. It was always waste.
        Woodland 20 perches long and as wide.

7   One outlier, KERMINCHAM. Godric held it. ½ hide paying tax.
     Land for 2 ploughs. It was and is waste.
     The value was 5s.

in NORTHWICH Hundred
8   SOMERFORD. Godric held it as a free man. ½ hide paying tax.
     Land for 1 plough. It was waste and still is.

Hᴀᴍᴏ teñ de comite *POTITONE* . Vluric tenuit 7 lib̃ hõ fuit.

Ibi . ıı . hidæ 7 dimiđ gelđ . Tra . ẽ . ııı . car̄ . In dñio . ẽ una . 7 uñ ſeruus.

7 ıııı . uilli . 7 ıııı . borđ . 7 uñ radman cũ . ı . car̄ . Val xx . ſot . Waſt fuit.

Iſđ Hamo . teñ *DONEHA* . Eluuard tenuit *IN BOCHELAV HD.*

7 lib̃ hõ fuit . Ibi . ı . hida gelđ . Tra . ẽ . ııı . car̄ . In dñio . ẽ una . 7 ıı . bo

uarij . 7 ıı . uilli 7 ı . borđ . 7 una ac̄ ſiluæ . 7 In ciuitate una dom.

T.R.E. ualb̃ . xıı . ſot . Modo . x . ſot . Waſt fuit.

Iſđ Hamo teñ *BOGEDONE* . Eluuard tenuit . 7 lib̃ hõ fuit . Ibi

una hida gelđ . Tra . ẽ . ıı . car̄ . Ibi . ıı . franciġ hñt . ı . car̄ . Ibi pbr

7 æcclã cui ptiñ dimiđ h̃ hida . Ibi moliñ redđ . xvı . denar̄.

Valet . ııı . ſoliđ . Waſt fuit 7 ita inuenit.

Iſđ Hamo teñ *HALE* . Eluuard tenuit . Ibi . ı . hida gelđ . Tra . ẽ . ıı . car̄

7 dimiđ . Ibi . ııı . uilli cũ . ı . radman hñt . ıı . car̄ . Ibi Silua . ı . leuũ lg̃.

7 dimiđ lat̄ . 7 Haia . 7 Aira accipitris . 7 dimiđ ac̄ p̃ti.

T.R.E. ualb̃ . xv . ſoliđ . Modo . xıı . ſoliđ . Waſt inueñ.

Iſđ Haimo teñ *BRAMALE* . Brun 7 Hacun p̃ . ıı . c̃õ tenuer̄ . 7 libi

hões fuer̄ . Ibi . ı . hida gelđ . Tra . ẽ . vı . car̄ . Ibi uñ radman 7 ıı . uilli

7 ıı . borđ hñt . ı . car̄ . Silua ibi dimiđ leuũ lg̃ . 7 tntđ lat̄ . 7 dimiđ

Haia . 7 una ac̄ p̃ti . T.R.E. ualb̃ . xxxıı . ſot . Modo . v . ſot . Waſta inueñ.

Iſđ Hamo teñ *ASCELIE* . Eluuard tenuit 7 lib̃ hõ fuit . *IN BOCHELAV HD.*

Ibi . ı . virg̃ tre gelđ . Tra . ẽ . ıı . boũ . Waſta fuit 7 eſt.

Iſđ Hamo teñ *ALRETVNE* . Æluuard tenuit . Ibi . una uirg̃ tre 7 dim̃ gelđ

## 13 Hamo (of Mascy) holds

In NANTWICH Hundred
1  PUDDINGTON from Earl Hugh. Wulfric held it; he was a free man.
2½ hides paying tax. Land for 3 ploughs. In lordship 1: 1 slave;
  4 villagers, 4 smallholders and 1 rider with 1 plough.
Value 20s; it was waste.

Hamo also holds

in BUCKLOW (East) Hundred
2  DUNHAM (Massey). Alfward held it; he was a free man. 1 hide
paying tax. Land for 3 ploughs. In lordship 1; 2 ploughmen;
  2 villagers and 1 smallholder.
  Woodland, 1 acre; 1 house in the City.
Value before 1066, 12s; now 10s; it was waste.

3  BOWDON. Alfward held it; he was a free man. 1 hide paying tax.
Land for 2 ploughs.
  2 Frenchmen have 1 plough. A priest and a church, to whom a
    half of this hide belongs.
  A mill which pays 16d.
Value 3s; it was waste; and he found it so.

4  HALE. Alfward held it. 1 hide paying tax. Land for 2½ ploughs.
  3 villagers with 1 rider have 2 ploughs.
  Woodland 1 league long and ½ wide; an enclosure; a hawk's
    eyrie; meadow, ½ acre.
Value before 1066, 15s; now 12s; found waste.

in MACCLESFIELD Hundred                                      266 d
5  BRAMHALL. Brown and Hakon held it as 2 manors; they were
free men. 1 hide paying tax. Land for 6 ploughs.
  1 rider, 2 villagers and 2 smallholders have 1 plough.
  Woodland ½ league long and as wide; ½ enclosure;
    meadow, 1 acre.
Value before 1066, 32s; now 5s; found waste.

in BUCKLOW (East) Hundred
6  ASHLEY. Alfward held it; he was a free man. 1 virgate of land
paying tax. Land for 2 oxen.
It was and is waste.

7  'ALRETUNSTALL'. Alfward held it. 1½ virgates of land paying tax.

Tra.ē.vi.boƀ.Waſta fuit 7 eſt. IN *DVDESTAN HD*.

Bigot ten de Hugone *FERENTONE*. Eduin tenuit. Ibi.iiii.

hidæ gelđ.Tra.viii.caſ.In dnĩo ſunt.ii.7 vii.uiłłi 7 iii.borđ cũ
ii.caſ. Ibi moliñ 7 piſcaria cũ.ii.piſcatoriƀ.7 una ač p̃ti.

T.R.E.ualƀ.xl.ſoliđ. Modo.vi.liƀ. Waſt inuen̄.

Iſđ Bigot ten *LAI*. Anſgot tenuit ut liƀ hō.Ibi.i.hida gelđ.

Tra.ē.ii.caſ.Ibi ſunt.ii.borđ 7 una ač p̃ti.Val.ii.ſol.Waſt fuit

Iſđ Big ten *TORENTVNE*.Steinchetel tenuit 7 liƀ hō fuit.Ibi.ii.

hidæ gelđ.Tra.ē.ii.caſ.In dnĩo.ē dimiđ.7 ii.uiłłi 7 borđ hñt
dimiđ caſ. Ibi æcc̃a 7 pƀr.7 i.ač p̃ti.

T.R.E.ualƀ.xx.ſoliđ.Modo.x.ſoliđ.Waſt inuen̄. *IN BOCHELAV HD*.

Iſđ Big ten *MOTBVRLEGE*.Dot tenuit 7 liƀ hō fuit.Ibi.i.hida 7 dimiđ
gelđ.Tra.ē.iiii.caſ. Ibi hŧ un tein.dimiđ caſ.7 i.ſeruũ.7 i.uiłł
7 ii.borđ.Ibi.i.ač p̃ti.7 Silua.ii.leuũ lḡ.7 tntđ laŧ.7 ii.hiæ.

T.R.E.ualƀ.xii.ſoliđ.Modo.v.ſoliđ.Waſt inuen̄. *IN HAMSTAN HD*.

Iſđ Big ten *NORDBERIE*.Brun tenuit 7 liƀ hō fuit.Ibi.i.hida
gelđ.Tra.ē.iiii.caſ.Ibi un radman cũ.iii.borđ hŧ.i.caſ.Ibi
una ač p̃ti.Silua.v.leuũ lḡ.7 iii.leuũ laŧ.7 ibi.iii.haiæ.

T.R.E.ualƀ.x.ſol. Modo.iii.ſol. Waſt inuen̄.

Iſđ Big ten *ALDREDELIE*.Goduin tenuit ut liƀ hō.Ibi.i.hida
gelđ.Tra.ē.viii.caſ.In dnĩo.ē una.cũ.ii.bouaſ.7 iii.uiłłi 7 un
radman cũ.i.caſ.Ibi.i.ač p̃ti.Silua.i.leuu 7 dimiđ lḡ.7 i.leuu lat.
7 ibi.ii.haiæ.ł.R.E.ualƀ.xx.ſoliđ.Modo.x.ſol.Waſt inuen̄.

Iſđ.Big ten *SVDENDVNE*.Brun tenuit.7 liƀ hō fuit.Ibi.i.hida
7 dimiđ gelđ.Tra.ē.vii.caſ.Ibi un francig hŧ dimiđ caſ.7 i.uiłł
7 i.borđ.cũ dimiđ caſ.Ibi Silua.i.leuu lḡ.7 dimiđ laŧ.

Land for 6 oxen. It was and is waste.

## 14 Bigot (of Loges) holds

In BROXTON Hundred

1 FARNDON from Earl Hugh. Earl Edwin held it. 4 hides paying tax.
Land for 8 ploughs. In lordship 2;
7 villagers and 3 smallholders with 2 ploughs.
A mill; a fishery with 2 fishermen; meadow, 1 acre.
Value before 1066, 40s; now £6; found waste.

Bigot also holds

2 LEA. Ansgot held it as a free man. 1 hide paying tax. Land for 2
ploughs.
2 smallholders.
Meadow, 1 acre.
Value 2s; it was waste.

3 THORNTON. Stenketel held it; he was a free man. 2 hides paying
tax. Land for 2 ploughs. In lordship ½.
2 villagers and [1] smallholder have ½ plough. A church and
a priest.
Meadow, 1 acre.
Value before 1066, 20s; now 10s; found waste.

in BUCKLOW (East) Hundred

4 MOBBERLEY. Dot held it; he was a free man. 1½ hides paying tax.
Land for 4 ploughs.
1 thane has ½ plough and 1 slave. 1 villager and 2 smallholders.
Meadow, 1 acre; woodland 2 leagues long and as wide.
2 enclosures.
Value before 1066, 12s; now 5s; found waste.

in MACCLESFIELD Hundred

5 NORBURY. Brown held it; he was a free man. 1 hide paying tax.
Land for 4 ploughs.
1 rider with 3 smallholders has 1 plough.
Meadow, 1 acre; woodland 5 leagues long and 3 leagues wide;
3 enclosures.
Value before 1066, 10s; now 3s; found waste.

6 ALDERLEY. Godwin held it as a free man. 1 hide paying tax.
Land for 8 ploughs. In lordship 1, with 2 ploughmen;
3 villagers and 1 rider with 1 plough.
Meadow, 1 acre; woodland 1½ leagues long and 1 league wide;
2 enclosures.
Value before 1066, 20s; now 10s; found waste.

7 SIDDINGTON. Brown held it; he was a free man. 1½ hides paying
tax. Land for 7 ploughs.
1 Frenchman has ½ plough; 1 villager and 1 smallholder with
⅓ plough.
Woodland 1 league long and ½ wide.

T.R.E.ualɓ xx̃ .ſoł.modo.v.ſoł.

Iſđ Biḡ teñ *Rodo*.Bernulf tenuit 7 liɓ hō fuit.Ibi dim̃ hida
geld.Tra.ē.ii.cař.Waſta.ē.7 ſic inueñ T.R.E.ualɓ viii.ſoł.
Silua.i.leuũ l͞g.7 dimiđ leuũ lat̃. *In Mildestvich hð.*

Iſđ Biḡ teñ *Cogeltone*.Goduin tenuit.Ibi.i.hida gelđ.Tra.ē
iiii.cař.Ibi ſunt.ii.cũ.ii.uiłłis 7 iiii.borđ.Silua ibi.i.leuũ l͞g.
7 una lat̃.7 ibi.ii.haiæ.Waſt fuit 7 ſic inueñ.modo uał.iiii.ſoł.

Iſđ Biḡ teñ *Sanbeco*.Dunning tenuit.7 liɓ fuit.Ibi.i.hida
gelđ.7 una v̄ 7 dimiđ ſimiliť gelđ.Tra.ē.ii.cař.Ibi.ē uñ franciḡ
cũ dim̃ cař.7 iii.ſeruis.7 ii.uiłłi cũ dimiđ cař.Ibi pɓr 7 æccła.
Silua dimiđ leuũ l͞g.7 xl.p̃tic lat̃.

T.R.E.ualɓ.iiii.ſoliđ.modo.viii.ſoliđ.

Iſđ Biḡ teñ *Svdtvne*.Aleſtan 7 Belam ꝑ.ii.m̃ tenueř.7 liɓi hōes
fueř.Ibi.iii.virg|træ gelđ.Tra.ē.ĩ.cař 7 dimiđ.In dñio.ē dimiđ
cař.7 ii.bouař.7 ii.uiłłi hñt dimiđ cař.

T.R.E.ualɓ.iiii.ſoliđ.Modo.iii.ſoliđ.Waſt fuit.

Iſđ Biḡ teñ *Wibaldelai*.Leuuin tenuit.7 liɓ fuit.Ibi.i.virg
træ gelđ.Tra.ē.i.cař.Ibi.i.radman h̃t dimiđ cař.7 ii.ſeruos cũ
uno uiłło.Vał.ii.ſoł.Waſt fuit 7 ſic inuenit.

Iſđ Biḡ teñ *Wevre*.Stenulf tenuit 7 liɓ fuit.Ibi.i.virg træ
gelđ.Tra.ē dimiđ cař.Ibi.ē cũ.i.radman 7 uno uiłło 7 ii.borđ.
Silua l͞g.i.q̃ʓ.7 tñtđ lat̃.7 ibi haia.Valuit.ii.ſoł.Modo.iii.ſoł.

Baldric ten de Hug̃ coᷝ*cocle*.Vlfac tenuit. *In Riseton hð.*
7 liɓ hō fuit.Ibi.i.hida gelđ.Tra.ē.i.cař.Ibi.ē ipſa in dñio.7 uñ
ſeruus.T.R.E.ualɓ.xl.ſoliđ.Modo ſimiliť.Waſt inuenit.

Toret tenuit *Alentvne*.Ibi.iii.hidæ gelđ. *In Exestan hð.*

Value before 1066, 20s; now 5s.

8    RODE. Bernwulf held it; he was a free man. ½ hide paying tax.
Land for 2 ploughs. It was waste and he found it so.
Value before 1066, 8s.
Woodland 1 league long and ½ league wide.

in NORTHWICH Hundred
9    CONGLETON. Godwin held it. 1 hide paying tax. Land for 4 ploughs.
2 are there, with
2 villagers and 4 smallholders.
Woodland 1 league long and as wide; 2 enclosures.
It was waste and he found it so; value now 4s.

10    SANDBACH. Dunning held it; he was free. 1 hide paying tax;
1½ virgates likewise paying tax. Land for 2 ploughs.
1 Frenchman with ½ plough and 3 slaves. 2 villagers with ½ plough.
A priest and a church.
Woodland ½ league long and 40 perches wide.
Value before 1066, 4s; now 8s.

11    SUTTON. Alstan and Beollan held it as 2 manors; they were free men.
3 virgates and 16 acres of land paying tax. Land for 1½ ploughs.
In lordship ½ plough; 2 ploughmen.
2 villagers have ½ plough.
Value before 1066, 4s; now 3s; it was waste.

12    WIMBOLDSLEY. Leofwin held it; he was free. 1 virgate of land
paying tax. Land for 1 plough.
1 rider has ½ plough and 2 slaves with 1 villager.
Value 2s; it was waste and he found it so.

13    WEAVER. Stenulf held it; he was free. 1 virgate of land paying tax.
Land for ½ plough. It is there, with
1 rider, 1 villager and 2 smallholders.
Woodland 1 furlong long and as wide; an enclosure.
The value was 2s; now 3s.

15  **Baldric holds**
In EDDISBURY (South)
1    *COCLE* from Earl Hugh. Wulfheah held it; he was a free man. 1 hide
paying tax. Land for 1 plough. It is there, in lordship; 1 slave.
Value before 1066, 40s; now the same; found waste.

16   **[Hugh son of Osbern]**
In MAELOR CYMRAEG Hundred
1    Thored, a free man, held ALLINGTON. 3 hides paying tax.

In *EITVNE* tenuit S Cedde.i.hiđ.⁊ in *SVTONE*.i.hiđ gelđ tenuit isđ Sēs.

Hos.iii.Ḿ q̓do Hugo recep:́erant wasti. Modo ten Hugo de eo.

⁊ hŧ dimiđ car̄ in dñio.⁊ iii.seruos.⁊ vii.uiłł ⁊ v.borđ ⁊ ii.franciḡ.

Int oms hn̄t.i.car̄ ⁊ dimiđ.Ibi molin̄ de.iiii.sot.⁊ dimiđ piscaria.

⁊ iiii.ac̄ p̓ti.Silua.ii.leuu lḡ.⁊ dimiđ lat̄.Ibi.ii.haiæ.Vat.xxx.sot.

Ibi.iiii.car̄ plus posseⁿ́.eē.   T.R.E.ualŧ.xx.soliđ.

### *IN DVDESTAN HĐ.*

GISLEBERTVS De Venables ten de Hugone *ECLESTONE*.

Eduin⁹ tenuit.⁊ liŧ hō fuit.Ibi.v.hidæ gelđ.Tra.ē.vi.car̄.

In dñio.ē una.⁊ ii.serui.⁊ iiii.uiłłi ⁊ i.borđ cū.i.car̄.Ibi nauis

⁊ rete.⁊ dimiđ ac̄ p̓ti.T.R.E.ualŧ.x.sot.Modo.l.sot.Wast fuit.

Isđ Gisłebt ten *ALBVRGHA*.Eduin⁹ tenuit.Ibi.ii.hidæ gelđ.

Tra.ē.iiii.car̄.Ibi.iii.uiłłi cū,vi.borđ hn̄t.i.car̄.

Silua ibi.ii.leuu lḡ.⁊ una lat̄.⁊ ii.ac̄ p̓ti.

T.R.E.ualŧ.xx.soliđ.modo.viii.soliđ. *IN RISETON HĐ.*

Isđ.G.ten *TORPELEI*.Vluiet tenuit ⁊ liŧ hō fuit.Ibi.ii.hidæ

gelđ.Tra.ē.iiii.car̄.In dñio.ē una.⁊ ii.serui.⁊ iiii.uiłłi ⁊ ii.borđ

cū.i.car̄.Silua.i.leuu lḡ.⁊ una lat̄.⁊ una ac̄ p̓ti.

T.R.E.ualŧ.xx.soliđ.modo.x.soliđ.Wast inuen.

Isđ.G.ten *WATENHALE*.Gleuuin⁹ tenuit.⁊ liŧ hō fuit.Ibi

una hida gelđ.Tra.ē.ii.car̄.Ibi.i.radman cū.i.uiłło ⁊ ii.borđ

hŧ.i.car̄.Ibi.ii.ac̄ p̓ti.Silua.i.leuu ⁊ dimiđ lḡ.⁊ una leuu lat̄.

Valuit ⁊ uat.v.soliđ.Wast inuen.   *IN ROELAV HVNĐ.*

Isđ.G.ten *HERFORD*.Dodo tenuit sic̄ liŧ hō.Ibi.ii.hidæ gelđ.

Tra.ē.ii.car̄.Ibi sunt.iiii.uiłłi ⁊ ii.borđ ⁊ faŧ.hn̄tes.i.car̄.

In Wich una salina redđ.ii.soliđ.⁊ alia dimidia salina wasta.

Ibi.i.ac̄ p̓ti.De hac tra ten un⁹ miles dimiđ hidā.⁊ ibi hŧ.i.

car̄.⁊ ii.bouar.⁊ iii.borđ.T.R.E.ualŧ.xx.sot.Modo.x.soliđ.

2   In EYTON St. Chad's held 1 hide, and in SUTTON the Saint also
held 1 hide paying tax. When Earl Hugh acquired these 3 manors
they were waste. Now Hugh son of Osbern holds from him and
has in lordship ½ plough; 3 slaves.
> 7 villagers, 5 smallholders and 2 Frenchmen have 1½ ploughs
> between them.
> A mill at 4s; ½ fishery; meadow, 4 acres; woodland 2 leagues long
> and ½ wide; 2 enclosures.

Value 30s. 4 more ploughs are possible; value before 1066, 20s.

## 17   Gilbert of Venables holds          267 a
In BROXTON Hundred

1   ECCLESTON from Earl Hugh. Edwin held it; he was a free man.
5 hides paying tax. Land for 6 ploughs. In lordship 1; 2 slaves;
> 4 villagers and 1 smallholder with 1 plough.
> A boat and a net; meadow, ½ acre.

Value before 1066, 10s; now 50s; it was waste.

Gilbert also holds

2   ALPRAHAM. Earl Edwin held it. 2 hides paying tax. Land for 4 ploughs.
> 3 villagers with 6 smallholders have 1 plough.
> Woodland 2 leagues long and 1 wide; meadow, 2 acres.

Value before 1066, 20s; now 8s.

in EDDISBURY (South) Hundred

3   TARPORLEY. Wulfgeat held it; he was a free man. 2 hides paying tax.
Land for 4 ploughs. In lordship 1; 2 slaves;
> 4 villagers and 2 smallholders with 1 plough.
> Woodland 1 league long and 1 wide; meadow, 1 acre.

Value before 1066, 20s; now 10s; found waste.

4   WETTENHALL. Glewin held it; he was a free man. 1 hide paying
tax. Land for 2 ploughs.
> 1 rider with 1 villager and 2 smallholders has 1 plough.
> Meadow, 2 acres; woodland 1½ leagues long and 1 league wide.

The value was and is 5s; found waste.

in EDDISBURY (North) Hundred

5   HARTFORD. Doda held it as 2 manors as a free man. 2 hides paying
tax. Land for 2 ploughs.
> 4 villagers, 2 smallholders and a smith who have 1 plough.
> In *Wich* 1 salthouse which pays 2s, and another ½ salthouse,
> derelict. Meadow, 1 acre.

1 man-at-arms holds ½ hide of this land and has 1 plough and
2 ploughmen;
> 3 smallholders.

Value before 1066, 20s; now 10s.

Iſđ.G.teñ *LIME*.Vluiet tenuit 7 liƀ fuit. *IN BOCHELAV HĐ*.

Ibi.ɪ.hida gelđ.Tra.ē.ɪɪ.caɼ.Ibi ſunt.ɪɪɪ.borđ.Ibi dimiđ

æcctā cū dimiđ virḡ træ.Siluæ dimiđ leuū lḡ.7 tñtđ lat.

T.R.E.ualƀ.x.ſot.Modo.xɪɪ.denaɼ.Waſꞇ inuen.

Iſđ.G.teñ *LEGE*.Vluiet 7 Dot ꝓ.ɪɪ.m̄ tenueɼ.7 liƀi hōes fueɼ.

Ibi.ɪ.hida gelđ.Tra.ē.ɪɪ.caɼ.Ibi.ɪ.hō ej hꞇ dimiđ caɼ.7 ɪɪɪ.

ſeruos.Ibi pƀr 7 æcctā cū.ɪ.uitto 7 ɪɪ.borđ hn̄s dimiđ caɼ.

Ibi Silua.ɪ.leuū lḡ.7 dimiđ leuū lat.7 ibi haia.

T.R.E.ualƀ.x.ſoliđ.Modo.v.ſoliđ.

Iſđ.G.teñ *WIMVNDISHA*.Dot tenuit.7 liƀ hō fuit.Ibi.ɪ.hida

7 dimiđ gelđ.Tra.ē.ɪɪ.caɼ.In dn̄io.ē una caɼ.cū.ɪ.ſeruo.

Ibi una aꞔ ſiluæ.7 aira accipitris.7 una dom in Wich.7 ɪ.borđ.

Vat.x.ſot.Waſꞇ fuit 7 ſic inuen.

Iſđ.G.teñ *MERA*.Vluiet tenuit 7 liƀ hō fuit.Ibi.ɪ.hida gelđ.

Tra.ē.ɪɪ.caɼ.Waſta fuit 7 eſt.Silua ibi dimiđ leuū lḡ.7 xL.ꝑtic

lat.Ibi.ɪɪ.aꞔ ꝑti.T.R.E.ualƀ.vɪɪɪ.ſoliđ.

Iſđ.G.teñ *PEVRE*.Dot tenuit.Ibi.ɪɪ.bouatæ træ gelđ.Waſta

fuit 7 eſt.

Iſđ.G.teñ *RODESTORNE*.Vluiet tenuit.Ibi.ɪ.uirg træ gelđ.Tra.ē

.ɪ.caɼ.Waſta fuit.Ibi.ɪɪ.aꞔ ſiluæ.T.R.E.ualƀ.ɪɪɪɪ.ſoliđ.

Iſđ.G.teñ *HOPE*.Eduin tenuit 7 liƀ hō fuit. *IN EXESTAN HĐ*.

Ibi.ɪ.hida gelđ.Tra.ē.ɪ.caɼ.7 ibi.ē cū.ɪɪ.uittis.7 ɪɪ.aꞔ ſiluæ.

Vat.vɪɪ.ſot.Waſꞇ fuit 7 ſic inuen. *IN MILDESTVIC HĐ*.

Gueñator

Gisleƀt ten.de com *NEVBOLD*.Vluiet tenuit.7 liƀ hō fuit.

Ibi.ɪ.hida 7 dimiđ gelđ.Tra.ē.v.caɼ.Ibi.ɪ.radman hꞇ.ɪ.caɼ.

7 pƀr.ɪ.caɼ.7 ɪɪɪ.uitti 7 ɪɪ.borđ.Ibi.ɪ.aꞔ ꝑti.7 Silua.ɪ.leuū

lḡ.7 tñtđ lat.7 ɪɪ.haiæ ibi.T.R.E.ualƀ.xx.ſot.modo.vɪɪɪ.ſot.

Iſđ.G.teñ *BRETONE*.Vluiet tenuit.Ibi.ɪɪ.hidæ gelđ.Tra.ē

ɪɪɪɪ.caɼ.In dn̄io.ē una.7 ɪɪ.bouar.7 ɪɪ.uitti 7 ɪɪɪ.borđ.

in BUCKLOW (East) Hundred

6 LYMM. Wulfgeat held it; he was free. 1 hide paying tax.
Land for 2 ploughs.
3 smallholders. ½ church with ½ virgate of land.
Woodland ½ league long and as wide.
Value before 1066, 10s; now 12d; found waste.

7 LEGH. Wulfgeat and Dot held it as 2 manors; they were free men.
1 hide paying tax. Land for 2 ploughs. 1 of (Gilbert's) men has
½ plough and 3 slaves.
A priest and a church, with 1 villager and 2 smallholders, who
has ½ plough.
Woodland 1 league long and ½ league wide; an enclosure.
Value before 1066, 10s; now 5s.

8 WINCHAM. Dot held it; he was a free man. 1½ hides paying tax.
Land for 2 ploughs. In lordship 1 plough, with 1 slave.
Woodland, 1 acre; a hawk's eyrie; 1 house in *Wich*.
1 smallholder.
Value, 10s; it was waste and he found it so.

9 MERE. Wulfgeat held it; he was a free man. 1 hide paying tax.
Land for 2 ploughs. It was and is waste.
Woodland ½ league long and 40 perches wide; meadow, 2 acres.
Value before 1066, 8s.

10 PEOVER. Dot held it. 2 bovates of land paying tax.
It was and is waste.

11 ROSTHERNE. Wulfgeat held it. 1 virgate of land paying tax.
Land for 1 plough. It was waste.
Woodland, 2 acres.
Value before 1066, 4s.

in MAELOR CYMRAEG Hundred

12 HOPE. Edwin held it; he was a free man. 1 hide paying tax.
Land for 1 plough. It is there, with
2 villagers.
Woodland, 2 acres.
Value 7s; it was waste and he found it so.

## 18 Gilbert Hunter holds

In NORTHWICH Hundred

1 NEWBOLD from the Earl. Wulfgeat held it; he was a free man.
1½ hides paying tax. Land for 5 ploughs. 1 rider has 1 plough.
A priest, 1 plough, 3 villagers and 2 smallholders.
Meadow, 1 acre; woodland 1 league long and as wide; 2 enclosures.
Value before 1066, 20s; now 8s.

Gilbert also holds

2 BRERETON. Wulfgeat held it. 2 hides paying tax. Land for 4 ploughs.
In lordship 1; 2 ploughmen;
2 villagers and 3 smallholders.

Ibi.i.ač p̄ti.Silua.i.leuu lḡ.7 dimiđ lať.7 moliñ de.xii.deñ.

De hac tra ten.ii.hões ej.i.hiđ.7 hn̄t.i.car.cū.ii.feruis.

7 ii.uiłłis.7 iiii.borđ.

Toť T.R.E. ualb.xx.fot.modo fimilit.Wasť inuen.

Ifđ.G.ten CINBRETVNE.Goduin tenuit 7 lib hō fuit.Ibi

iii.hidæ gelđ.Tra.ē.v.car.In dnīo.ē una.7 ii.ferui.

7 iii.borđ.Ibi.i.ač p̄ti.Silua dimiđ leuu lḡ.7 tntđ lať.

7 ibi haia.Valet.x.fot.Wasť fuit 7 inuenit.

Ifđ.G.ten DENEPORT.Goduin tenuit.Ibi dimiđ hida gelđ.

Tra.ē.i.car.Ibi.ē cū uno radman.7 ii.bouař.7 iii.borđ.

7 una ač filuæ.Vat.iii.foliđ.Wasť inuenit.

267 b

Ifđ Giflebť ten WITTNE.Dot tenuit 7 lib hō fuit.

Ibi.i.hida 7 dimidia gelđ.Tra.ē.ii.car.

Ibi.i.francig hť.i.car.7 ii.bouař 7 i.borđ.Ibi moliñ

de.iii.foliđ. Vat.vii.foliđ.Wasť inueñ.

Ifđ.G.ten BLACHENHALE. IN WARMVNDESTROV HĐ.

Goduin tenuit.7 lib hō fuit.Ibi.iiii.hidæ:i.virg min

7 gelđ.Tra.ē.v.car.Ibi.iiii.radmans 7 ii.borđ.hn̄t.ii.

car.Silua ibi.ii.leuu lḡ.7 una leuu lať.Ibi Haia.

7 aira Accipitris:T.R.E.ualb.x.fot.Modo:xii.foliđ.


IN MILDESTVIC HĐ.

GOZELIN ten de Hugone NEVTONE.Grifin tenuit

7 lib hō fuit.Ibi.i.hida gelđ.Tra.ē.iii.car.In dnīo.ē

una.7 ii.bouař.Pbr cū.i.borđ hť.i.car.Ibi dimiđ ač

p̄ti:T.R.E.ualb.iiii.fot.Modo.x.fot.

Ifđ Gozet ten CROSTVNE.Goduin tenuit 7 lib hō fuit.

Ibi.i.hida gelđ.Tra.ē.i.car.quæ ibi.ē cū.i.radman

7 ii.feruis.7 ii.uiłłis 7 uno borđ.Valuit.iiii.fot.M.x.fot.

Ifđ Gozet ten STABLEI.Oftebrand tenuit IN BOCHELAV HĐ.

7 lib hō fuit.Ibi.ii.bouatæ træ gelđ.Tra.ē dimiđ car.Wafta fuit 7 ē.

Meadow, 1 acre; woodland 1 league long and ½ wide;
a mill at 12d.
2 of (Gilbert's) men hold 1 hide of this land and have 1 plough, with 2 slaves;
2 villagers and 4 smallholders.
Total value before 1066, 20s; now the same; found waste.

3 KINDERTON. Godwin held it; he was a free man. 3 hides paying tax. Land for 5 ploughs. In lordship 1; 2 slaves;
3 smallholders.
Meadow, 1 acre; woodland ½ league long and as wide; 1 enclosure.
Value 10s; it was waste and he found it so.

4 DAVENPORT. Godwin held it. ½ hide paying tax. Land for 1 plough. It is there, with 1 rider and 2 ploughmen;
3 smallholders.
Woodland, 1 acre.
Value 3s; found waste.

5 WITTON. Dot held it; he was a free man. 1½ hides paying tax.    267 b Land for 2 ploughs.
1 Frenchman has 1 plough, 2 ploughmen and 1 smallholder.
A mill at 3s.
Value 7s; found waste.

in NANTWICH Hundred
6 BLAKENHALL. Godwin held it; he was a free man. 4 hides, less 1 virgate, paying tax. Land for 5 ploughs.
4 riders and 2 smallholders have 2 ploughs.
Woodland 2 leagues long and 1 league wide; an enclosure.;
a hawk's eyrie.
Value before 1066, 10s; now 12s.

## 19   Jocelyn holds
In NORTHWICH Hundred
1 NEWTON from Earl Hugh. Gruffyd held it; he was a free man.
1 hide paying tax. Land for 3 ploughs. In lordship 1; 2 ploughmen.
A priest with 1 smallholder has 1 plough.
Meadow, ½ acre.
Value before 1066, 4s; now 10s.

Jocelyn also holds
2 CROXTON. Godwin held it; he was a free man. 1 hide paying tax.
Land for 1 plough which is there, with 1 rider; 2 slaves;
2 villagers and 1 smallholder.
The value was 4s; now 10s.

in BUCKLOW (East) Hundred
3 TABLEY. Uhtbrand held it; he was a free man. 2 bovates of land paying tax. Land for ½ plough. It was and is waste.

Rannvlfvs ten de Hugone *BLACHEHOL*. Toret tenuit.
7 liber hō fuit. Ibi. 11. hidæ geld. Tra. ē. 1111. car. In dūio funt. 1i.
7 1111. bouar. 7 1111. uilli. 7 1111. bord hñt. 1. car. Ibi piscaria.
T.R.E. ualb. x1111. sot. Modo. xl. sot.   *In ROELAV HVND.*
Rannulf ten *WENITONE*. Leuenot tenuit 7 lib hō fuit. Ibi
dimid hida. geld. Tra. ē dimid car. Ibi. ē un radman 7 i. uills.
Rannulf ten de comite *TATVNE*. *In BOCHELAV HD.* Val. 11. sot.
Leuuin tenuit. Ibi. v1. pars hidæ geld. Tra. ē dimid car. Ipsa. ē
ibi cū. 1. radman 7 11. seruis. 7 11. uillis 7 1111. bord. Silua ibi. 1. leuu
lg. 7 tntd lat. In Wich. 1. dom wasta. Valet. 111. solid.
Isd. R. ten *PEVRE*. Erniet tenuit 7 lib fuit. Ibi dimid hida geld.
Tra. ē. 1. car. Ibi qdā hō ej ht. 11. boues. 7 11. seruos. 7 11. uillos
Silua ibi dimid leuu lg. 7 xl. ptic lat. 7 aira accipitris.
T.R.E. ualb. xv. sot. Modo. 1111. sot. Wast fuit
Ipse. R. ten *WAREFORD* 7 Godid de eo. Ipsa tenuit 7 liba fuit.
Ibi dimid hida geld. Tra. ē. 1. car. Ibi ht. 11. boues 7 1111. seruos 7 11.
ancill. Val. 111. solid. Wast fuit.
Isd. R. ten *PEVRE*. de. 11. bouatis træ geld. Tra. ē dimid car.
Isd R. ten *CEPMVNDEWICHE* de dimid hida geld. Tra. ē dim car.
Godid tenuit. 7 liba femina fuit. h tra wasta fuit 7 est.
Isd. R. ten *ALRETVNE*. de dimid uirg træ geld. Godid tenuit.
Terra. ē. 11. boum. Wasta fuit 7 est.
Isd. R. ten *SENELESTVNE*. Leuenot tenuit. Ibi. 1. virg træ
geld. Tra. ē dimid car. Wasta fuit 7 est.   *In TVNENDVNE HD.*
Isd. R. ten *COCHESHALLE*. Vluiet tenuit 7 lib hō fuit. Ibi dimid
hida geld. Tra. ē. 1. car. De pastura exeuñ. 111. solid. Wasta. ē tra.

## 20 Ranulf (Mainwaring) holds

In WIRRAL Hundred
1 BLACON from Earl Hugh. Thored held it; he was a free man.
2 hides paying tax. Land for 4 ploughs. In lordship 2; 4 ploughmen.
4 villagers and 4 smallholders have 1 plough.
A fishery.
Value before 1066, 14s; now 40s.

In EDDISBURY (North) Hundred
2 WINNINGTON. Leofnoth held it; he was a free man. ½ hide
paying tax. Land for ½ plough.
1 rider and 1 villager.
Value 2s.

In BUCKLOW (East) Hundred
3 TATTON from the Earl. Leofwin held it. A sixth part of a hide
paying tax. Land for ½ plough. It is there, with 1 rider; 2 slaves;
2 villagers and 4 smallholders.
Woodland 1 league long and as wide; 1 unoccupied house in *Wich.*
Value 3s.

4 Ranulf also holds PEOVER. Erngeat held it; he was free.
½ hide paying tax. Land for 1 plough.
One of (Ranulf's) men has 2 oxen; 2 slaves and 2 villagers.
Woodland ½ league long and 40 perches wide; a hawk's eyrie.
Value before 1066, 15s; now 4s; it was waste.

5 Ranulf holds WARFORD himself. Godgyth holds from him. She held
it herself, and was free. ½ hide paying tax. Land for 1 plough.
She has 2 oxen; 4 male and 2 female slaves.
Value 3s; it was waste.

Ranulf also holds

6 PEOVER, at 2 bovates of land paying tax. Land for ½ plough.

7 'CHAPMONSWICHE', at ½ hide paying tax. Land for ½ plough.
Godgyth held it; she was a free woman.
This land was and is waste.

8 OLLERTON, at ½ virgate of land paying tax. Godgyth held it.
Land for 2 oxen.
It was and is waste.

9 SNELSON. Leofnoth held it. 1 virgate of land paying tax.
Land for ½ plough.
It was and is waste.

in BUCKLOW (West) Hundred
10 COGSHALL. Wulfgeat held it; he was a free man. ½ hide paying tax.
Land for 1 plough.
From the pasture comes 3s. The land is waste.

Iſd.R.ten *Hoiloch*.Morcar tenuit; *In Mildestvich Hᴅ.*

Ibi.ɪɪɪ.hidæ gelđ.Tra.ē.ɪɪɪɪ.cař.In dñio.ē una.7 ɪɪɪɪ.ſerui

7 ɪɪ.radmans cū.ɪ.cař.Silua ibi.ɪɪɪ.leuu lḡ.7 una lat.

T.R.E.7 poſt waſt fuit.Modo ual.xx.ſolid.

Iſd.R.ten *Tadetvne*;Godid tenuit.Ibi.ɪ.hida 7 una v gelđ.
Tra.ē.ɪɪ.cař.Ibi.ɪ.francig hȓ.ɪ.cař.7 ɪɪ.bouař.7 ɪ.radman
cū dimiđ cař 7 ɪɪɪɪ.borđ.Silua ibi xʟ.ptic lḡ 7 una ač lat.
7 ibi haia.T.R.E.7 poſt.waſt fuit.Modo ual.x.ſolid.

*In Dvdestan Hᴅ.*

R uenator ADVLFVS ten de Hugone *Stapleford*;Vlſi tenuit.
7 lib hō fuit.Ibi.ɪɪ.hidæ gelđ.Tra.ē.ɪɪɪ.cař.In dñio.ē una.
7 un radman 7 ɪɪ.uilli 7 v.borđ cū.ɪɪɪ.cař.Silua ibi.ɪɪ.ačs
lḡ.7 una lat.Ibi molinū.

Valuit 7 ualet.xvɪ.ſolid.

267 c

~~Rainald ten de Hugone~~ com ~~Gressord.~~ *In Exestan Hᴅ.*
~~Toret tenuit 7 lib hō fuit.~~ ~~Ibi.ɪ.hida 7 dimiđ gelđ.~~
★ ~~Tra.ē.ɪɪ.cař.Ibi.ɪ.uills cū.ɪɪ.~~ ~~borđ~~ ~~hȓ.ɪ.cař.Val.xx.ſol.~~
~~De ſilua quæ.ē.ɪɪɪɪ.leuu lḡ.7 ɪɪ.lat.hȓ qtū ptiñ ad.ɪ.hid 7 dim.~~

Iſd Rainald ten *Erpestoch*.Rees tenuit ſiē lib hō.
Ibi dimiđ hida gelđ.Tra.ē.ɪ.cař.Ipſa ibi.ē cū.ɪ.radman
7 uno uill 7 uno borđ.

·T.R.E.uuaſt fuit.7 poſt ualuit.x.ſol.Modo.ɪx.ſolid.


*In Dvdestan Hᴅ.*

Ilbertvs ten de Hugone com *Wavretone*.Ernuin tenuit.
7 lib hō fuit.Ibi.ɪɪɪ.hidæ gelđ.Tra.ē.ɪɪɪɪ.cař.In dñio.ē una.
7 ɪɪɪ.francig cū.ɪɪɪ.uillis hñt.ɪɪɪ.cař.

T.R.E.ualb.xx.ſol.7 poſt.vɪ.ſol.Modo xvɪ.ſol.

in NORTHWICH Hundred

11   WHEELOCK. Earl Morcar held it. 3 hides paying tax. Land for
4 ploughs. In lordship 1; 4 slaves;
    2 riders with 1 plough.
    Woodland 3 leagues long and 1 wide.
Before 1066 and later it was waste; value now 20s.

12   TETTON. Godgyth held it. 1 hide and 1 virgate paying tax.
Land for 2 ploughs.
    1 Frenchman has 1 plough and 2 ploughmen. 1 rider with
      ½ plough and 3 smallholders.
    Woodland 40 perches long and 1 acre wide; an enclosure.
Before 1066 and later it was waste; value now 10s.

## 21   Ralph Hunter holds

In BROXTON Hundred

1   STAPLEFORD from Earl Hugh. Wulfsi held it; he was a free man.
2 hides paying tax. Land for 3 ploughs. In lordship 1;
    1 rider, 2 villagers and 5 smallholders with 3 ploughs.
    Woodland 2 acres long and 1 wide; a mill.
The value was and is 16s.

## 22   Reginald (Balliol) holds                267 c

In MAELOR CYMRAEG Hundred

1   *GRESFORD from Earl Hugh. Thored held it; he was a free man.
1½ hides paying tax.* Land for 2 ploughs.
    *1 villager with 2 smallholders has 1 plough.*
*Value 20s.*
    Of the woodland, *which is 4 leagues long and 2 wide, he has
      what belongs to 1½ hides.*

2   Reginald also holds ERBISTOCK. Rhys held it as a free man. ½ hide
paying tax. Land for 1 plough. It is there, with
    1 rider, 1 villager and 1 smallholder.
Before 1066 it was waste; value later 10s; now 9s.

## 23   Ilbert holds

In BROXTON Hundred

1   WAVERTON from Earl Hugh. Ernwin held it; he was a free man.
3 hides paying tax. Land for 4 ploughs. In lordship 1.
    3 Frenchmen with 3 villagers have 3 ploughs.
Value before 1066, 20s; later 6s; now 16s.

Iſđ Ilbť teñ *ETONE*. Alnod 7 Ernuin ꝑ. II. Ⱦ tenueꝛ.7 liƀi

hões fueꝛ.Ibi.II.hidæ gelđ.Ťra.ē.III.caꝛ.Ibi.ē uñ uiłłs

cū.I.caꝛ.T.R.E.ualƀ.xx.ſoł.Modo.IX.ſoł 7 IIII.denaꝛ.Vasť fuit.

Iſđ Ilbť teñ *CLOTONE*.Stenulf tenuit *IN RISETON HVNÐ*.

7 liƀ hõ fuit.Ibi.III.hidæ gelđ.Ťra.ē.VI.caꝛ.Ibi ſunt.VI.uiłłi

7 II.borđ 7 IIII.radmans hñtes.V.caꝛ.Valuit 7 uał.XII.ſoł.

*IN DVDESTAN HVNÐ*.

Osbernvs filius Tezzonis teñ de Hugone comite *HANLEI*.

Grinchel tenuit 7 liƀ hõ fuit.Ibi.I.hida gelđ.Ťra.ē.IIII.

caꝛ.In dñio.ē una caꝛ 7 dimiđ.cū.I.ſeruo.7 II.uiłłi 7 I.borđ

hñt dimiđ caꝛ.T.R.E.ualƀ.XIII.ſoł 7 III.deñ.Modo.xv.ſoł.

Iſđ Osƀn teñ *COLBORNE*.Eduin tenuit 7 liƀ hõ fuit.Ibi.I.

hida gelđ.Ťra.ē.III.caꝛ.In dñio.ē una.7 uñ uiłłs 7 uñ borđ.

Ibi dimiđ aꝗ ꝑti.              Valuit 7 uał.xvi.ſoliđ.

Iſđ Osƀn teñ *PONTONE*.7 Rogeꝛ de eo. *IN WILAVESTON HÐ*.

Gamel tenuit 7 liƀ hõ fuit.Ibi.II.hidæ gelđ.Ťra.ē.IIII.caꝛ.

In dñio.ē una.7 II.ſerui.7 uñ radman 7 I.uiłłs 7 pƀr 7 IIII.borđ

cū.I.caꝛ int oñs.

T.R.E.ualƀ xxv.ſoł.7 poſt wasť fuit.Modo uał.xxv.ſoł.

Iſđ.O.teñ *WENITONE* Hunding tenuit *IN ROELAV HVNÐ*.

7 liƀ hõ fuit.Ibi dimiđ hida gelđ.Ťra.ē dimiđ caꝛ.Ibi eſt

uñ radman cū.I.uiłło              Vał.II.ſoliđ.

Iſđ.O.teñ *LIME*.Eduuard tenuit 7 liƀ *IN BOCHELAV HÐ*.

hõ fuit.Ibi.I.hida gelđ.Ťra.ē.IIII.caꝛ.Eduuard teñ de eo.

Ibi hƚ.I.caꝛ.7 II.bouar.7 II.uiłł 7 IIII.borđ 7 dimiđ æccła

cū pƀro cū dimiđ v træ ꝗeta.Silua dimiđ leuū łḡ.7 tñtđ

lať.T.R.E.ualƀ.x.ſoliđ.modo.vIII.ſoł.Wasť inueñ.


267 c

2    Ilbert also holds HATTON. Alnoth and Ernwin held it as 2 manors.
they were free men. 2 hides paying tax. Land for 3 ploughs.
   1 villager with 1 plough.
Value before 1066, 20s; now 9s 4d; it was waste.

In EDDISBURY (South) Hundred
3    Ilbert also holds CLOTTON. Stenulf held it; he was a free man.
3 hides paying tax. Land for 6 ploughs.
   6 villagers, 2 smallholders and 4 riders who have 5 ploughs.
The value was and is 12s.

## 24  Osbern son of Tezzo holds

In BROXTON Hundred
1    HANDLEY from Earl Hugh. Grimkel held it; he was a free man.
1 hide paying tax. Land for 4 ploughs. In lordship 1½ ploughs,
with 1 slave.
   2 villagers and 1 smallholder have ½ plough.
Value before 1066, 13s 3d; now 15s.

Osbern also holds

2    GOLBORNE. Edwin held it; he was a free man. 1 hide paying tax.
Land for 3 ploughs. In lordship 1;
   1 villager and 1 smallholder.
   Meadow, ½ acre.
The value was and is 16s.

in WIRRAL Hundred
3    POULTON. Roger holds from him. Gamel held it; he was a free man.
2 hides paying tax. Land for 4 ploughs. In lordship 1; 2 slaves;
   1 rider, 1 villager, a priest and 4 smallholders with 1 plough
     between them.
Value before 1066, 25s; later it was waste; value now 25s.

in EDDISBURY (North) Hundred
4    WINNINGTON. Hunding held it; he was a free man. ½ hide paying
tax. Land for ½ plough.
   1 rider with 1 villager.
Value 2s.

in BUCKLOW (East) Hundred
5    LYMM. Edward held it; he was a free man. 1 hide paying tax.
Land for 4 ploughs. Edward holds from him. He has:
1 plough and 2 ploughmen.
   2 villagers and 4 smallholders.
   ½ church with a priest, with an exempted ½ virgate of land.
   Woodland ½ league long and as wide.
Value before 1066, 10s; now 8s; found waste.

Iſd.O.teñ *WARBVRGETONE*. Rauene tenuit 7 libꝰ hõ fuit.

Ibi dimiđ hida gelđ. Tra.ē.ɪ.caꝛ. Ibi uñ radman 7 ɪɪ.uiłłi 7 uñ

borđ cũ dimiđ caꝛ.    Valuit.v.ſoł.Modo.ɪɪ.ſolid.Waſt fuit.

Iſd.O.teñ *DVNTVNE*. Eduuard tenuit. libꝰ hõ fuit *IN TVNENDVNE HD*.

Ibi dimiđ hida gelđ. Eduuard teñ de Osbno. Ibi.ē uñ radman

7 uñ uiłłs 7 ɪɪɪ.borđ cũ.ɪ.caꝛ 7 dimiđ.

T.R.E.ualb.xɪɪ.denaꝛ. Modo.ɪɪ.ſolid.

Iſd.O.teñ *EPLETVNE*. Dot tenuit 7 libꝰ hõ fuit.Ibi.ɪ.

hida gelđ.Tra.ē.ɪɪɪɪ.caꝛ. Waſta fuit 7 eſt.T.R.E.ualb.xvɪ.

ſoł. Silua ibi dimiđ leuu lɡ̄.7 xʟ.ꝑtiċ laꝛ.

Iſd.O.teñ *GROPENHALE*.7 Eduuard de eo. Ipſe 7 Dot ꝑ.ɪɪ.

manerijs tenueꝛ 7 libi hões fueꝛ. Ibi.ɪ.hida 7 dimiđ virg

træ gelđ. Tra.ē.ɪɪ.caꝛ. In dñio.ē una 7 dimiđ.7 ɪɪ.ſerui.

7 uñ uiłłs 7 ɪɪɪ.borđ. Silua ibi.ɪ.leuu lɡ̄.7 xʟ.ꝑtiċ laꝛ.

Ibi.ɪɪ.Haiæ.T.R.E.ualb.v.ſolid.modo.vɪ.ſoł.Waſt fuit.

267 d

Nɪɢᴇʟʟᴠs teñ de Hugone comite *ALTETONE. IN RISETON HD*.

Donning tenuit 7 libꝰ hõ fuit.Ibi dimiđ hida gelđ.Tra.ē.ɪ.

caꝛ.Redđ de firma.v.ſoł 7 ɪɪɪɪ.deñ.T.R.E.ualb.xx.ſoł.

waſt inuenit.                    *IN WILAVESTON HD*.

Iſd Nigel teñ *GRAVESBERIE*. Dunning tenuit.Ibi.ɪɪ.hidæ gelđ.

Tra.ē.ɪɪɪ.caꝛ. In dñio.ē una.7 ɪɪ.ſerui.7 ɪɪɪ.uiłłi 7 ɪɪ.francig

7 uñ borđ cũ.ɪ.caꝛ int oms.

T.R.E.ualb.xxv.ſoł.7 poſt.x.ſolid.Modo.xx.ſolid.

Iſd Nigel teñ *STORTONE*.Dunning tenuit.Ibi.ɪɪ.hidæ gelđ.

Tra.ē.ɪɪɪ.caꝛ. In dñio.ē dimiđ caꝛ.7 uñ ſeruus.7 v.uiłłi 7 ɪɪɪ.

borđ cũ.ɪ.caꝛ 7 dimiđ.T.R.E.ualb.xv.ſoł.modo.xx.ſoł.Waſt fuit.


Tᴇᴢᴇʟɪɴ teñ de Hugone com *SVMREFORD*.Raueſue 7 Chetel

7 Morfar ꝑ.ɪɪɪ.ꟼ tenueꝛ.Duo libi hões fueꝛ.Morfar ñ poterat

recedere a dño ſuo. Ibi.ɪ.virg tre gelđ. In.ɪɪɪ.partes erat diuiſa.

Tra.ē.ɪɪɪ.caꝛ. Ibi.ē uñ radman hñs.ɪ.caꝛ 7 ɪɪ.ſeruos.

6   WARBURTON. Raven held it; he was a free man. ½ hide paying tax.
Land for 1 plough.
    1 rider, 2 villagers and 1 smallholder with ½ plough.
The value was 5s; now 2s; it waste.

in BUCKLOW (West) Hundred
7   DUTTON. Edward held it; he was a free man. ½ hide paying tax.
Edward holds from Osbern.
    1 rider, 1 villager and 3 smallholders with 1½ ploughs.
Value before 1066, 12d; now 2s.

8   APPLETON. Dot held it; he was a free man. 1 hide paying tax.
Land for 4 ploughs. It was and is waste.
Value before 1066, 16s.
    Woodland ½ league long and 40 perches wide.

9   GRAPPENHALL. Edward holds from him. He and Dot held it as
2 manors; they were free men. 1 hide and ½ virgate paying tax.
Land for 2 ploughs. In lordship 1½; 2 slaves;
    1 villager and 3 smallholders.
    Woodland 1 league long and 40 perches wide; 2 enclosures.
Value before 1066, 5s; now 6s; it was waste.

## 25   Nigel (of Burcy) holds                                267 d

In EDDISBURY (South) Hundred
1   OULTON from Earl Hugh. Dunning held it; he was a free man.
½ hide paying tax. Land for 1 plough. It pays 5s 4d in revenue.
Value before 1066, 20s; found waste.

In WIRRAL Hundred
2   Nigel also holds GREASBY. Dunning held it. 2 hides paying tax.
Land for 3 ploughs. In lordship 1; 2 slaves;
    3 villagers, 2 Frenchmen and 1 smallholder with 1 plough
      between them.
Value before 1066, 25s; later 10s; now 20s.

3   Nigel also holds STORETON. Dunning held it. 2 hides paying tax.
Land for 3 ploughs. In lordship ½ plough; 1 slave;
    5 villagers and 3 smallholders with 1½ ploughs.
Value before 1066, 15s; now 20s; it was waste.

## 26              [The Earl's Men]

In MACCLESFIELD Hundred
1   Tesselin holds SOMERFORD from Earl Hugh. Ravenswart, Ketel
and Morfar held it as 3 manors; two of them were free men;
Morfar could not withdraw from his lord. 1 virgate of land paying
tax; it was divided into 3 parts. Land for 3 ploughs.
    1 rider who has 1 plough; 2 slaves.

Silua ibi.xL.ptic̄ lḡ.7 tntđ laꝉ.Valb̄.vi.ſoꝉ.modo.iiii.ſoꝉ.

Oᴅᴀʀᴅ ten de com̄ *Dᴠ̄ᴠɴᴇ*.Rauene    Iɴ *Tᴠɴᴇɴᴅᴠ̄ɴᴇ HĐ*.
tenuit 7 lib̄ hō fuit.Ibi.i.virḡ trǣ 7 dimiđ gelđ.Tra.ē.i.caꝛ̄.
Ibi.ē un radman cū.i.ſeruo.Silua.ii.leuū lḡ.7 dimiđ laꝉ.
Ibi aira Accipitris.T.R.E.ualb̄.v.ſoꝉ.Modo.xii.denaꝛ.

Mᴠɴᴅʀᴇᴛ ten de com̄ *Bᴇʀᴛɪɴᴛᴠɴᴇ*.Dūning tenuit.
Ibi dimiđ hida gelđ.Tra.ē.i.caꝛ̄.Ipſa ibi.ē cū.i.radman 7 uno
ſeruo.7 i.borđ.T.R.E.ualb̄.iii.ſoꝉ.Modo.ʟxiiii.den.

Uʟᴠɪᴇᴛ ten de com̄ *Bᴇʀᴛɪɴᴛᴠɴᴇ*.Leuenot tenuit.
Ibi dimiđ hida gelđ.Tra.ē.i.caꝛ̄.Waſta.ē.Valuit.ii.ſoliđ.

Unus ſeruie̦s comitis ten unā trā in hoc *HᴠɴĐ Tᴠɴᴇɴᴅᴠɴᴇ*.
Ħ tra nunq̄ fuit hidata.Ibi hꝉ.i.caꝛ̄.cū.i.bouaꝛ.Vaꝉ.iiii.ſoꝉ.

Dᴠɴɴɪɴɢ ten de com̄ *Cʜɪɴɢᴇsʟɪᴇ*.Ipſemet Iɴ *Rᴏᴇʟᴀᴠ HĐ*
tenuit ſīc lib̄ hō.Ibi.i.hida gelđ.Tra.ē.ii.caꝛ̄.In dn̄io.ē una.
7 v.ſerui.7 un uiꝉꝉs 7 iii.borđ.Ibi piſcaria 7 dimiđ.Ibi Silua
una leuū lḡ.7 una laꝉ.Hanc poſuit com̄ in ſua foreſta.
7 ibi aira accipitris.7 iiii.haiæ capreoꝉ.
T.R.E.ualb̄.xxx.ſoꝉ.modo.vi.ſoꝉ.

Lᴇᴠʀɪᴄ ten de com̄ *Eʟᴠᴇʟᴅᴇʟɪᴇ*.Ernui tenuit 7 lib̄ hō fuit.
Ibi dimiđ hida gelđ.Tra.ē.iiii.caꝛ̄.In dn̄io.ē una cū.i.uiꝉꝉo
7 ii.borđ.Silua dimiđ leuū lḡ.7 dimiđ laꝉ. *Iɴ Hᴀᴍᴇsᴛᴀɴ HĐ*.

Vʟᴠʀɪᴄ ten *Bᴏᴛᴇʟᴇɢᴇ*.Ipſemet tenuit ſīc lib̄ hō.Ibi.i.hida
gelđ.Tra.ē.v.caꝛ̄.Waſta.ē p̄ter.vii.ac̄s ſeminatas.
Silua ibi.iii.leuū lḡ.7 una laꝉ.7 haia ibi.7 ii.ac̄ p̄ti 7 dimiđ.
T.R.E.ualb̄.xxx.ſoliđ.Modo.ii.ſoliđ.

Gᴀᴍᴇʟ ten đe com̄ *Cᴇᴅᴅᴇ*.Pat ej tenuit ut lib̄ hō.Ibi.ii.
hidæ gelđ.Tra.ē.vi.caꝛ̄.In dn̄io.ē una.7 ii.bouaꝛ.7 iiii.uiꝉꝉi
7 iii.borđ cū.ii.caꝛ̄.Silua ibi.i.leuū lḡ.7 dimiđ laꝉ.7 Haia
7 aira accipitris.7 una ac̄ p̄ti.Valuit 7 uaꝉ.x.ſoliđ.
Toꝉ ꝏ̃ hꝉ.ii.leuū lḡ.7 una laꝉ.

Woodland 40 perches long and as wide.
The value was 6s; now 4s.

### In BUCKLOW (West) Hundred

2 Odard holds DUTTON from the Earl. Raven held it; he was a free
man. 1½ virgates of land paying tax. Land for 1 plough.
   1 rider with 1 slave.
   Woodland 2 leagues long and ½ wide; a hawk's eyrie.
Value before 1066, 5s; now 12d.

3 Mundret holds BARTINGTON from the Earl. Dunning held it.
½ hide paying tax. Land for 1 plough. It is there, with
   1 rider, 1 slave and 1 smallholder.
Value before 1066, 3s; now 64d.

4 Wulfgeat holds BARTINGTON from the Earl. Leofnoth held it.
½ hide paying tax. Land for 1 plough. It is waste.
The value was 2s.

5 One of the Earl's servants holds land in this Hundred of Bucklow
(West). This land was never hidated. He has 1 plough with 1
ploughman.
Value 4s.

### In EDDISBURY (North) Hundred

6 Dunning holds KINGSLEY from the Earl. He held it himself as a
free man. 1 hide paying tax. Land for 2 ploughs. In lordship 1;
5 slaves;
   1 villager and 3 smallholders.
   1½ fisheries; woodland 1 league long and 1 wide, which the
      Earl put in his Forest; a hawk's eyrie; 4 deer parks.
Value before 1066, 30s; now 6s.

7 Leofric holds ALVANLEY from the Earl. Ernwy held it; he was a
free man. ½ hide paying tax. Land for 4 ploughs. In lordship 1;
   1 villager and 2 smallholders.
   Woodland ½ league long and ½ wide.
[Value ...]

### In MACCLESFIELD Hundred

8 Wulfric holds BUTLEY. He held it himself as a free man. 1 hide
paying tax. Land for 5 ploughs. It is waste, except for 7 acres sown.
   Woodland 3 leagues long and 1 wide; an enclosure; meadow,
      2½ acres.
Value before 1066, 30s; now 2s.

9 Gamel holds CHEADLE from the Earl. His father held it as a free man.
2 hides paying tax. Land for 6 ploughs. In lordship 1; 2 ploughmen;
   4 villagers and 3 smallholders with 2 ploughs.
   Woodland 1 league long and ½ wide; an enclosure; a hawk's eyrie;
      meadow, 1 acre.
The value was and is 10s.
The whole manor is 2 leagues long and 1 wide.

Iſđ Gamel ten̅ MOTRE . Paᵗ ej tenuit . Ibi . 1 . hida 7 dimiđ gelđ.

Tra . e̅ . IIII . caꝝ . Waſta . e̅ . Ibi Silua . III . leuū lḡ . 7 II . laᵗ . 7 II . haiæ.

7 aira Accipitris.

VLVRIC ten̅ de com̅ ALRETVNE . Ipſemet tenuit . ut lib̅ ho̅.

Ibi . II . partes uni hidæ gelđ . Tra . e̅ . III . caꝝ . Ibi . e̅ una cū . I.

bouaꝝ . 7 uno uitto 7 II . borđ . Ibi . I . ac̅ pᵗi . 7 III . ac̅ ſiluæ.

Vaꝉ . v . ſoliđ . Waſᵗ fuit T.R.E. IN MILDESTVIC HVNĐ.

MORAN ten̅ de com̅ LECE . Colben tenuit . ut lib̅ ho̅ . Ibi

dimiđ hida gelđ . Tra . e̅ . I . caꝝ . Ibi . e̅ in dn̅io . 7 II . bouaꝝ . 7 I . borđ.

Ibi dimiđ ac̅ pᵗi . Vaꝉ . VIII . ſoliđ . Waſᵗ fuit T.R.E.

268 a          IN BOCHELAV HĐ.

RANNVLFVS 7 Bigot ten̅ de com̅ NORWORDINE.

Vluiet tenuit ꝑ uno M̅ . 7 lib̅ ho̅ fuit . Ibi . I . hida gelđ.

Tra . e̅ . II . caꝝ . Waſta . e̅ . Ibi æccta 7 II . qͬrenᵗ ſiluæ.

Vaꝉ . III . ſoꝉ . T.R.E. ualb̅ . x . ſoꝉ.

GISLEBERTVS 7 Rannulf 7 Hamo ten̅ SVNDRELAND.

7 BAGELEI . Eluuard 7 Suga 7 Vdeman 7 Pat tenueꝝ

ꝑ . IIII . M̅ . 7 libi hoͤs fueꝝ . Ibi . I . hida gelđ . Tra . e̅

un̅ caꝝ 7 dimiđ . Waſta . e̅ tota . T.R.E. ualb̅ . III . ſoꝉ.

HVGO 7 Osb̅n 7 Rainald ten̅ GRETFORD . IN EXTAN HĐ.

Thoret tenuit ut lib̅ ho̅ . Ibi . XIII . hidæ gelđ.

Tra . e̅ . XII . caꝛ . Hugo hᵫ . v . hiđ . Osb̅n VI . hiđ 7 dim̅.

Rainald . I . hiđ 7 dimiđ . In dn̅io . e̅ . I . caꝝ 7 dimiđ.

Æccta 7 pb̅r ibi . 7 VII . uitti 7 XII . borđ 7 un̅ francig̅.

Int om̅s hn̅t . II . caꝝ 7 dimiđ.

In toto M̅ Silua . IIII . leuū lḡ . 7 II . laᵗ . 7 II . airæ accipit̅.

Osb̅n hᵫ molin̅ annonā ſuæ curiæ molenᵗe.      ⌐int om̅s

Toᵗ T.R.E. uuaſᵗ erat . 7 uuaſᵗ recep̅ . Modo uaꝉ . LXV . ſoꝉ.

De hac tra huj M̅ jacuit , I . hida T.R.E. in æccta S̅ CEDDE.

dimiđ in cheſpuiͨ 7 dimiđ in Radenoure . Hoc teſtat̅

comitat̅ . ſed neſcit quom̅ æccta ꝑdiderit.

10    Gamel also holds MOTTRAM. His father held it. 1½ hides paying
tax. Land for 4 ploughs. It is waste.
    Woodland 3 leagues long and 2 wide; 2 enclosures;
      a hawk's eyrie.

11    Wulfric holds OLLERTON from the Earl. He held it himself as a free
man. Two parts of 1 hide paying tax. Land for 3 ploughs.
1 is there, with 1 ploughman.
    1 villager and 2 smallholders.
    Meadow, 1 acre; woodland, 3 acres.
Value 5s; it was waste before 1066.

   In NORTHWICH Hundred
12    Moran holds LACH (Dennis) from the Earl. Colben held it as a free man.
½ hide paying tax. Land for 1 plough. It is there in lordship;
2 ploughmen;
    1 smallholder.
    Meadow, ½ acre.
Value 8s; it was waste before 1066.

27               **[Shared Lands]**             268 a

   In BUCKLOW (East) Hundred
1    Ranulf and Bigot hold NORTHENDEN from the Earl. Wulfgeat held
it as 1 manor; he was a free man. 1 hide paying tax. Land for
2 ploughs. It is waste.
    A church.
    Woodland, 2 furlongs.
Value 3s; before 1066, 10s.

2    Gilbert, Ranulf and Hamo hold SUNDERLAND and BAGULEY.
Alfward, Sucga, Woodman and Pat held it as 4 manors; they were
free man. 1 hide paying tax. Land for 1½ ploughs.
It is all waste; value before 1066, 3s.

   In MAELOR CYMRAEG Hundred
3    Hugh, Osbern and Reginald hold GRESFORD. Thored held it as a
free man. 13 hides paying tax. Land for 12 ploughs. Hugh has 5
hides; Osbern 6½ hides; Reginald 1½ hides. In lordship 1½ ploughs.
    A church and a priest, 7 villagers, 12 smallholders and
      1 Frenchman. Between them they have 2½ ploughs.
     In the whole manor, woodland 4 leagues long and 2 wide; 2
       hawk's eyries. Osbern has a mill which grinds corn for his hall.
Before 1066 it was all waste, and they acquired it waste; value
    now 65s between them.
     Before 1066 1 hide of this manor lay (in the lands of)
St. Chad's Church; ½ in *Chespuic* and ½ in Radnor. The County
testifies this, but does not know how the church lost [the land].

Hᴠɢᴏ 7 Wilts teñ de com̄ *Rode*. *In Mildestvic* ʜᴅ́.

Godric 7 Rauefua p̱.ɪɪ. Ⓜ̃ tenueř 7 liɓi hōēs fueř.

Ibi.ɪ.hida gelð.Tra.ē.ɪɪɪ.cař.Wafta.ē.p̃t qð uⁿ

★ radman h̄ fub eis  cař dimið.Val.ɪɪ.folið.T.R.E.

ualɓ.xx.fol.Silua ibi.ɪɪ.leuü lḡ.7 una laŧ.7 ɪɪ.haiæ.

7 aira Accipitris.


ꝙ Iₙ eoð *Mildestvic hvnd́*.erat tciü *Wich* qð uocat̓ *Norvvich*.

7 erat ad firmā p̱.ᴠɪɪɪ.liɓ.Ipfæ leges 7 c̄fuetudines erant ibi

quæ erant in alijs Wichis.7 rex 7 comes fimiliŧ partiebant̓

redditiones

Oͫs teini qui in ifto Wich habeɓ falinas.p̱ toŧ annū ñ dabaꝗ̃

in die ueneris bulliones falis.Quifꝗs ex alia fcira carrū ad

ducebat cū.ɪɪ.boɓ︜ aut cū pluriɓ︜ dabat de theloneo.ɪɪɪɪ.

denar.Ex eadē fcira homo dabat de carro.ɪɪ.denarios

infra tciam noc̄tē quā reuerfus erat unde uenerat.Si tcia

nox tranfibat.xʟ.folið em̄dabat.De alia fcira homo

de sūma caballi.ɪ.denar dabat.De ead uero fcira.unā

minutā.infra tciā noc̄tē ut dic̄tū eft.

Homo maneⁿs in ipfo hunð.fi carro ducebat fal ad uen

dendū p̱ eunð comitatū.de uno q́q︜ carro daɓ uñ denar.

q́tꝗt uiciɓ︜ oneraret eū.Si æquo portabat fal ad uendenð.

ad feftū 🜊 ᴍᴀʀᴛɪɴɪ dabat.ɪ.denar.Qui in ipfo tmino

ñ reddeɓ.xʟ.fol em̄daɓ.Cætera oīa in his Wichis sŧ fimilia.

Iftud qᵈdo Hugo recep̓.erat waft.Modo ual.xxxv.folið.

In NORTHWICH Hundred

4   Hugh and William hold (Odd) RODE from the Earl. Godric and
Ravenswart. held it as 2 manors; they were free man. 1 hide
paying tax. Land for 3 ploughs. It is waste, except that 1 rider
has [..]½ ploughs under them.
Value 2s; before 1066, 20s.
    Woodland 2 leagues long and 1 wide; 2 enclosures;
      a hawk's eyrie.


## [The Salt Works]

†   *(Directed to its proper place by transposition signs)*

## S3   (Northwich)

1   Also in Northwich Hundred was a third *Wich,* called NORTHWICH.
It was at a revenue of £8. The same laws and customs were (kept)
there as in the other two *Wiches,* and the King and the Earl
shared the returns similarly.

2   None of the thanes who had salthouses in this *Wich* paid the
Friday salt-boilings at any time of the year. Anyone from
another shire who brought a cart with 2 or more oxen paid 4d
toll; a man from the same shire paid 2d a cart, by the third
night after his return home; if the third night passed, he paid
a fine of 40s. A man from another shire paid 1d for a
packhorse load; but a man from the same shire paid 1 farthing
by the third night, as stated.

3   If a man dwelling in this Hundred carted salt through the same
county for sale, he paid 1d for each cart each time he loaded it;
if he carried salt on a horse for sale, he paid 1d at Martinmas;
anyone who did not pay by that date was fined 40s. All the other
[customs] in these *Wiches* are similar.

4   This *[Wich]* was derelict when Earl Hugh acquired it; value now 35s.

Tᴇᴘᴏʀᴇ Regis Eᴅᴡᴀʀᴅɪ erat in *Wᴀʀᴍᴠɴᴅᴇꜱᴛʀᴏᴠ Hᴰ*

unū Wich . in quo erat puteus ad ſal faciendū . 7 ibi eraꝗ̃

. ᴠɪɪɪ . ſalinæ . int regē 7 comitē Eduinū . ita q̄d de omibƺ

exitibƺ 7 redditionibƺ ſalinarū habeꝛ rex . ɪɪ . partes.

7 comes tciã . Ipſe ũ comes p̄ter has habeꝛ unã ſalinã

ꝓpriã . quæ adjacebat ſuo ℳ *ᴀᴄᴀᴛᴏɴᴇ* . De hac ſalina p tot anã

habeꝛ comes ſal ſufficient ſuæ domui . Siq̄d autē inde

uenderẽt.' de theloneo habeꝛ rex . ɪɪ . denar . 7 com̃ tciũ.

In eod̄ Wich habeꝛ ſalinas plurimi hoẽs patriæ . de

q̄bƺ erat tal c̄ſuetudo . Ab aſcenſione dn̄i uſqƺ ad feſtū ſc̄i

Martini.' poterat q̄ſqƺ hn̄s ſalinã portare ſal ꝓpũ ad ſuã

domũ . Qui ũ inde aliq̄d uenderet ſiue ibi ſiue in comitatu

ceſtrenſi.' dabat theloneũ regi 7 comiti . Poſt feſtū S̄ Mar

tini q̄ſq̄s inde portaret ſal uel ꝓpũ uel empticiũ.' dabat

theloneũ . excepta ſalina comitis ſup̄dicta ſua c̄ſuetud̄ utente.

Illæ . ᴠɪɪɪ . p̄dictæ ſalinæ regis 7 comit̄ . in ipſa ebdomada qua

bulliebant 7 exercebant . in die ueneris reddeꝛ . xᴠɪ . bullio

nes . ex q̄bƺ . xᴠ . facieꝛ unã ſūmã ſalis . Alioƺ hōum ſa

linæ . ab aſcenſione dn̄i uſqƺ ad feſtū S̄ Mᴀʀᴛɪɴɪ . n̄ dabaꝗ̃

has bullitiones in die ueneris . Tranſacta ũ feſtiuit̄ S̄ ᴍᴀʀ

ᴛɪɴɪ . uſqƺ ad aſcenſionẽ dn̄i.' dabant om̄s c̄ſuetud̄ bullitionis.

ſic ſalinæ regis 7 comitis.

Om̄s iſtæ ſalinæ 7 cōmunes 7 dn̄icæ . cingebant ex una p⟨⟩rte

quodã flumine . 7 q̄da foſſato ex alia parte.

Qui infra hanc metã forisfeciſſet.' poterat em̄dare p . ɪɪ.

ſolid̄ . aut p . xxx . bulliones ſalis . Excepto homicidio uel

furto de quo ad mortē iudicabaꞇ latro . H̄ ſi ibi fiebant.'

em̄dabant ſic p totã ſciram.

Siq̄s ex præſcripto circuitu ſalinarū alicubi p totū comitaꞇ

detuliſſet theloneũ.' ꝗbat inde referebat . 7 p xʟ . ſolid̄ ibid̄ē

em̄dabat . ſi liꝛ hō erat . Si n̄ erat liꝛ.' p . ɪɪɪɪ . ſolid̄.

In NANTWICH Hundred

1    Before 1066 there was a *Wich,* where there was a saltpit and 8
salthouses, divided between the King and Earl Edwin, so that the
King had two parts of all income and returns from the salthouses
and the Earl one third. But as well as these the Earl had a
salthouse of his own, attached to his manor of Acton. From this
salthouse the Earl had salt sufficient for his household for the
whole year; but if any of it were sold, the King had two pence
of the toll, the Earl the third penny.

2    In the same *Wich* many of the men of the district had salthouses,
which were subject to the following custom:

3    From  Ascension Day to Martinmas anyone who had a salthouse
might carry his own salt to his house, but if he sold any of it, either
there or anywhere else throughout Cheshire, he paid toll to the
King and the Earl.
      After Martinmas anyone who carried salt, whether his own or
for sale, paid toll, except for the aforesaid salthouse of the Earl,
which kept its own custom.

4    In a week in which these said 8 salthouses of the King and the Earl
were at work boiling, they paid on the Friday 16 boilings, 15 of
which make a packload of salt; other men's salthouses did not pay
these Friday boilings between Ascension Day and Martinmas, but
from Martinmas to Ascension Day they paid all boiling customs,
like the salthouses of the King and the Earl.

5    All these salthouses, both of the commons and of the lords, were
bounded on one side by a river and on the other by a dyke.
Anyone who incurred a penalty within these boundaries could pay
a fine of 2s, or of 30 boilings of salt, except for homicide, or for a
theft for which the thief was condemned to death. Those who
committed such offences were punished as in the rest of the shire.

6    If anyone were proved to have taken the toll (which he should
have paid) outside the prescribed boundaries of the salthouses,
to anywhere else in the county, he returned and paid a fine, of
40s if he were a free man, of 4s if he were not free;

Si ũ in aliã fcirã ipsũ theloneũ afportabat: ubi calũnia
bat ibid emdabat.                          ꝸ ejufđ hunđ.

T.R.E . reddeƀ . xxi . liƀ de firma iſtud Wich cũ omĩbʒ placitis
Qdo Hugo recepit: erat uuaſtũ p̃ter unã tanℏ falinã .

Modo ten eunđ Wich Wiłłs malbedeng de comite cũ omĩƀ
cſuetudinibʒ ibid p̃tĩtibʒ . 7 toℏ ipſũ HVND . qđ app̃ciaℏ . xL . ſoℏ .
de qƀʒ denaꝛ ponunℏ fup̃ trã ipſius Wiłłi . xxx . ſoℏ . Reliɋ
x . folid fup̃ trã ep̃i 7 fup̃ tras Ricardi 7 Giſłeƀti . q̃s hñt
7 Wich . e ad firmã ꝑ . x . liƀ.                  ꝸ in eod Hund.

In MILDESTVICH HVND erat aliud Wich . inℏ regẽ 7 comĩℏℏ.
Non eraɴ ibi dñicæ falinæ . fed æedẽ leges habebanℏ ibi
7 cſuetudines . quæ in fup̃iori Wich diđæ fuɴ . 7 eod m̃ partici
pabanℏ rex 7 comes . Hoc Wich erat ad firmã ꝑ . viii . liƀ.
7 Hvndret in quo jaceƀ ꝑ . xL . ſolid . Rex . ii . partes . tciã comes.
Qdo Hugo recep̃: waſtũ fuit . Modo ten ipſe comes.
7 eſt ad firmã ꝑ . xxv . ſolid . 7 duabʒ caretedes falis.

HVndret ũ: ualet . xL . ſoℏ.

De his duobʒ Wichis . ɋcunɋ emptũ ſal carro portabat:
de theloneo . iiii . deɴ dabat . fi ad carrũ . iiii . boues aut plus
habeƀ . Si . ii . boues: ii . denaꝛ thelon dabat . fi . ii . ſũmæ ſaℏ
eraɴ . ꝸ Homo de alio hunđ . de ſũma caballi daƀ . ii . denaꝛ.
Homo ũ de eod hunđ: ñ nifi obolũ dabat ꝑ ſũma falis.

ꝸ Qui carrũ in tantũ onerabat ut axis frangereℏ infra unã
leuũ circa utrunɋ Wich: daƀ . ii . ſolid miniſtro regis
uel comitis . fi infra leuuã poſſet confequi.

Similiℏ qui caballũ ita onerabat ut dorſũ frangeret.
daƀ . ii . ſolid . infra leuuã cſecuℏ . Extra leuuã nichil.

Qui de una ſũma ſal facieƀ duas: xL . ſoℏ emdaƀ . fi minis
ter eũ poſſet confequi . Si ñ eſſet inuenℏ: nil ꝑ aliũ emdaƀ.

Hões pedites de alio Hund ſal ibi emtes: de viii . oneribʒ
ꝓ hõum dabaɴ . ii . deń . Hões ejđ Hund: ꝑ . viii . oneribʒ unũ
                                     ꝸ denariũ.

268 b

but if he took it into another shire, he paid the fine where he was charged.

7 Before 1066 this *Wich* paid £21 in revenue, with all the pleas of this Hundred. When Earl Hugh acquired it, it was derelict, except for a single salthouse; now William Malbank holds this *Wich* from the Earl, with all the customary dues that belong to it, and the whole of this Hundred, which is assesssed at 40s, of which money 30s is imposed upon the land of William himself, the other 10s upon the Bishop's land and upon the lands which Richard (of Vernon) and Gilbert (of Venables) have in this Hundred; the *Wich* is at a revenue of £10.

## S2 (Middlewich)

1 In Northwich Hundred there was another *Wich,* (divided) between the King and the Earl. Although there were no lord's salthouses there, they had the same laws and customs, as set down in the above *Wich,* and the King and Earl shared in the same way. This *Wich* was at a revenue of £8, and the Hundred in which it lay at 40s; the King had two parts, the Earl the third. When Earl Hugh acquired it, it was derelict; now the Earl holds it himself, and it is at a revenue of 25s and 2 cartloads of salt; but the value of the Hundred is 40s.

2 Whoever carted purchased salt from these two *Wiches* paid 4d in toll if he had four or more oxen to his cart; if two oxen, he paid 2d toll, if there were two packloads of salt.
   A man from another Hundred paid 2d for a packhorse load, but a man from the same Hundred paid only ½d for a packload of salt.
   Anyone who so overloaded a cart that the axle broke within one league of either *Wich* paid 2s to the officer of the King or the Earl, if he could be caught within the league; similarly, anyone who so overloaded a horse that he broke its back paid 2s, if caught within the league; beyond the league, nothing.

3 Anyone who made two packloads of salt out of one paid a fine of 40s, if the officer could catch him; if he were not found he paid no fine through anyone else.

4 Men on foot from another Hundred who bought salt there paid 2d on 8 manloads; men of the same Hundred paid 1d on 8 loads.

† (S3 is added at the foot of column 268 a, after 27,4, directed to its proper place by transposition signs)

*In Wales all land, except those parts of Gwynedd granted to Robert of Rhuddlan, was held from the King by Earl Hugh; the customary chapter numbers, headings and list of landholders were omitted. In the translation the name of each chief landholder who held from Earl Hugh is printed bold at the beginning of his chapter, with its number; the list of landholders is given opposite.*

268 d

Hᵉᵒᵐ̃vɢo ten in dñio *HAORDINE*. *IN ATISCROS HVND*.

Eduin tenuit.Ibi.III.hidæ geld.Tra.ē.IIII.car.7 dimiđ

In dñio funt.II.car.7 IIII.ferui.Ibi æccła ad quā ꝑtin dim car træ.

7 Ibi.IIII.uiłłi 7 VI.borđ.cū.II.car.Ibi dimiđ aĉ ꝑti.Silua.II.leuū

lḡ.7 una lat. Vał.XL.folid.In ciuitate.II.mafuræ waftæ jbi ꝑtin.

Iꝑfe coɱ̃ ten *RADINTONE*.Eduin tenuit.Ibi.I.hida geld.Tra.ē

.I.car.Wast fuit 7 ē.

Roꝑt de Roeleɴ ten de coɱ̃ *BROCHETVNE* Leuenot tenuit 7 liƀ hō fuit.

Ibi.I.virg 7 dim.gelđ.Tra.ē dimiđ car.quæ ibi.ē cū.I.uiłło.

Prati.I.virg 7 dim.Vał.III.foł.7 hɫ̃ tciā partē filuæ.I.leu lḡ 7 lat.

# LAND OF EARL HUGH AND HIS MEN IN WALES

**FD** In ATI'S CROSS Hundred
(FLINTSHIRE, Deeside)

1 Earl Hugh himself
2 Robert of Rhuddlan
3 William Malbank
4 William son of Nigel
5 Hugh son of Osbern
6 Osbern son of Tezzo
7 Hamo (of Mascy)
8 Ralph Hunter
9 The Earl's Forest

**FT** In ATI'S CROSS Hundred
(FLINTSHIRE, Tegeingl)

1 Earl Hugh himself
2 Robert of Rhuddlan
3 The Earl's Men

**G** In NORTH WALES
(Gwynedd)

1 Robert of Rhuddlan

---

**FD 1**        **EARL HUGH holds**        268 d

In ATI'S CROSS Hundred

1 HAWARDEN in lordship. Earl Edwin held it. 3 hides paying tax.
Land for 4½ ploughs. In lordship 2 ploughs; 4 slaves;
a church, to which belongs ½ carucate of land.
4 villagers and 6 smallholders with 2 ploughs.
Meadow, ½ acre; woodland 2 leagues long and 1 wide.
Value 40s.
2 unoccupied dwellings in the City belong to there.

2 The Earl holds RADINGTON himself. Earl Edwin held it. 1 hide
paying tax. Land for 1 plough. It was and is waste.

### [From Earl Hugh]

## FD 2    Robert of Rhuddlan holds

1 BROUGHTON from the Earl. Leofnoth held it; he was a free man.
1½ virgates paying tax. Land for ½ plough, which is there, with
1 villager.
Meadow, 1½ virgates.
Value 3s.
He has a third part of a wood 1 league long and wide.

Iſd.R.ten ibi.i.m̃ de dimiđ hida gelđ.Vlmer liƀ h̄o tenuit.

Tra.ē dim car.Hanc h̄t ibi.i.radman cū.i.uilło 7 uno borđ.

Iſd.R.ten VLFEMILTONE.7 Azelin de eo.Leuenot̄/Val.iii.ſol.
tenuit.liƀ h̄o fuit.Ibi.i.hida gelđ.Tra.ē.i.car.Ibi ſunt.ii.uilłi
7 un borđ.cū.vi.boƀ.Silua.i.leuu lḡ.7 tn̄tđ lat̄.Val.x.ſolid.

Iſd.R.ten LATBROC.Leuenot 7 Vlƀert p.ii.m̃ tenuer̄.7 liƀi fuer̄.
Ibi dimiđ hida gelđ.Tra.ē.i.car.Hanc hn̄t ibi.ii.radmans
cū.ii.borđ.Silua.i.leuu lḡ.7 tn̄tđ lat̄.Val.x.ſolid.

Iſd.R.ten BACHELIE.7 Roger de eo.Erne tenuit.Ibi.i.hida gelđ.
Tra.ē.i.car.Hanc hn̄t ibi.ii.uilłi 7 iiii.borđ.Val.viii.ſolid.

Iſd.R.ten COLESELT.7 Eduin de eo.qui 7 tenuit ut liƀ h̄o.
Ibi.i.hida gelđ.Tra.ē.i.car.Ipſa.ē ibi cū.i.radman 7 iiii.uilłis
7 ii.borđ.Val.x.ſolid.Valuit.vi.ſol.

Wilłs Malbedeng 7 Ricard de eo ten CLAITONE.Rauechel
tenuit 7 liƀ h̄o fuit.Ibi.i.hida gelđ.Tra.ē.i.car.Ibi.ē in dn̄io
cū.ii.borđ.Ibi.i.ac̄ p̄ti.Silua.i.leuu lḡ.7 tn̄tđ lat̄.Val.x.ſol.

Iſd.W.ten WEPRE.Ernui tenuit 7 liƀ fuit.Ibi tcia pars hidæ
gelđ.Tra.ē tciæ partis car.Hanc h̄t ibi.i.radman cū.i.uilło.

Wilłs.F.Nigelli ten MERLESTONE.Erne /Val.x.ſol.
tenuit.Anſger ten de Wilło 7 h̄t ibi dim car.Ibi.i.virg træ gelđ.
Ibi.i.ſeruus.ē.Wast̄ fuit.Modo ual.iiii.ſol.

Robert also holds

2   One manor there, at ½ hide paying tax. Wulfmer, a free man,
held it. Land for ½ plough. 1 rider has it, with
    1 villager and 1 smallholder.
Value 3s.

3   GOLFTYN. Ascelin holds from him. Leofnoth held it; he was a
free man. 1 hide paying tax. Land for 1 plough.
    2 villagers and 1 smallholder with 6 oxen.
    Woodland 1 league long and as wide.
Value 10s.

4   LEADBROOK. Leofnoth and Wulfbert held it as 2 manors; they
were free. ½ hide paying tax. Land for 1 plough. 2 riders have it, with
    2 smallholders.
    Woodland 1 league long and as wide.
Value 10s.

5   BAGILLT. Roger holds from him. Arni held it. 1 hide paying tax.
Land for 1 plough.
    2 villagers and 4 smallholders have it.
Value 8s.

6   COLESHILL. Edwin, who also held it as a free man, holds from him.
1 hide paying tax. Land for 1 plough. It is there, with
    1 rider, 4 villagers and 2 smallholders.
The value is 10s; it was 6s.

## FD 3   William Malbank holds

1   'CLAYTON'. Richard holds from him. Ravenkel held it; he was a
free man. 1 hide paying tax. Land for 1 plough. It is there,
in lordship, with
    2 smallholders.
    Meadow, 1 acre; woodland 1 league long and as wide.
Value 10s.

2   William also holds WEPRE. Ernwy held it; he was free. A third part
of 1 hide paying tax. Land for a third part of a plough. 1 rider
has it, with
    1 villager.
Value 10s.

## FD 4   William son of Nigel holds

1   MARLSTON. Arni held it. Asgar holds it from William and has
½ plough. 1 virgate of land paying tax. 1 slave.
It was waste; value now 4s.

Hᴠɢᴏ.F.Osɓni ten̄ Bʀᴏᴄʜᴇᴛᴏɴᴇ.Rauesuard tenuit.7 liɓ fuit.
Ibi.ɪ.virg̃ tre 7 dɪm̃ geld̃ Tra.ē dɪm̃ car̃.Hanc h̄t ibi.ɪ.radman
cū.ɪ.uitlo 7 ɪɪ.borđ.Silua ibi.ɪ.leuu l̄g.7 una lat̄.Val̄.ᴠ.ſol̄.

Iſđ.H.ten̄ Cʟᴀᴠᴇɴᴛᴏɴᴇ.Oſmer tenuit.7 liɓ h̄o fuit.Ibi.ɪɪ.hidæ
geld̃.Tra.ē.ɪɪ.car̃.Vna.ē in dn̄io.7 ɪɪ.bouar̃.7 ɪɪɪɪ.uilti h̄nt aliã.
cū.ɪɪɪ.borđ.Ad̃ hoc m̄ ptin̄ in ciuitate.ᴠɪɪɪ.burg̃ſes.7 ɪɪɪɪ.ult̄ aquā.
7 reddt.ɪx.ſol̄.7 ɪɪɪɪ.den̄.7 jn Noruuich.ɪ.ſalina de.xɪɪ.den̄.
Ibi.ɪɪɪ.ac̃ p̃ti.Valuit 7 ual̄.xʟ.ſol̄.Waſt̄ inuen̄.

Iſđ.H.ten̄ Eᴅʀɪᴛᴏɴᴇ.7 Ricard de eo.Elmer 7 Rauechet p.ɪɪ.m̄
tenuer̄.7 liɓi h̄oes fuer̄.Ibi.ɪ.hidā geld̃.Tra.ē.ɪ.car̃.Hæc ibi
ē cū.ɪɪ.radmans.7 ɪɪɪ.borđ.Ibi.ɪ.ac̃ p̃ti.Val̄.x.ſoliđ.
Huj træ.ɪ.hidā ten̄ Osɓn̄.F.tezon.7 Hugo.F.Norman dɪm̃ hiđ.

Osʙᴇʀɴ̄.F.Tezonis ten̄ Dᴏᴅᴇsᴛᴠɴᴇ.Eduin̄ tenuit.Ibi.ɪɪ.hidæ
geld̃.Tra.ē.ɪɪ.car̃.In dn̄io.ē una 7 dɪm̃.cū.ɪɪɪ.bouar̃.7 ɪɪɪɪ.uilti
cū.ɪɪɪ.borđ h̄nt dɪm̃ car̃.Huic m̄ ptin̄.xᴠ.burg̃ſes in ciuitate
7 reddt.ᴠɪɪɪ.ſol̄.Silua.ɪ.leuu l̄g.7 tn̄tđ lat̄.Val̄.xʟ.ſoliđ.

Hᴀᴍᴏ ten̄ Esᴛᴏɴᴇ.Eduin̄ 7 Toret p.ɪɪ.m̄ tenuer̄.7 liɓi fuer̄.
Ibi.ɪ.hida geld̃.Tra.ē.ɪ.car̃.H̄ ibi.ē cū.ɪɪ.radmans.7 ɪɪ.uiltis
7 ɪɪɪ.borđ.Silua ibi.ɪ.leuu l̄g.7 tn̄tđ lat̄.Val̄.x.ſoliđ.
De hac tra ten̄ Ran̄n̄.ɪ.uirg̃.

Iſđ Hamo ten̄ Cᴀsᴛʀᴇᴛᴏɴᴇ.7 Oſmund de eo.Eduin̄ tenuit ſic̄
liɓ h̄o.Ibi dimiđ hida geld̃.Tra.ē.ɪ.car̃.Dimiđ h̄nt ibi.ɪɪ.uilti
cū.ɪ.borđ.Silua.ɪ.leuu l̄g.7 tn̄tđ lat̄.Val̄.ᴠ.ſoliđ.

## FD 5 Hugh son of Osbern holds

1    BROUGHTON. Ravenswart held it; he was free. 1½ virgates of land paying tax. Land for ½ plough. 1 rider has it, with
     1 villager and 2 smallholders.
     Woodland 1 league long and 1 wide.
   Value 5s.

Hugh also holds

2    CLAVERTON. Osmer held it; he was a free man. 2 hides paying tax. Land for 2 ploughs. In lordship 1; 2 ploughmen.
     4 villagers have the other plough, with 3 smallholders.
     To this manor belong 8 burgesses in the City and 4 across the river, who pay 9s 4d; and in Northwich 1 salt-house at 12d.
     Meadow, 3 acres.
   The value was and is 40s; found waste.

3    KINNERTON (?). Richard holds from him. Aelmer and Ravenkel held it as 2 manors; they were free men. 1½ hides paying tax. Land for 1 plough. It is there, with
     2 riders and 3 smallholders.
     Meadow, 1 acre.
   Value 10s.
     Osbern son of Tezzo holds 1 hide of this land, and Hugh son of Norman ½ hide.

## FD 6 Osbern son of Tezzo holds

1    DODLESTON. Earl Edwin held it. 2 hides paying tax. Land for 2 ploughs. In lordship 1½, with 3 ploughmen.
     4 villagers with 3 smallholders have ½ plough.
     To this manor belong 15 burgesses in the City; they pay 8s.
     Woodland 1 league long and as wide.
   Value 40s.

## FD 7 Hamo (of Mascy) holds

1    ASTON. Edwin and Thored held it as 2 manors; they were free. 1 hide paying tax. Land for 1 plough. It is there, with
     2 riders, 2 villagers and 3 smallholders.
     Woodland 1 league long and as wide.
   Value 10s.
     Ranulf holds 1 virgate of this land.

2    Hamo also holds LLYS EDWIN. Osmund holds from him. Edwin held it as a free man. ½ hide paying tax. Land for 1 plough.
     2 villagers with 1 smallholder have ½ (plough).
     Woodland 1 league long and as wide.
   Value 5s.

R<sup>uenator</sup>ADVLFVS ten de com̃ BROCHETVNE . Vlfac tenuit 7 lib̃ hõ fuit.

Ibi . I . virg træ geld . Tra . ẽ . I . car̃ . H̃ ibi . ẽ in dñio cũ . II . feruis.

Ibi . I . virg p̃ti . Val . v . fol.

RADVLF ten SVTONE . Sberne tenuit 7 lib̃ hõ fuit . Ibi . I . hida

geld . Tra . ẽ . I . car̃ . H̃ ibi . ẽ cũ . I . radman 7 IIII . bord̃ . Val . v . folid̃.

Silua ibi dim̃ leuu lg̃ . 7 IIII . acs lat̃.

Harũ . xx . hidar̃ oms filuas h̃ comes in forefta fua pofitas.

Vnde M̃ funt multũ pejorata.

H̃ forefta h̃ . x . leuu long̃ . 7 III . leuu lat̃ . Ibi fuɴ̃ . IIII . airæ.

f accipitrũ.

## IN ATISCROS HVND.

HVGO COMES ten de rege ROELEND . Ibi T.R.E

jacebat ENGLEFELD . 7 tot̃ erat Waft . Eduin com̃ teneb̃.

Q̃do Hugo recep̃ fimilit̃ erat Waft . Modo h̃ in dñio

Medietatẽ caftelli qd̃ ROELENT uocat̃ . 7 cap̃ eft huj træ

Ibi h̃ . VIII . burg̃fes . 7 medietatẽ æcclæ 7 monetæ . 7 medietatẽ

mineriæ ferri ubicunq̃ in hoc M̃ inuenta fuerit . 7 medie

tatẽ Aquæ de Cloit . 7 de Molinis 7 pifcarijs quæ ibi fient.

in ea fcilicet parte fluminis quæ p̃tin ad feudũ comitis.

7 medietatẽ foreftarũ quæ ñ p̃tineb̃ ad aliq̃ uillã ifti M̃.

7 medietatẽ thelonei . 7 medietatẽ uillæ quæ uocat̃ BREN.

Ibi . ẽ Tra . III . car̃ . 7 ibi funt in dñio cũ . VII . feruis . Ad BREN

p̃tin hæ . v . træ . Cauber Keuend . Brennehedui . Leuuarludæ.

7 dimid̃ Peintret . Val . III . lib̃.

Ad hoc M̃ ROELENT jaceɴ̃ hæ Bereuuichæ.

Diffaren . Bodugan . Chiluen 7 Maineual . In his . ẽ tra . I . car̃

tant̃ . 7 Silua . I . leuu lg̃ . 7 dimid̃ lat̃ . Ibi . I . francig 7 II . uilti

h̃nt . I . car̃.

## FD 8    Ralph Hunter holds

1   BROUGHTON from the Earl. Wulfheah held it; he was a free man.
1 virgate of land paying tax. Land for 1 plough. This is there,
in lordship, with 2 slaves.
    Meadow, 1 virgate.
Value 5s.

2   Ralph also holds SOUGHTON.   Esbern held it; he was a free man.
1 hide paying tax. Land for 1 plough. This is there, with
    1 rider and 4 smallholders.
Value 5s.
    Woodland ½ league long and 4 acres wide.

## FD 9    [The Earl's Forest]

1   Of these 20 hides the Earl has all the woodland, which he has
put in his forest; whence the manors have greatly deteriorated.
The forest is 10 leagues long and 3 leagues wide; there are
4 hawk's eyries.

## FT 1    EARL HUGH holds    269 a

In ATI'S CROSS Hundred

1   RHUDDLAN from the King. Before 1066 ENGLEFIELD  lay there;
it was all waste. Earl Edwin held it. When Earl Hugh acquired it
it was likewise waste. Now he has in the lordship half of the
castle called Rhuddlan, which is the head of this land. He has
there 8 burgesses; half of the church and the mint; half the iron
mines, wherever found on this manor; half the waters of the
Clwyd; of the mills and fisheries made there, namely on the part
of the river that belongs to the Earl's Holding; half of the forests
which did not belong to any other village of this manor; half of
the toll, and half the village called BRYN. Land for 3 ploughs
They are there, in lordship, with 7 slaves.
    These 5 lands belong to Bryn: CWYBR, CEFN DU, BRYN HEDYDD, .
LLEWERLYDD  and half PENTRE.
Value £3.

2   These outliers lay in the manor of Rhuddlan: DYSERTH, BODEUGAN,
CILOWEN, MAEN - EFA. In them land for 1 plough only.
    Woodland 1 league long and ½ wide.
    1 Frenchman and 2 villagers have 1 plough.

Itē Widhulde Blórat Dinmerſch 7 Brenuuen. Tra.e͛.ɪ.car.quā
hn̄t ibi.ɪɪ.uiłłi 7 ɪ.ſeruie͛ſ comit. Silua.ɪ.leuu lḡ.7 dim̄ lat̄.

In Treuelefneu 7 Schiuiau.e͛ tra.ɪ.car.q̄ hn̄t ibi.ɪɪɪ.uiłłi
Silua.xʟ.p̄tic lḡ.7 tntd̄ lat̄.                    ſuiłłi.7 una ac̄ ſiluæ.

In Leſthunied 7 Moclitone 7 Leſſecóit.e͛ tra.ɪ.car.q̄ hn̄t ibi.ɪɪɪ.

In Brunford 7 Helchene 7 Vlchenol.e͛ tra.ɪ.car.quā hn̄t
ibi.v.uiłłi.Silua.ɪ.leuu lḡ.7 ɪɪ.ac̄r lat̄.

In Folebroc.e͛ tra.ɪ.car.quā hn̄t ibi.ɪɪɪ.uiłłi 7 ɪɪ.bord̄.Silua
dimid̄ leuu lḡ.7 xʟ.p̄tic lat̄.

In Meretone 7 Caldecote 7 tcia par|de Widford.e͛ tra.ɪ.car.
quā hn̄t ibi p̄br cū.vɪ.uiłłis.7 æceła.Silua dimid̄ leuu lḡ.7 xx.
p̄tic lat̄.Odin ten de comite.                    ſp̄tic lat̄

In Aſketone 7 Cheſlilaued.e͛ tra.ɪ.car.Marcud ten de comite.
7 ibi ſunt.ɪɪɪ.uiłłi 7 ɪ.bord̄.cū.x.bob̃ arantes.

Om̄s hæ Bereuuich Waſtæ fuer̄.T.R.E.7 qdó com̄ recepit.
Modo int̄ om̄s uał.cx.ſolid̄.


Rotbertvs de Roelent ten de Hugone medietatē
ejd̄ caſtelli 7 burgi in quo ht̄ ipſe.Ro.x.burḡſes.7 medietatē
æcclæ 7 monetæ.7 minariæ ferri ibid̄ inuentæ.7 medietatē
aquæ de Cloith.7 de piſcarijs 7 molinis ibid̄ faćtis 7 faciendis.
7 medietatē thelonei 7 foreſtarū quæ n̄ p̄tin ad aliq̄ uillā
ſup̄dićti m̄.7 medietatē uillæ quæ uocat Bren.cū his
bereuuichis.Lauarludon.Penegors.Reuuordui.Tredueng
7 paruū Cauber.In his.e͛ tra ad.ɪɪɪ.car tant̄.7 ibi ſunt in
dn̄io.cū.vɪ.ſeruis.7 molin̄ ibi redd̄.ɪɪɪ.modios annonæ.
Vał.ɪɪɪ.lib̄.

3 Also *WIDHULDE*, BLORANT, TREMEIRCHION, and BRYNGWYN.
Land for 1 plough, which
2 villagers and 1 of the Earl's servants have.
Woodland 1 league long and ½ wide.

4 In TRELLYNIAU and YSCEIFIOG land for 1 plough, which
3 villagers have.
Woodland 40 perches long and as wide.

5 In LLSTYN HUNYDD, MECHLAS and LLYS Y COED land for 1 plough, which
3 villagers have.
Woodland, 1 acre.

6 In BRYNFORD, HALKYN and *ULCHENOL* land for 1 plough, which
5 villagers have.
Woodland 1 league long and 2 acres wide.

7 In FULBROOK land for 1 plough, which
3 villagers and 2 smallholders have.
Woodland ½ league long and 40 perches wide.

8 In MERTYN, CALCOT and a third part of WHITFORD land for 1 plough, which
a priest with 6 villagers have. A church
Woodland ½ league long and 20 perches wide.
Odin holds from the Earl.

9 In AXTON and GELLILYFDY land for 1 plough. Marchiud holds from the Earl.
3 villagers and 1 smallholder who plough with 10 oxen.

10 Before 1066, and when Earl Hugh acquired them, all these outliers were waste.
Value now 110s between them.

## [FROM EARL HUGH]

### FT 2 Robert of Rhuddlan holds

1 half of this castle and Borough from the Earl Hugh, wherein
Robert himself has 10 burgesses; half of the church and the
mint, and of the iron mines found there; half of the waters of
the Clwyd; of the fisheries and mills there, made or to be made;
half of the toll; and of the forests which do not belong to any
other village of the said manor; half of the village called BRYN
with these outliers:
LLEWERLLYD, 'PEN-Y-GORS', RHYD ORDDWY, *TREDVENG* and CWYBR BACH
In them land for 3 ploughs only. They are there, in lordship,
with 6 slaves.
A mill which pays 3 measures of corn
Value £3.

In diſſard 7 Boteuuarul 7 Ruargor. Tra.ē.ɪ.car. Ibi.ē in dnĩo
7 ɪɪ.ſerui.7 æccła cū pͮbro.7 ɪɪ.uiłłi 7 molĩn de.ɪɪɪ.ſoł.7 ɪɪ.borđ.
Silua.ɪ.leuu lḡ.7 dimiđ lať.7 ibi aira accipitris.Vał.xxx.ſoł.
In Raduch 7 Pengdeſlion.ē tra.ɪ.car.Ibi.ē in dnĩo cū.ɪɪɪ.uiłł.
In Riuelenoit.ē tra.ɪ.car.7 ibi.ē in dnĩo.   ⌐Vał.x.ſoliđ.
cū.ɪɪ.ſeruis.7 v.borđ.Vał.xx.ſoliđ.
In Cairos 7 Lanuuile 7 Charcan.ē tra.ɪ.car.7 ibi.ē ipſa
cū.ɪ.ſeruo.7 vɪ.borđ.Silua.xʟ.ptic̃ lḡ.7 xʟ.lať.Vał.xv.ſoł.
In Meincatis 7 Treueri.7 Coiwen.ē tra.ɪ.car.7 ibi.ē in dnĩo cū.ɪɪ.
ſeruis.7 ɪɪɪɪ.borđ.7 ɪɪ.uiłłis.  Vał.xxv.ſoł.
In Inglecroſt.7 Brunfor 7 Alchene.ē tra.ɪ.car.Ibi.ē in dnĩo cū
eccła 7 pͮbro 7 ɪɪɪ.borđ.Ibi molĩn de.v.ſoł.Silua dim leuu lḡ.7 xʟ.
pticas lať.Vał.x.ſoliđ.
In Widford 7 putecain.ē tra.ɪ.car.Ibi.ē cū.ɪɪ.uiłłis 7 xɪɪ.int̃
ſeruos 7 anciłł.Ibi piſcaria 7 Silua dim leuu lḡ.7 xʟ.ptic lať.
                                   ⌐Vał.xx.ſoł.
269 b
In *MOSTONE*.ē tra.ɪ.car.Ibi.ē cū.ɪɪɪɪ.uiłłis.7 vɪɪɪ.borđ.Silua
una leuu lḡ.7 xʟ.ptic lať.Vał.xx.ſoliđ.
In *PICHETONE* 7 Melchaneſtone.ē tra.ɪ.car.7 Ibi.ē cū.ɪɪ.uiłłis
7 ɪɪ.borđ.Silua dimiđ leuu lḡ.7 xʟ.ptic lať.Vał.xv.ſoliđ.

2   in DYSERTH, *BOTEUUARUL* and 'RHIWARGOR' land for 1 plough.
It is there, in lordship; 2 slaves;
  a church with a priest and 2 villagers.
  A mill at 3s.
  2 smallholders.
  Woodland 1 league long and ½ wide; a hawk's eyrie.
Value 30s.

3   In HIRADDUG and *PENGDESLION* land for 1 plough. It is there,
in lordship, with
  3 villagers.
Value 10s.

4   In TRELAWNYD land for 1 plough. It is there, in lordship, with
2 slaves;
  5 smallholders.
Value 20s.

5   In CAERWYS, LLAN ELWY and CYRCHYNAN land for 1 plough. It is
there, with 1 slave;
  6 smallholders.
  Woodland 40 perches long and 40 wide.
Value 15s.

6   In *MEINCATIS,* TREFRAITH and *COIWEN* land for 1 plough. It is
there, in lordship, with 2 slaves;
  4 smallholders and 2 villagers.
Value 25s.

7   In *INGLECROFT,* BRYNFORD and HALKYN land for 1 plough. It is
there, in lordship, with
  a church, and a priest and 3 smallholders.
  A mill at 5s; woodland ½ league long and 40 perches wide.
Value 10s.

8   In WHITFORD and BYCHTON land for 1 plough. It is there, with
  2 villagers and 12 male and female slaves.
  A fishery; woodland ½ league long and 40 perches wide.
Value 20s.

9   In MOSTYN land for 1 plough. It is there, with          269 b
  4 villagers and 8 smallholders.
  Woodland 1 league long and 40 perches wide.
Value 20s.

10  In PICTON and *MELCHANESTONE* land for 1 plough. It is there, with
  2 villagers and 2 smallholders.
  Woodland ½ league long and 40 perches wide.
Value 15s.

In Danfrond Calſtan 7 Weſbie.ē tra.ɪ.cař.Ibi ſunt.ɪɪ.radmans.

7 Tual q̇dā francig cū.vɪɪ.borđ.7 una æccła.Val.xv.ſolid.

In Cancarnacan 7 Weneſcol.ē tra.ɪ.cař.7 ibi.ē in dnio.cū.ɪɪ.francig.

7 ɪɪ.uiłłis.7 una æccła waſta.Val.xv.ſolid.

In Gronant 7 Vlueſgraue.tra.ē.ɪ.cař.Hæc ibi.ē cū.ɪɪ.uiłłis

★ 7 v.borđ.                    Val.xvɪ.cař.

In Wenfeſne.ē tra.ɪ.cař.7 ibi.ē in dnio.cū.ɪɪ.ſeruis.Val.xL.ſol.

In Preſtetoñe 7 Rūeſtoch.ē tra.ɪ.cař.7 ibi.ē in dnio.cū.ɪɪ.bouař.

7 ɪɪ.uiłłis.7 ɪɪɪɪ.borđ.Ibi.ē æccła.    Val.xx.ſolid.

In Dicolin 7 Rahop 7 Witeſtan.ē tra.ɪ.cař.7 ipſa ibi.ē.cū.ɪɪ.

uiłłis.7 ɪɪ.borđ.Silua ibi.ɪ.leuū lḡ.7 dimiđ lat.Val.xɪɪ.ſol.

Oms hæ Bereuuich ſup̄dictæ de Englefeld.jaceb T.R.E.in Roeleɴ.

7 tc erant waſtæ.7 Q̇do recep̄ Hugo.erant waſtæ.

Terra huj ꝏ ROELEND 7 Englefeld uel aliarū Bereuuicharū ſup̄dictař

ibi p̄tintiū.nunq̇ geldauit.neq̷ hidata fuit.

In ipſo ꝏ ROELEND ē factū nouit caſtellū.ſimilit Roeleɴ appellať.

Ibi.ē nouū burgū 7 in eo.xvɪɪɪ.burgſes.int Comit 7 Robtū

ut ſup̄dictū.ē.Ipſis burgſibȝ annueř leges 7 c̄ſuetudines

quæ ſunt in Hereford 7 in bretuill.ſcilicet qđ p̷ tot annū

de aliq̇ forisfactura n̄ dabunt niſi.xɪɪ.denař.p̄t homici

diū 7 furtū 7 Heinfař præcogitata.            ⌐ꝓ.ɪɪɪ.ſolid.

Ipſo anno huj deſcriptionis.datū.ē ad firmā huj burgi theloneū

11  In *DANFROND,* KELSTON and GWESBYR land for 1 plough.
    2 riders and Tual, a Frenchman, with 7 smallholders.
    A church.
    Value 15s.

12  In CARN-YLCHAN and GWAUNYSGOR land for 1 plough. It is there,
    in lordship, with
    2 Frenchmen and 2 villagers.
    A derelict church.
    Value 15s.

13  In GRONANT and GOLDEN GROVE land for 1 plough. This is there, with
    2 villagers and 5 smallholders.
    Value 16 [s].

14  In *WENFESNE* land for 1 plough. It is there, in lordship, with
    2 slaves.
    Value 40s.

15  In PRESTATYN and MELIDEN land for 1 plough. It is there, in lordship,
    with 2 ploughmen;
    2 villagers and 4 smallholders.
    A church.
    Value 20s.

16  In DINCOLYN, GOP and *WITESTAN* land for 1 plough. It is there, with
    2 villagers and 2 smallholders.
    Woodland 1 league long and ½ wide.
    Value 12s.

17  All the above Englefield outliers lay in Rhuddlan
    before 1066 and were then waste; and were waste when Earl
    Hugh acquired them.

18  Neither the land of this manor of Rhuddlan and Englefield, nor
    the above outliers belonging thereto ever paid tax; nor was it
    hidated.

19  In the manor of Rhuddlan itself a castle has been newly built,
    likewise called Rhuddlan. There is a new Borough and 18
    burgesses in it, divided between the Earl and Robert, as stated
    above. They accorded these burgesses the laws and customs which
    are observed in Hereford and Breteuil, namely that throughout
    the whole year they pay only 12d for any penalty apart from
    homicide, theft and premeditated breaking and entry. In the
    year of this survey the toll of this Borough was granted at a
    revenue of 3s.

Redditio Hugonis ex Roeleꝣ 7 Englefeld . ē apꝑciata . vi . lib

7 x . ſoliđ . Rotɓti pars: xvii . liɓ 7 iii . ſoliđ . *IN ATISCROS HĎ*

*B<sup>c</sup>ISOPESTREV* fuit ꝏ Eduini . T.R.E. Nunꝗ geldaú nec

hidaꞇ fuit . Tc ̄erat waſꞇ . 7 ꝗdo Hugo recep: ſimiliꞇ waſꞇ .

Modo tē Hugo . F . norman de comite medietatē huj ꝏ

7 totā Legge . 7 Sudfell . Tra . ē . i . caꝛ . quæ ibi . ē in đnio . cū . ii .

borđ . 7 i . aꞇ ꝓti ibi . Val . x . ſoliđ .

Aliā medietatē huj ꝏ 7 medietatē de mulintone 7 totū

Wiſelei . tē de com ̄Odin . Tra . ē . i . caꝛ . quæ ibi . ē cū . ii .

ſeruis . 7 uno borđ . Val . x . ſoliđ . *BEREWICH EꝨĎ MANꝚ .*

ꝼHendrebifau 7 Weltune 7 Munentone 7 Horſepol 7 Mulintone .

tē Hugo . F . Norman de comite . Tra . ē . ii . caꝛ .

Ipſæ . ii . caꝛ ibi ſunt cū . iii . uilꞇis 7 ii . borđ . Val . xviii . ſoliđ .

ꝼBruncot . tē Warmund de com . Tra . ē . i . caꝛ . Ibi . ē un

uilꞇs cū dimiđ caꝛ . 7 ii . boɓ . Val . x . ſoliđ .

ꝼRiſteſelle . tē Rađ de com . Tra . ē . i . caꝛ . Ipſa ibi . ē cū

iiii . borđ . Val . viii . ſoliđ .

ꝼQuiſnan . tē Wilꞇs de com . Tra . ē . i . caꝛ . Ipſa . ē ibi

cū pɓro 7 ii . uilꞇis . Silua ibi . i . leúu lꞧ . 7 dimiđ laꞇ .

★ Val . x . ſol . Omis ƕ tra ꝑtin ad Biſcopeſtreu . 7 Waſta f . . .

In hoc eođ ꝏ ē ſilua una ꝼNunꝗ geldauit . nec hidata fuit .

longituđ . i . leúu . 7 latituđ dimiđ leúu . Ibi . ē aira accipitris .

Hanc ſiluā ƕ com in foreſta ſua poſitā .

20  Earl Hugh's returns from Rhuddlan and Englefield are
    assessed at £6 10s; Robert's at £17 3s.

**FT 3**                **[The Earl's Men]**

In ATI'S CROSS Hundred
1   Before 1066 BISTRE was a manor of Earl Edwin's. It never paid
    tax, nor was it hidated. It was then waste, and was likewise waste
    when Earl Hugh acquired it. Now Hugh son of Norman holds
    half of this manor from the Earl, and all of *LEGGE and SUDFELL*.
    Land for 1 plough, which is there, in lordship, with
        2 smallholders.
        Meadow, 1 acre.
    Value 10s.
        Odin holds the other half of the manor from the Earl and half
    of *MULINTONE* and all of *WISELEI*. Land for 1 plough, which is
    there, with 2 slaves;
        1 smallholder.
    Value 10s.

**Outliers of this manor**
2   Hugh son of Norman holds from the Earl HENDREBIFFA, *WELTUNE*,
    *MUNENTONE*, the two 'HORSEPOOLS' and half of *MULINTONE*.
    Land for 2 ploughs. These 2 ploughs are there, with
        3 villagers and 2 smallholders.
    Value 18s.

3   Warmund Hunter holds BRYNCOED from the Earl. Land for 1 plough.
        1 villager with ½ plough and 2 oxen.
    Value 10s.

4   Ralph holds RHOS ITHEL from the Earl. Land for 1 plough.
    It is there, with
        4 smallholders.
    Value 8s.

5   William holds GWYSANEY from the Earl. Land for 1 plough. The
    plough is there, with
        a priest and 2 villagers.
        Woodland 1 league long and ½ wide.
    Value 10s.

6   All this land belongs to Bistre. It was waste. It never paid tax,
    nor was it hidated .
        In this manor the woodland is 1 league in length and
        ½ league in width; there is a hawk's eyrie. The Earl has this
        woodland, which he has put into his forest.

In eoð *ATISCROS* Hð Habuit . Rex Grifin . i . maneriū

Biſcopeſtreu . 7 in dnĩo . i . car̄ habeƀ . 7 Hōes ej̄ . vi . car̄.

Q̃do ipſe rex ibi uenieƀ,'reddeƀ ei unꝗꝗ car̄ . cc . heſthas.

7 unā cuuā plenā ceruiſia . 7 unā butiri Ruſcā.


Rotbert de Roeleſ ten de rege *NORTWALES* ad firmā ꝑ . xl . liƀ.

p̄t illā trā quā rex ei dederat in feudo . 7 p̄t tras epiſcopat.

Iſð Robꞇ calūniaꞇ uñ *HVND ARVESTER* . qð ten Rogerius.

Walenſes teſtificanꞇ iſtū *HVND* . ēē . de his *NORTWALIS*.

In feudo qð ipſe Robꞇ ten de rege *Ros* 7 *REWENIOV* . ſuꞇ xii . leuuæ

træ long . 7 iiii . leuū lat . Tra . ē . xx . car̄ tanꞇ . Apꝑciata . ē . xii . liƀ.

Om̃is alia tra . ē in Siluis 7 moris . nec poteſt arari.

7    In this Hundred of Ati's Cross King Gruffydd had 1 manor at
     BISTRE . He had 1 plough in lordship; his men, 6 ploughs.
     When the King came there himself every plough paid him
     200 loaves(?), a barrel of beer and a vessel of butter.


**G**    **Robert of Rhuddlan holds**

1    NORTH WALES  from the King at a revenue of £40, except for
     the land which the King gave him as a holding, and except
     for the land of the Bishopric. .

2    Robert also claims a Hundred, ARWYSTLI, which Earl Roger
     (of Montgomery) holds. The Welshmen testify that this
     Hundred is one of the  (Hundreds) of North Wales.

3    In the Holding which Robert holds himself from the King
     RHOS and RHUFONIOG   are 12 leagues of land long and 4 leagues wide.
     Land for 20 ploughs only.
     It is assessed at £12.
         All the other land is in woods and moors and cannot be
     ploughed.

Terrā infra Scriptā Tenvit Rogeri Pictavensis,
*Inter Ripā 7 Mersham.*      *In Derbei Hvndret,*
*Ibi* Habuit Rex Edward uñ m̄ *Derbei* nominatū.

cū . vi . Bereuuick . Ibi . iiii . hidæ . Tra . ē . xv . car . Foreſta

.ii . leuu lḡ . 7 una lat . 7 aira Accipitris.

Vctred tenƀ . vi . Maner . Rabil Chenulueſlei . Cherchebi

Croſebi . Magele . Achetun . Ibi . ii . hidæ

Siluæ . ii . leuū lḡ . 7 lat . 7 ii . airæ accipitr .

Dot teneƀ Hitune 7 Torboc . Ibi . i . hida qeta ab om̄i c̄ſuetud præt

gelđ . Tra ē . iiii . car . Valƀ . xx . ſoł .      ƒ Reddeƀ . iiii . ſolid .

Bernulf teneƀ Stocheſtede . Ibi . i . uirg træ 7 dimiđ caruc træ .

Stainulf tenƀ Stocheſtede . Ibi . i . virg tre . 7 dimiđ car tre . Vłƀ

Quinq taini tenƀ Sextone . Ibi . i . hida . Valƀ . xvi . ſoł . ƒ iiii . ſoł .

Vctred tenƀ Chirchedele . Ibi dimiđ hida qeta ab om̄i c̄ſuetud

p̄t gelđ . Valƀ . x . ſolid .      ƒ viii . ſoł .

Wineſtan teneƀ Waletone . Ibi . ii . car tre 7 iii . bouatæ . Valƀ

Elmær tenƀ Liderlant . Ibi dimiđ hida . Valƀ . viii . ſoł .

Tres taini teneƀ Hinne p . iii . m̄ . Ibi dimiđ hida . Valƀ . viii . ſoł .

Aſcha tenþ Torentun . Ibi dimiđ hida . Valƀ . viiii ſoł .

# [SOUTH LANCASHIRE]

**R1** **Roger of Poitou** held the undermentioned land 269 c

## Between the RIBBLE and the MERSEY

In (West) DERBY Hundred

1 King Edward had 1 manor named (West) DERBY, with 6 outliers.
4 hides. Land for 15 ploughs.
Forest 2 leagues long and 1 wide; a hawk's eyrie.

2 Uhtred held 6 manors: ROBY, KNOWSLEY, KIRKBY, CROSBY, MAGHULL
and AUGHTON. 2 hides.
Woodland 2 leagues long and wide; 2 hawk's eyries.

3 Dot held HUYTON and TARBOCK. 1 hide exempt from all
customary dues except tax. Land for 4 ploughs.
The value was 20s.

4 Bernwulf held TOXTETH. 1 virgate of land and ½ carucate of land.
It paid 4s.

5 Steinulf held TOXTETH. 1 virgate of land and ½ carucate of land.
The value was 4s.

6 Five thanes held SEFTON. 1 hide.
The value was 16s.

7 Uhtred held KIRKDALE. ½ hide exempt from all customary dues
except tax.
The value was 10s.

8 Winstan held WALTON. 2 carucates of land and 3 bovates (of land).
The value was 8s.

9 Aelmer held (Down) LITHERLAND. ½ hide.
The value was 8s.

10 Three thanes held INCE as 3 manors. ½ hide.
The values was 8s.

11 Aski held THORNTON. ½ hide.
The value was 8s.

Tres taini tenƀ *MELE* .p. iii. maneꝛ. Ibi dimid hida.|Valƀ. viii. ſoł.

Vɑ̃red tenƀ Vluentune. Ibi. ii. car tꞃæ. 7 dimid leuu ſiluæ.

Edelmund teneƀ *ESMEDVNE*. Ibi una ⎰ Valƀ. lxii. den.

car tꞃæ. Valƀ. xxxii. denaꞃ. ⎰ viii. ſoł.

Tres taini teneƀ Alretune .p. iii. ꝏ. Ibi dimid hida. Valƀ

Vɑ̃red tenƀ Spec. Ibi. ii. caruc tꞃæ. Valƀ. lxiiii. denaꞃ.

Quattuor radmans tenƀ Cildeuuelle .p. iiii. ꝏ. Ibi dimid

hida. Valƀ. viii. ſoł. Ibi pƀr erat hn̄s dimid car tꞃæ in elemos.

Vlƀt tenƀ Wibaldeſlei. Ibi. ii. caruc tꞃæ. Valƀ. lxiiii. den.

Duo taini teneƀ Vuetone .p. ii. ꝏ. Ibi. i. car tꞃæ. Vlƀ. xxx. den.

Leuing tenƀ Wauretreu. Ibi. ii. caruc tꞃæ. Valƀ. lxiiii. den.

Quattuor taini tenƀ Boltelai .p. iiii. ꝏ. Ibi. ii. car tꞃæ.

Valƀ. lxiiii. den. Pƀr habƀ. i. car tꞃæ ad æccłam Waletone.

Vɑ̃red teneƀ Achetun. Ibi. i. car tꞃæ. Valƀ. xxxii. denaꞃ.

Tres taini tenƀ Fornebei .p. iii. ꝏ. Ibi. iiii. car tꞃæ. Valƀ

Tres taini teneƀ Emuluesdel. Ibi. ii. car tꞃæ. ⎰ x. ſoł.

Valƀ. lxiiii. denaꞃ.

★ Stemulf tenƀ Hoiland. Ibi. ii. car tꞃæ. Valƀ. lxiiii. den.

Vɑ̃red teneƀ Daltone. Ibi. i. caruc tre. Valƀ. xxxii. denaꞃ.

Iſd Vɑ̃red *SCHELMERESDELE*. Ibi. i. car tꞃæ. Valƀ. xxxii. den.

Iſd Vɑ̃red tenƀ Literland. Ibi. i. caruc tꞃæ. Valƀ. xxxii. den.

Wiƀt tenƀ *ERENGERMELES*. Ibi. ii. car tꞃæ. Valƀ. viii. ſoł.

H̄ tra ꝺeta fuit p̄t geld.

12   Three thanes held (Raven) MEOLS as 3 manors. ½ hide.
The value was 8s.

13   Uhtred held (Little) WOOLTON. 2 carucates of land.
     Woodland, ½ league.
The value was 64d.

14   Aethelmund held SMITHDOWN. 1 carucate of land.
The value was 32d.

15   Three thanes held ALLERTON as 3 manors. ½ hide.
The value was 8s.

16   Uhtred held SPEKE. 2 carucates of land.
The value was 64d.

17   Four riders held CHILDWALL as 4 manors. ½ hide.
The value was 8s.
     A priest who had ½ carucate of land in alms.

18   Wulfbert held *WIBALDSLEI*. 2 carucates of land.
The value was 64d.

19   Two thanes held (Much) WOOLTON as 2 manors. 1 carucate of land.
The value was 30d.

20   Leofing held WAVERTREE. 2 carucates of land.
The value was 64d.

21   Four thanes held BOOTLE as 4 manors. 2 carucates of land.
The value was 64d.
     A priest had 1 carucate of land at Walton church.

22   Uhtred held AUGHTON. 1 carucate of land.
The value was 32d.

23   Three thanes held FORMBY as 3 manors. 4 carucates of land.
The value was 10s.

24   Three thanes held AINSDALE. 2 carucates of land.
The value was 64d.

25   Steinulf held UPHOLLAND. 2 carucates of land.
The value was 64d.

26   Uhtred held DALTON. 1 carucate of land.
The value was 32d.

27   Uhtred also held SKELMERSDALE. 1 carucate of land.
The value was 32d.

28   Uhtred also held (Up) LITHERLAND. 1 carucate of land.
The value was 32d.

29   Wigbert held ARGARMELES. 2 carucates of land.
The value was 8s.
     This land was exempt  apart from tax.

Quinq̑ taini tenḃ Otegrimele . Ibi dim̄ hida . Valḃ . x . ſoł.

Vȼred tenḃ *LATVNE* . cū . 1 . bereuuich . Ibi dimid hida.

Silua . 1 . leuū łḡ . 7 dimid lat̄ . Valḃ . x . ſoł 7 viii . denar̄.

Vȼred tenḃ Hirletun 7 dimid Merretun . Ibi dim̄ hida.

Valḃ . x . ſoł . 7 viii . denar̄. ⸗ 7 dimid leuū lat̄ . Valḃ . x . ſoł.

Godeue tenḃ Melinge . Ibi . 11 . car̄ træ . Silua . 1 . leuū łḡ.

Vȼred tenḃ Leiate . Ibi . vi . bouat̄ træ . Silua . 1 . leuū łḡ.

7 11 . q̄ł lat̄ . Valḃ . Lxiiii . denar̄. ⸗ . 11 . ſolid.

Duo taini tenḃ . vi . bouat̄ træ ᵱ . 11 . M̄ in Holand . Valḃ

Vȼred tenḃ Acrer . Ibi dimid car̄ træ . Waſta fuit.

Teos tenḃ Bartune . Ibi . 1 . caruc̄ træ . Valḃ . xxxii . den̄.

Chetel tenḃ Heleſhale . Ibi . 11 . caruc̄ træ . Valḃ . viii . ſoł.

⸗ Om̄is h̄ ira geldaḃ . 7 xv . Maner̄ . nil reddeḃ niſi geld . R.E.

Hoc M̄ Derbei cū his ſuᵱdictis hid reddeḃ regi . E.

de firma . xxvi . liḃ 7 11 . ſolid . Ex his . 111 . hidæ cra͛

libere . quar̄ censū ᵱdonauit teinis q̄i eas teneḃ.

Iſtæ reddeḃ . iiii . liḃ . 7 xiiii . ſolid . 7 viii . denar̄.

269 d

O m̄s iſti taini habuer̄ c̄ſuetud redde . 11 . oras denario͛

de unaq̄q̄ caruc̄ træ . 7 facieḃ ᵱ c̄ſuetud domos regis

7 quæ ibi ᵱtineḃ ſī uiłłi . 7 piſcarias . 7 in ſilua haias

7 ſtabilituras . 7 qui ad hæc n̄ ibat q̄do debeḃ . 11 . ſoł em̄daḃ.

7 poſtea ad oᵱ uenieḃ 7 oᵱabat̄ donec ᵱfect̄ erat.

Vn̄ quiſq̄ eo͛ uno die in Auguſto mitteḃ meſſores

ſuos ſecare ſegetes regis . Si non ᵱ . 11 . ſoł em̄dabat.

⸗ Siq̄s liḃ h̄ō faceret furtū . Aut foreſtel aut heinfara.

aut pace regis infringeḃ xl . ſoł em̄dabat.


⸗ Siq̄s facieḃ ſanguinē aut raptū de femina . uel | re

maneḃ de ſiremot ſine rationabili excuſatione

ᵱ . x . ſolid em̄daḃ . ⸗ Si de Hund remaneḃ . aut n̄ ibat

ad placit̄ ubi ᵱᵱoſit jubeḃ ᵱ . v . ſoł em̄daḃ.

30 Five thanes held (North) MEOLS. ½ hide.
The value was 10s.

31 Uhtred held LATHOM with 1 outlier. ½ hide.
   Woodland 1 league long and ½ wide.
The value was 10s 8d.

32 Uhtred held HURLSTON and half MARTON. ½ hide.
The value was 10s 8d.

33 Godiva held MELLING. 2 carucates of land.
   Woodland 1 league long and ½ league wide.
The value was 10s.

34 Uhtred held LYDIATE. 6 bovates of land.
   Woodland 1 league long and 2 furlongs wide.
The value was 64d.

35 Two thanes held 6 bovates of land in DOWNHOLLAND as 2 manors.
The value was 2s.

36 Uhtred held ALTCAR. ½ carucate of land.
It was waste.

37 Teos held BARTON. 1 carucate of land.
The value was 32d.

38 Ketel held HALSALL. 2 carucates of land.
The value was 8s.

39 All this land paid tax; 15 manors did not pay King Edward
anything except tax. This manor of Derby with the above hides
paid King Edward a revenue of £26 2s. Three of these hides
were free, for he remitted their dues to the thanes who held them;
these paid £4 14s 8d.

40a All these thanes customarily paid 2 ora of pence for each carucate 269 d
of land. As a customary due they used to build the King's
buildings and whatever belonged to them, as though they were
villagers, fisheries, woodland enclosures and stag-beats.
Anyone who did not go to this (work) when he should was fined
2s, and afterwards came to the work and worked until it was
done. Each one of them sent his harvesters for one day in August
to cut the King's corn; if he did not he was fined 2s.

b If any free man committed theft, highway robbery, breaking and
entry or a breach of the King's peace he was fined 40s.

c If anyone drew blood, raped a woman or stayed away from the
Shire Moot without reasonable excuse he was fined 10s.

d If he stayed away from the Hundred, or did not go to the (hearing
'of) pleas where the Reeve ordered, he was fined 5s.

Si cui jubeꝧ in ſuū ſeruitiū ire 7 ñ ibat.ꞌ IIII.ſoł em̄daꝧ.

Siꝙs de tra regis receꝺe uoleꝧ.daꝧ.XL.ſoł 7 ibat quo uoleꝧ.

Siꝙs trā patris ſui mortui haꝧe uoleꝧ.ꞌ XL.ſoliꝺ releuabat.

Qui noleꝧ.ꞌ 7 trā 7 om̄em pecuniā patris mortui rex haꝧeꝧ.

Vꞇred tenuit Croſebi 7 Chirchedele ꝓ.I.hida.7 erat ꝙeta
ab om̄i c̄ſuetuꝺ p̄t has.VI.pace infraꞇa.Foreſtel.Heinfara.
7 pugna quæǁſacram̄tū faꞇū remaneꝧ.7 ſi conſtrict juſticia
ꝓpoſiti alicui debiꞇ ſolueꝧ.7ǀtminū a ꝓpoſito daꞇ ñ attendeꝧ.
Ħ ꝑ.XL.ſoł em̄daꝧ.Geldū ū regis ſīc hōes patriæ ſolueꝧ.

In Otringemele 7 Herleſhala.7 Hiretun.erant.III.hidæ ꝙetæ
a geldo carucataꞃ træ.7 a forisfaꞇura ſanguinis.7 femine
uiolentia.Alias ū c̄ſuetuꝺ reddeꝧ om̄s.

De iſto c̄ō DERBEI ten modo dono Roᵍ piꞇau hi hōes trā.
Goisfriꝺ.II.hiꝺ 7 dimiꝺ caꞃ.Roger.I.hiꝺ 7 dimiꝺ.Wiłłs unā
hiꝺ 7 dimiꝺ.Wariñ dimiꝺ hiꝺ.Goisfriꝺ.I.hiꝺ.Tetbalꝺ hidā
7 dimiꝺ.Robert.II.car træ.Gißleꝧ.I.caruc træ.

Hi hn̄t in dn̄io.IIII.caꞃ.7 XLVI.uiłł.7 I.radman 7 LXII.borꝺ.
7 II.ſeruos 7 III.ancilł.Int om̄s hn̄t.XXIIII.car.

Silua eoꝛ.III.leuū 7 dim long.7 I.leuū 7 dim̄ 7 XL.ꝑtic latit.
7 ibi.III.airæ accipitꞃ.

Toꞇ ualet.VIII.liꝧ 7 XII.ſoł. In unaꝙꝙ; hida.ſuꝥ.VI.caruc træ.
Dn̄ium ū huj c̄ō qꝺ teneꝧ Rogeri.uał.VIII.liꝧ.Suꝥ ibi m̄ in
dn̄io.III.caꞃ.7 VI.bouaꞃ.7 un radman 7 VII.uiłłi.

In NEWETON.T.R.E.fueꞃ.V.hidæ.     IN NEWETON HD.
Ex his una erat in dn̄io.Æccła ipsi c̄ō haꝧeꝧ.I.caruc træ.
7 Sc̄s Oſuuolꝺ de ipſa uilla.II.caruc tre haꝧeꝧ ꝙetas ꝑ om̄a.
Huj c̄ō aliā tram.XV.hōes quos drenchs uocabant ꝓ.XV.c̄ō.
teneꝧ.ſed huj c̄ō bereuuicħ erant.7 int om̄s XXX.ſoliꝺ reddꝧ.
Silua ibi.X.leuū łg.7 VI.leuū 7 II.ꝙrent laꞇ.7 ibi airæ accipiꞇ.

e  If the Reeve ordered anyone to perform his service and he
did not he was fined 4s.

f  If anyone wished to leave the King's land he paid 40s and
went where he would.

g  If anyone wished to have his dead father's land he paid 40s
death duty; if he did not wish to, the King had his dead father's
land and all his goods.

41  Uhtred held CROSBY and KIRKDALE as 1 hide and was exempt from
all customary dues except these six; breach of the peace, highway
robbery, breaking and entry, a combat which persisted after an
oath had been taken, if a man, after he had been constrained
thereto by the Reeve's judgment, did not pay anyone what he
owed  or did not heed a boundary set by the Reeve.'For these
the fine was 40s. But Uhtred paid the King's tax like the men
of the district.

42  In NORTH MEOLS, HALSALL and HURLSTON were 3 hides exempt from
tax on carucates of land, from the fines for bloodshed and for
violation of women, but they paid all the other customary dues.

43  These men now hold land of this manor of Derby by gift of
Roger of Poitou. Geoffery holds 2 hides and ½ carucate; Roger
1½ hides; William 1½ hides; Warin ½ hide; Geoffrey 1 hide;
Theobald 1½ hides; Robert 2 carucates of land and Gilbert 1
carucate of land. They have 4 ploughs in lordship;
    46 villagers, 1 rider, 62 smallholders, 2 male and 3 female
      slaves. They have 24 ploughs between them.
    Their woodland, 3½ leagues long and 1½ leagues and 40
      perches wide; 3 hawk's eyries.
Total value £8 12s.

44  In each hide there are 6 carucates of land.

45  But the value of the lordship of this manor which Roger held is £8.
Now in lordship 3 ploughs; 6 ploughmen;
    1 rider and 7 villagers.

R2  In NEWTON Hundred
1    Before 1066 there were 5 hides in NEWTON, of which 1 was in
lordship. The church of the manor had 1 carucate of land.
ST. OSWALD'S of the village had 2 carucates of land exempt from
all (payments). 15 of the men whom they call *drengs* held the
rest of the land of this manor as 15 manors, but they were
outliers of this manor. They paid 30s between them.
    Woodland 10 leagues long and 6 leagues and 2 furlongs wide;
      hawk's eyries.

Huj⁹ HVND hōēs liɓi p̄t. ii.era𝔫 in ead c̄ſuetuđ qua hōēs derberiæ.
7 plus illis. ii. dieƀӡ in Auguſto meteba𝔫 in culturis regis.
Illi duo habeƀ. v. carucat træ.7 forisfacturā ſanguinis 7 feminæ
uiolentiā paſſæ.7 paſnagiū ſuoӡ hominū. Alias habeƀ rex.
Toɫ hoc ꝏ reddeƀ de firma regi. x. liɓ.7 x. ſoliđ.
Modo ſunt ibi.vi. drenghs.7 xii. uiɫɫi 7 iiii. borđ. Inɫ om̄s.ix. car̄
hn̄t. Valet. iiii. liɓ. hoc dn̄ium.    IN WALINTVNE HVND.
Rex. E. tenuit WALINTVNE. cū. iii. Bereuuich. Ibi. i. hida.
Ad ipsū ꝏ p̄tineƀ. xxxiiii. drengh.7 totiđ ꝏ habeƀ.
In quiƀӡ erant xl.ii. carucatæ træ.7 una hida 7 dimidia.
Scs Elfin teneƀ. i. caruc̄ træ đeta ab om̄i c̄ſuetuđ p̄t geldū.
Toɫ ꝏ cū HVND reddeƀ regi de firma. xv. liɓ.ii. ſoɫ min⁹.
Modo ſunt in dn̄io. ii. car̄.7 viii. hōēs cū. i. car̄.
Hōēs iſti ten ibi trā. Roger. i. caruc træ. Tetbald. carucat
7 dimiđ. Wariñ. i. car̄. Radulf. v. car̄. Wiɫɫs. ii. hiđ 7 iiii. car̄ træ.
Adelard. i. hiđ 7 dimiđ caruc̄. Oſmund. i. car̄ træ.
Vaɫ hoc toɫ. iiii. liɓ 7 x. ſoɫ. Dn̄ium uaɫ. iii. liɓ 7 x. ſoɫ.

270 a

Rex. E. tenuit BLACHEBVRNE. Ibi. ii. hidæ IN BLACHEBVRN ᒣ HVND·
7 ii. caruc̄ træ. Æccɫa habeƀ habeƀ. ii. bouatas de hac tra. ᒣ c̄ſuetuđ.
7 æccɫa S MARIÆ habeƀ in Wallei. ii. caruc̄ træ. đetas ab om̄i
★ In eod ꝏ Silua. i. leuu l̄g.7 tn̄tđ laɫ.7 ibi erat aira ac    ciris.
Ad hoc ꝏ uel HVND. adjaceƀ. xxviii. liɓi hōēs. tenentes
v. hiđ 7 dimiđ 7 xl. carucat træ p̱. xxviii. Manerijs.
Silua ibi. vi. leuu l̄g.7 iiii. leuū laɫ.7 era𝔫 in ſup̱dictis
c̄ſuetudiniƀӡ.
In eod HVND habeƀ rex. E. Hunnicot de. ii. car̄ tre.7 Wale
tune de. ii. car̄. træ.7 Peniltune de dimiđ hida.
Toɫ ꝏ cū HVND reddeƀ regi de firma. xxxii. liɓ 7 ii. ſoliđ.
Hanc trā totā deđ Rogerius pictauenſis Rogerio de Buſli.
7 Alƀto Greſlet.7 ibi ſunt tot hōēs qui hn̄t. xi. car̄ 7 dimiđ.
quos ipſi c̄ceſſeꝝ. eē. đetos uſqz ad. iii. annos.7 idō n̄ ap̄pciaɫ m̄.

2      All but two of the free men of this Hundred were subject to the
same customs as the men of (West) Derby, but they reaped for
two days more in August in the King's fields. These two had 5
carucates of land, the fines for bloodshed and violence to
women, and the pasturage of their men. The King had the other
(fines). The whole manor paid £10 10s in revenue to the King.
    Now there are 6 *drengs*, 12 villagers and 4 smallholders; between
     them they have 9 ploughs.
Value of this lordship £4.

### R3 In WARRINGTON Hundred
1      King Edward held WARRINGTON with 3 outliers. 1 hide. To the
manor itself belonged 34 *drengs* and they had as many manors, in
which there were 42 carucates of land and 1½ hides.
ST. ELFIN'S held 1 carucate of land exempt from all customary
dues except tax. The whole manor with the Hundred paid £15
less 2s in revenue to the King. Now 2 ploughs in lordship; 8 men
with 1 plough.
    These men hold land there: Roger 1 carucate of land; Theobald
1½ carucates; Warin 1 carucate; Ralph 5 carucates; William 2
hides and 4 carucates of land; Aethelhard 1 hide and ½ carucate;
Osmund 1 carucate of land.
Total value £4 10s; value of the lordship £3 10s.

### R4 In BLACKBURN Hundred          270 a
1      King Edward held BLACKBURN. 2 hides and 2 carucates of land.
The Church had 2 bovates of this land and ST. MARY'S Church
had 2 carucates of land in WHALLEY exempt from all customary
dues.
    In the same manor woodland 1 league long and as wide;
     a hawk's eyrie.
    To this manor or Hundred were attached 28 free men who
held 5½ hides and 40 carucates of land as 28 manors.
    Woodland 6 leagues long and 4 leagues wide.
    They were (subject to) the aforesaid customs.

2      In the same Hundred King Edward had at HUNCOAT 2 carucates
of land; at WALTON 2 carucates of land and at PENDLETON ½ hide.
The whole manor with the Hundred paid £32 2s in revenue to
the King.
    Roger of Poitou gave all this land to Roger of Bully and
Albert Grelley. There are as many men as have 11½ ploughs,
to whom they granted exemption from dues for 3 years. It
is therefore not now assessed.

Rex . E . tenuit SALFORD . Ibi . III . hidæ. *IN SALFORD HVND*.

7 XII . caruc̄ træ Waſtæ.7 Foreſta . III . leuu lḡ.7 tn̄t̄d lat.

7 ibi plures haiæ 7 aira accipitris.                      ⌐ad Salford.

Radecliue teneƀ rex . E . ꝓ Ḿ.Ibi . I . ĥida.7 alia hid̄ ꝑtineɳs

Æcc̄la S̄ MARIE.7 æcc̄la S̄ Michael teneƀ in Mameceſtre.

una caruc̄ træ . q̄et̄a aƀ om̄i c̄ſuetud̄ p̄t geld̄.

Ad hoc Ḿ uel *HVND* ꝑtineƀ.XXI. bereuuick̄ . teneƀ

totid̄ taini ꝓ totid̄ Maner . In quiƀȝ era ꬱ. XI . hidæ 7 dimid̄.

7 X . caruc̄ træ 7 dimid̄.

Siłuæ ibi . IX . leuu 7 dim lḡ.7 V . leuu 7 una q̄r̄ent lat.

Vn̄ eoȝ Gamel teneɳs . II . hid̄ in Recedh̄a . habeƀ ſuas c̄ſue

tudines q̄etas . p̄ter . VI . has . Furt̄u . Heinfare . Foreſtel.

Pacel̄ regis infrac̄ta . tmin̄u frac̄t̄u aƥpoſito ſtabilit̄u . pugn̄a

poſt ſacram̄t̄u fac̄t̄u remanent̄e . Ħ em̄dab̄ . XL . ſolid̄.

Aliquæ har̄u trar̄u era ꬱ q̄etæ ab om̄i c̄ſuetud̄ p̄t geld̄.

7 aliqtæ a geldo ſu ꬱ q̄etæ.

To̅t̄ Ḿ Salford cu̅ *HVND* reddeƀ . XXX.VII . liƀ 7 IIII . ſoł.

Modo ſunt in Ḿ in dn̄io . II . car̄.7 VIII . ſerui 7 II . uiłł cu̅.I.car̄.

Valet . C . ſolid̄ hoc dn̄ium.

De hac tra huj Ḿ ten milites dono Rogerij pic̄tau.

Nigellus . III . hid̄.7 dimid̄ caruc̄ træ . Warin . II . car̄ træ.

7 alt̄ Warin . I . caruc̄ 7 dimid̄ . Goisfrid . I . caruc̄ træ . Gamel

˄II . car̄ træ . In his ſunt . III . taini . 7 IX. bord̄ 7 XXX . uiłłi 7 pƀr 7 X.

ſerui . In̄t om̄s hn̄t . XXII . car̄ . Valet . VII . liƀ.

Rex . E . tenuit *LAILAND* . Ibi . I . hida *IN LAILAND HVND*.

7 II . caruc̄ træ . Silua . II . leuu lḡ.7 una lat.7 aira Accipitr̄.

Ad hoc Ḿ ꝑtineƀ . XII . car̄ træ quas teneƀ . XII . hȏes liƀi ꝓ

totid̄ Maner . In his . VI . hidæ .7 VIII . caruc̄ træ.

Siluæ ibi . VI . leuu lḡ.7 III . leuu 7 una q̄rent lat.

270 a

**R5** In SALFORD Hundred
1    King Edward held SALFORD. 3 hides and 12 carucates of waste
     land.
          Forest 3 leagues long and as wide; several enclosures;
          a hawk's eyrie.

2    King Edward held RADCLIFFE as a manor. 1 hide and another hide
     which belongs to Salford. ST. MARY'S Church and ST. MICHAEL'S
     Church hold 1 carucate of land in MANCHESTER exempt from all
     customary dues except tax.

3    To this manor or Hundred belonged 21 outliers. As many thanes
     held them for as many manors. In them were 11½ hides and
     10½ carucates of land.
          Woodland 9½ leagues long and 5 leagues and 1 furlong wide.
          One of them, Gamel, who held 2 hides in ROCHDALE, had his own
     exempt customary dues, except for these six: theft,
     breaking and entry, highway robbery, breach of the King's peace,
     breach of a boundary fixed by a Reeve and a combat persisting
     after an oath had been taken. For these the fine was 40s.

4    Some of these lands were exempt from all customary dues except
     tax, and some are exempt from tax.

5    The whole manor of SALFORD with the Hundred paid £37 4s.
     Now in lordship 2 ploughs; 8 slaves;
          2 villagers with 1 plough.
     Value of this lordship 100s.

6    The following men-at-arms hold of this manor this land by the
     gift of Roger of Poitou. Nigel 3 hides and ½ carucate of land,
     Warin 2 carucates of land, another Warin 1½ carucates, Geoffrey
     1 carucate of land, Gamel 2 carucates of land.
          On these lands are 3 thanes, 30 villagers, 9 smallholders,
          10 slaves and a priest. They have 22 ploughs between them.
     Value £7.

**R6** In LEYLAND Hundred
1    King Edward held LEYLAND. 1 hide and 2 carucates of land.
          Woodland 2 leagues long and 1 wide; a hawk's eyrie.
          To this manor belonged 12 carucates of land which 12 free
     man held as as many manors. In them 6 hides and 8 carucates of
     land.
          Woodland 6 leagues long and 3 leagues and 1 furlong wide.

Hōes huj ꝏ 7 de Salford ñ opabant p̄ c̄suetud̄ ad aulā regis̄.
neꝗ meteba ͛ſ in Augusto . Tantm̄ . I . haiā in ſilua facieb̄.

7 habeb̄ ſanguinis forisfacturā . 7 feminæ paſſæ uiolent.

De alijs c̄ſuetudinibꝫ alioꝗ ſupioꝗ Manerioꝗ era ͛ſſ c̄ſortes̄.
Tot̄ ꝏ Lailand cū *HVND* reddeb̄ de firma regi . XIX . lib̄.
7 XVIII . ſolid̄ 7 II . denar.

De hac t ͛ra huj ꝏ ten Girard hid̄ 7 dimid̄ . Rob̄t . III . car̄ træ.
Radulf . II . car̄ træ . Roger . II . car̄ træ . Walter . I . car̄ træ.

Ibi ſunt . IIII . radmans . p̄br 7 XIIII ↄuilli 7 VI . bord̄ . 7 II . bouar.
Int ōs hn̄t . VIII . car̄ . Silua . III . leuū lḡ . 7 II . leuū lat.

7 ibi . IIII . airæ Accipitrū . Valet tot̄ . L . ſolid̄ . Ex parte . ē waſta.

Rex . E . tenuit *PENEVERDANT* . Ibi . II . car̄ træ . 7 reddeb̄ . X . den.

Modo . ē ibi caſtellū . 7 II . car̄ ſunt in dn̄io . 7 VI . burḡſes . 7 III.
radmans . 7 VIII . uilli 7 IIII . bouar . Int ōs hn̄t . IIII . car̄ . Ibi
dimid̄ piſcaria . Silua 7 airæ accipitrū . ſīc T.R.E . Val̄ . III . lib̄.

270 b

In his . VI . *HVND* Derbie Neutōne Walintuñe . Blacheburne
Salford 7 Lailand ſunt . c . qt . XX ꝉManerij . In qꝫ ſunt
qt XX . hidæ geld̄ una min.

T.R.E . ualb̄ . CXLV . lib̄ 7 II . ſolid̄ 7 II . denar.

Qdo Rogeri pictaueñſis de rege recep̄. ualb̄ . CXX . lib̄.

Modo tenet Rex . 7 h̄t in dn̄io . XII . car̄ . 7 IX . milites
ſeudū tenentes . Int eos 7 eoꝗ hōes . ſunt . CXV . car̄ 7 III . boues.

Dn̄ium qd̄ tenuit Rogerius̄. app̄ciat . XXIII . lib̄ 7 X . ſolid̄.

Qd̄ dedit militibꝫ. XX lib̄ 7 XI . ſolid̄ app̄ciatuR.

270 a, b

2   The men of this manor, and of Salford, did not do customary
work at the King's Hall, nor did they reap in August. Nevertheless
they made 1 enclosure in the woodland. They had the fines for
bloodshed and for violence to women. They shared the other
customs of the other manors above.

3   The whole manor of Leyland with the Hundred paid £19 18s 2d
in revenue to the King.

4   Of this manor's land Gerard holds 1½ hides, Robert 3 carucates of
land, Ralph 2 carucates of land, Roger 2 carucates of land and
Walter 1 carucate of land.
4 riders, a priest, 14 villagers, 6 smallholders, 2 ploughmen.
They have 8 ploughs between them.
Woodland 3 leagues long and 2 leagues wide; 4 hawk's eyries.
Total value 50s.
It is partly waste.

5   King Edward held PENWORTHAM . 2 carucates of land. It paid 10d.
Now there is a castle. 2 ploughs in lordship;
6 burgesses, 3 riders, 8 villagers and 4 ploughmen. They have
4 ploughs between them.
½ fishery; woodland and hawk's eyries as before 1066.
Value £3.

R7                                                        270 b
1   In these six Hundreds of (West) Derby, Newton, Warrington
Blackburn, Salford and Leyland there are 188 manors in which
there are 80 hides less 1 paying tax.
Value before 1066 £145 2s 2d; value when Roger of Poitou
acquired them from the King £120.
Now the King holds them. He has 12 ploughs in lordship and
9 men-at-arms who hold a Holding. They and their men have
115 carucates and 3 oxen between them.
The lordship which Roger held is assessed at £23 10s; what he gave
to the men-at-arms is assessed at £20 11s.

Ⓜ In Mellinge 7 Hornebi 7 Wennigetun . Vlf . ıx . caᷓ ad glđ.

Ⓑ Ibidē ħɓ Orme . ı . caᷓ 7 dim̄ ad gld.

Ⓜ In Tornetun 7 in Borch . Orm . vı . caᷓ ad gld.

## *AGEMVNDRENESSE.*

In *PRESTVNE* , comes Toſti . vı . caᷓ ad gld . Ibi ptiñ he traͤ.

Eſtun .ᴵᴵ·ᶜ Lea .ᴵ·ᶜ Saleuuic .ᴵ·ᶜ Clistun .ᴵᴵ·ᶜ Neutune .ᴵᴵ·ᶜ Frecheltun .ᴵᴵᴵᴵ·ᶜ Rigbi .ⱽᴵ·ᶜ

Chicheham .ᴵᴵᴵᴵ·ᶜ Treueles .ᴵᴵ·ᶜ Weſtbi .ᴵᴵ·ᶜ Pluntun .ᴵᴵ·ᶜ Widetun .ᴵᴵᴵ·ᶜ Pres .ᴵᴵ·ᶜ Wartun, .ᴵᴵᴵᴵ·ᶜ

Lidun .ᴵᴵ·ᶜ Meᵣetun .ⱽᴵ·ᶜ Latun .ⱽᴵ· Staininghe .ⱽᴵ·ᶜ Carlentun .ᴵᴵᴵᴵ·ᶜ Biſcopham .ⱽᴵᴵᴵ ᶜ

Rushale .ᴵᴵ·ᶜ Brune .ᴵᴵ·ᶜ Torentun .ⱽᴵ·ᶜ Poltun .ᴵᴵ·ᶜ Singletun .ⱽᴵ·ᶜ Greneholf .ᴵᴵᴵ·ᶜ

Egleſtun .ᴵᴵᴵᴵ·ᶜ alia Egleſtun .ᴵᴵ·ᶜ Edelesuuic .ᴵᴵᴵ·ᶜ Inscip .ᴵᴵ·ᶜ Sorbi .ᴵᴵ·ᶜ Aschebi .ᴵ·ᶜ

Micheleſcherche .ᴵ·ᶜ Catrehala .ᴵᴵ·ᶜ Clactune .ᴵᴵ ᶜ Neuhuſe .ᴵ·ᶜ Pluntun .ⱽ·ᶜ

Broctun .ᴵ·ᶜ Witingheham .ᴵᴵ·ᶜ Bartun .ᴵᴵᴵ·ᶜ Guſanſarghe .ᴵ·ᶜ Halctun .ᴵ·ᶜ

Trelefelt .ᴵ·ᶜ Watelei .ᴵ·ᶜ Chipinden .ᴵᴵᴵ·ᶜ Actun .ᴵ·ᶜ Fiſcuic .ᴵ·ᶜ Grimeſarge .ᴵᴵ·ᶜ

Ribelcastre .ᴵᴵ·ᶜ Bileuurde .ᴵᴵ·ᶜ Sueneſat .ᴵ ᶜ Fortune .ᴵ·ᶜ Crimeles .ᴵ·ᶜ Che

reſtanc .ⱽᴵ·ᶜ Rodeclif .ᴵᴵ·ᶜ alia Rodeclif .ᴵᴵ·ᶜ tcia Rodeclif .ᴵᴵᴵ·ᶜ Hameltune .ᴵᴵ·ᶜ

Stalmine .ᴵᴵᴵᴵ·ᶜ Preſſouede .ⱽᴵ·ᶜ Midehope .ᴵᶜ·ᶜ

Om̄s haͤ uille iacent ad Preſtune . 7 ııı . ecclaͤ . Ex his . xvı .

a paucis incoluntᷠ . ſʒ quot ſint habitantes ignoratur.

Reliqua ſunt waſta . Rogᷓ pict habuit.

# [NORTH LANCASHIRE with WESTMORLAND and CUMBERLAND]

*included in the Survey of Yorkshire, from which the relevant entries are
here reproduced, since the north-western counties did not exist in 1086.
Subsequently, all places named were in Lancashire, except those marked
[C] for Cumberland, [W] for Westmorland, or [Y] for Yorkshire.*

## LAND OF THE KING IN YORKSHIRE      299 a

### WEST RIDING      301 b

**Y1**

M. In MELLING, HORNBY and WENNINGTON, Ulf, 9 c. taxable    301 c
B. There Orm also had 1½ c. taxable.
M. In THORNTON [Y] and (Nether) BURROW, Orm, 6 c. taxable.

**Y2**       AMOUNDERNESS      301 d

In PRESTON, Earl Tosti, 6 c. taxable.

These lands belong there

ASHTON 2 c., LEA 1 c., SALWICK 1 c., CLIFTON 2 c., NEWTON
2 c., FRECKLETON 4 c., RIBBY 6 c., KIRKHAM 4 c., TREALES
2 c., WESTBY 2 c., (Field) PLUMPTON 2 c., WEETON 3 c., PREESE
2 c., WARTON 4 c., LYTHAM 2 c., MARTON 6 c., LAYTON 6 c.,
STAINING 6 c., CARLETON 4 c., BISPHAM 8 c., ROSSALL 2 c.,
BURN 2 c., THORNTON 6 c., POULTON (le Fylde) 2 c., SINGLETON
6 c., GREENHALGH 3 c., ECCLESTON 4 c., the other (Little)
ECCLESTON 2 c., ELSWICK 3 c., INSKIP 2 c., SOWERBY 1 c., ASCHEBI 1 c.,
ST MICHAEL'S (on Wyre) 1 c., CATTERALL 2 c., CLAUGHTON 2 c.,
NEWSHAM 1 c., (Wood) PLUMPTON 5 c., BROUGHTON 1 c.,
WHITTINGHAM 2 c., BARTON 4 c., GOOSNARGH 1 c., HAIGHTON
1 c., THRELFALL 1c., WHEATLEY 1 c., CHIPPING 3 c., AIGHTON
1 c., FISHWICK 1 c., GRIMSARGH 2 c., RIBCHESTER 2 c.,
DILWORTH 2 c., SWAINSEAT 1 c., FORTON 1 c., CRIMBLES 1 c.,
GARSTANG 6 c., (Upper) RAWCLIFFE 3 c., HAMBLETON 2 c.,
STALMINE 4c., PREESALL 6 c., MYTHOP 1 c.

All these villages and 3 churches belong to Preston. 16 of them
have a few inhabitants, but how many is not known. The
rest are waste. Roger of Poitou had them.

Ⓜ In *HALTVN* . habuit——comes Tofti . vɪ . caŕ træ ad gld.

In Aldeclif . Tiernun . Hillun . Loncaſtre . Chercaloncaſtre.

Hotun . Neutun . Ouretun . Middeltun . Hietune . Heſſam.

Oxeneclif . Poltune . Toredholme . Schertune . Bare . Sline.

Bodeltone . Chellet . Stopeltièrne . Neuhuſe . Chreneforde.

Om̄s hæ uillæ ꝑtin ad Haltune.


Ⓜ In *WITETVNE* . ħƀ comes Tofti . vɪ . car̂ tre ad gld.

In Neutune . Ergune . Gherſinȼtune . Hotun . Cantesfelt.

Irebi . Borch . Lech . Borctune . Bernulfeſuuic . Inglestune.

★ Caſtretune . Berebrune . Sedberge . Tiernebi.

.xɪɪ. Oms hæ uillæ ꝑtin ad Witetune.

Ⓜ In *OVSTEVVIC* . 7 Heldetune . Clapeham . Middeltun . Manz

ſerge . Cherchebi . Lupetun . Preſtun . Holme . Bortun . Hotune.

Wartun . Claȼtun . Catun . Hæc habuit Torfin . ꝓ xɪɪ . Maner̂.

.ɪɪɪɪ. In his ſunt xL.ɪɪɪ . carucate ad gld.

Ⓜ In *BENETAIN* . Wininȼtune . Tathaim . Fareltun . Tuneſtalle.

Chetel ħƀ . ɪɪɪɪ . Ⓜ . 7 ſunt in eis . xvɪɪɪ . car̂ ad gld . 7 ɪɪɪ . æcclæ.

Ⓜ In *HOVGVN* . ħƀ comes Tofti . ɪɪɪɪ . car̂ tre ad gld.

In Chiluestreuic . Sourebi . Hietun . Daltune . Warte . Neutun.

Walletun . Suntun . Fordebodele . Roſſe . Hert . Lies . alia Lies.

Glaſſertun . Steintun . Cliuertun . Ouregraue . Meretun . Penni

getun . Gerleuuorde . Borch . Berretſeige . Witinghā . Bodele.

Santacherche . Hougenai . Oms hæ uillæ iacent ad Hougun.

**Y3**

M. In **HALTON**   Earl Tosti had 6 c., of land taxable.

In ALDCLIFFE 2 c., THURNHAM 2 c., HILLAM 1 c., LANCASTER 6 c., KIRK LANCASTER 2 c., HUTTON 2 c., NEWTON 2 c., OVERTON 4 c., MIDDLETON 4 c., HEATON 2 c., HEYSHAM 4 c., OXCLIFFE 2 c., POULTON (le Sands) 2 c., TORRISHOLME 2 c., SKERTON 6 c., BARE 2 c., SLYNE 6 c., BOLTON (le Sands) 4 c., KELLET 6 c., STAPLETON TERNE 2 c., NEWSHAM 2 c., CARNFORTH 2 c.

All these villages belong to Halton.

**Y4**

M. In **WHITTINGTON**  Earl Tosti had 6 c., of land taxable.

In NEWTON 2 c., ARKHOLME 6 c., GRESSINGHAM 2 c., HUTTON (Roof) [W] 3 c., CANTSFIELD 3 c., IREBY 3 c., (Over) BURROW 3 c., LECK 3 c., BURTON [Y] 1 c., BARNOLDSWICK [Y] 1 c., INGLETON [Y] 6 c., CASTERTON [W] 3 c., BARBON [W] 3 c., SEDBERGH [Y] 3 c., THIRNBY 2 c.

All these villages belong to Whittington.

**Y5**

12 M. In AUSTWICK [Y], *HELDETUNE [Y]*, CLAPHAM [Y], MIDDLETON [W], MANSERGH [W], KIRKBY (Lonsdale) [W], LUPTON [W], PRESTON [W], HOLME [W], BURTON [Y], (Priest) HUTTON, WARTON, CLAUGHTON, CATON.

Thorfin had them as 12 manors. There are 43 c., taxable in them.

**Y6**

4 M. In BENTHAM, WENNINGTON, TATHAM, FARLETON, TUNSTALL.

Ketel had 4 manors. There are 18 c., taxable and 3 churches in them.

**Y7**

M. In **MILLOM** [C]  Earl Tosti had 4 c., of land taxable.

In KILLERWICK 3 c., SOWERBY 3 c., HEATON 4 c., DALTON 2 c., WART 2 c., NEWTON 6 c., WALTON 6 c., *SUNTUN* 2 c., FORDBOOTLE 2 c., ROOSE 6 c., HART 2 c., LEECE 6 c., another LEECE 6 c., GLEASTON 2 c., STAINTON 2 c., CRIVELTON 4 c., ORGRAVE 3 c., MARTIN 4 c., PENNINGTON 2 c., KIRKBY IRELETH 2 c., BROUGHTON 6 c., BARDSEA 4 c., WHICHAM [W] 4 c., BOOTLE [C] 4 c., KIRKSANTON [C] 1 c., MILLOM (Castle?) [C] 6 c.

All these villages belong to Millom.

ᴹ☩In *STERCALAND*.Mimet.Cherchebi.Helſingetune.
Steintun.Bodelforde.Hotun.Bortun.Daltun.Patun.
H̄ habuit Gilemichel.In his ſuꝗ.xx.car̕ træ ad gld.

ᴹ☩In Cherchebi.Duuan.vi.car̕ ad gld.

ᴹ☩In Aldinghā.Ernulf.vi.car̕ ad gld.

ᴵᴹ☩In Vlureſtun.Turulf.vi.car̕ ad gld.

In Bodeltun.vi.car̕.In Dene.i.car̕.

ᴹ☩ 327 c
7 B.In *HOLECHER* 7 Bretebi ħƀ Orm.viii.car̕ træ ad gld.

332 b
ᴹ☩In *LANESDALE*.7 *COGREHĀ*.ħƀr Vlf 7 Machel
ii.car̕ ad gld.

ᴹ☩In *ESTVN*.Cliber.Machern 7 Ghilemichel ħƀr.vi.car̕
ad gld.In Ellhale.ii.car̕.In Scozforde.ii.car̕.

ᴹ☩In *BIEDVN*.ħƀ comes Toſti.vi.car̕ ad gld.Nc̄ ħt̄ Rog̕
piĉtau̕.7 Ernuin ſub eo.In jaiant̕.Fareltun̕.prestun.
Bereuuic.Hennecaſtre.Eureshaim.Lefuenes.

## Y8

9
M. In **STRICKLAND** [W], MINT [W], KIRKBY (Kendal) [W],
HELSINGTON [W], STAINTON [W], 'BOTHELFORD' [W],
(Old) HUTTON [W], BURTON [W], DALTON[W], PATTON [W].

302 a

Gillemichael had them. There are 20 c., of land taxable in them.

## Y9

M. In 'KIRKBY' (Cartmel), Dwan, 6 c., of land taxable.
M. In ALDINGHAM, Arnulf, 6 c., of taxable.
M. In ULVERSTON, Thorulf, 6 c., taxable.
In BOLTON, 6 c. In DENDRON, 1 c.

## Y10

M.
& B. In **HOLKER** and BIRKBY Orm has 8 c., of land taxable.

327 c

## Y11     LAND OF ROGER OF POITOU

332 b

2
M. In **LONSDALE** and **COCKERHAM** Ulf and Machel had 2 c., taxable.

## Y12

3
M. In **ASHTON** Gilbert and Machern and Gillemichael had 6 c., taxable.
In ELLEL 2 c. In SCOTFORTH 2 c.

## Y13

M. In **BEETHAM** [W] Earl Tosti had 6 c., taxable. Now Roger of Poitou
has them, and Ernwin the priest under him.

In YEALAND 4 c., FARLETON [W] 4 c., PRESTON (Richard) [W]
3 c., BORWICK 2 c., HINCASTER [W] 2 c., HEVERSHAM [W] 2 c.,
LEVENS [W] 2 c.

# NOTES

ABBREVIATIONS used in the notes.

DB.. Domesday Book. DG.. H.C. Darby and G.R. Versey *Domesday Gazeteer* (Cambridge 1975). EPNS.. English Place-Name Society Survey (44-47, Cheshire; 20-22, Cumberland; 42-43, Westmorland). MS.. Manuscript. PNDB.. O. von Feilitzen *Pre-Conquest Personal Names of Domesday Book*. PNL.. E. Ekwall *The Place-Names of Lancashire*. Tait.. James Tait *The Domesday Survey of Cheshire*. TaitF.. James Tait *Flintshire in Domesday Book* (Flintshire Historical Society xi, 1925).

The manuscript is written on leaves, or folios, of parchment (sheep-skin), measuring about 15 inches by 11 (38 by 28 cm). There are two columns to each page, four to each folio. The folios were numbered in the 17th century, and the four columns of each are here lettered a,b,c,d. The manuscript emphasises chapters and headings by the use of red ink. Underling indicates deletion.

*CESTRESCIRE* in red, at the top of each page, centred over the two columns; folios 268d-269b, the Welsh sections, omit the heading.

*INT(ER) RIPA ET MERSHAM* in red, at the top of folio 269c,d centred over the two columns.

*EVRICSCIRE* in red, at the top of folio 301d, centred over the two columns.

| | |
|---|---|
| C 3 | **100s.** DB uses the old English currency system which endured for a thousand years until 1971. The pound contained 20 shillings, each of 12 pence, abbreviated as £(ibrae), s(olidi), d(enarii). |
| C 11-13 | The lines were copied into the MS in the wrong order, but their proper order was indicated by inserting the letters a.b.c.d. into the MS at the beginning of the lines. |
| C 22 | **TIMBER.** A quantity of furskins, usually varying between 40 and 60. |
| B 2 | MS 'diem lunis' for 'lunae', Monday. |
| B 6 | MS. Marginal 'R', perhaps for reclamatio, a claim or counter-claim. |
| | **ST. CHAD'S** of Lichfield. The Bishop's see was transferred from Lichfield to Chester in 1075, and St. John's Church remained the diocesan cathedral until its transfer to Coventry in 1095. |
| B 9 | **RADMAN.** Literally a man who rides (a horse); free men who performed riding services as messengers or escorts. |
| A | **ST. WERBERGH'S.** A church of secular canons refounded as a Benedictine monastery by Earl Hugh in 1093. |
| A 21 | **WILLIAM** Malbank who held the remaining third of Wepre. See FD3,2. |
| 1,1 | **WICH.** An area of salt-workings; possibly Nantwich. The identifications of DG are followed unless otherwise stated. See below 1,8; 8,16; 9,17; 17,5; 17,8; 20,3. |
| | **SALTHOUSE.** 'Salina' comprehends all kinds of salt workings from the coastal salt pans to the boilers of Worcestershire and Cheshire, with their associated sheds and buildings. 'Salthouse' is the most comprehensive term. |
| 1,2 | **KENARDSLIE.** Lost in Whitegate parish, perhaps near Earnslow Grange, EPNS iii, 207. |
| 1,8 | **A PRIEST.** The remainder of the Frodsham entry is interrupted by the addition of Ollerton, exdent in the MS to signal its later addition. |
| 1,10 | **ALDREDELIE.** Lost within the forest of Delamere and in Kingsley, EPNS iii, 239. |
| 1,11 | **DONE.** Lost in the forest of Delamere, perhaps near Utkinton, EPNS iii, 161. |
| 1,20 | **ALRETONE.** Possibly located at Harewood Hill (54 67), EPNS iii, 211. |
| 1,22 | Hugh son of Norman, William Malbank, Walter of Vernon, Hamo of Mascy, Robert and Robert, probably either of Rhuddlan, or son of Hugh, or Cook. |
| 1,31 | **HOFINCHEL.** Lost in Macclesfield Hundred. Wincle seems unlikely, EPNS i, 282. |
| | **LAITONE.** Possibly in the region of Low and Old Leighton (95 87), EPNS i, 282. |
| 2,2 | **SALTHOUSE.** At Fulwich in Iscoyd and Wigland, EPNS iv, 51. |
| 2,3 | **ORA.** Literally an ounce, in Scandinavia a monetary unit and coin still in use; in DB valued at 16 or 20 pence, here at 16 pence, giving 12 ora = 16 shillings. |
| 2,4 | **MALPAS.** Probably created by the Norman castle; *Depenbech* may have been in the region of Hough Farm, EPNS iv, 39. |

| | |
|---|---|
| 2,9 | 2 (½?). Farley 'ii hidae 7  geld' (2 and  hides paying tax); MS '7 dimid' (and a half), partially erased, by accident or on purpose, but plainly legible. |
| 2,19 | Farley error, 2 for 3 ploughs. |
| 2,29 | MS 'iii bord cum i villo', probably in error for 'iii bord cum i car', villager written for plough, see note FT2,13 below. |
| 2,30-1 | ROBERT, probably son of Hugh, but perhaps intending a different Robert. |
| 3 | ROBERT OF RHUDDLAN cousin of Earl Hugh, on whose death without issue in 1088, most of his lands reverted to the Earldom. |
| 5,14 | RICHARD OF VERNON. Omitted in its proper place, added at the foot of the column, with Richard's name repeated in full to signal the error; corrected by Farley with marginal pointing hands. |
| 6,2 | CALVINTONE Lost in Broxton Hundred, EPNS iv, 2. |
| 7,4 | LUVEDE, perhaps in error for Leofede, PNDB 322. |
| 8,5 | 'tra iiii bou geld', land for 4 bovates paying tax rather than 4 oxen. See 1,33 'iiii bovatis trae geld.' |
| 8,16 | NANTWICH. Identified in S1,1 below. See note 1,1. |
| 9,3 | HANDBRIDGE. The three entries (9,3;10,2;12,1) contain the only references to carucates in the county, although there are taxable bovates at Chester (B11), Sutton (1,33), Pool (8,5), Peover (17,10) and Tabley (19,3). There is clear evidence of Scandinavian settlement in the place-names of the Wirral. The Handbridge entries may reflect a period of Danish supremacy during the early expansion of Chester; but the nomenclature of the district reveals only an occasional Scandinavian form in the spellings of Netherleigh/Overleigh, and a Scandinavian name, Arni, for the TRE tenant of Netherleigh and Handbridge. |
| 9,17 | AITARD, probably for Ailard, a form of Aethelhard. |
| 9,28-9 | WILLIAM, probably son of Nigel, whose heirs held Alderley; but the compiler, writing 'Wills' in place of the 'Isdem W df the preceding entries, may have been unsure of the identity of this William. The next entry (Lach) was subsequently divided into two moieties, Lach Dennis held by Colben, a Dane, and Lach Malbank held by William Malbank. This entry may well belong in chapter 8, under William Malbank. |
| 10 | HUGO DE MARA perhaps named from 'Mara' (Delamere) in Cheshire, but possibly connected with William and Wigot de Mara of Wiltshire and East Anglia, probably ancestors of the Delamere and de la Mere families of those counties, who may have come from one or other of the places named La Mare, by the lower Seine. |
| 11 | HUGO following the 'Isd(em) H' of the preceding entries, marks a different landholder; Hugh son of Norman (of Mold) held Lawton and Goostrey and subsequently granted them to St. Werbergh's. |
| 11,5-8 | HUGO following the 'Isd(em) H' of the preceding entries; in the MS 11,5-8 are written with a different pen, though by the same hand, and are exdent to mark a different landholder. The heirs of Hugh son of Norman held these lands. |
| 12,2 | MS 'ipse' for 'ipsae', these. |
| 13,7 | ALRETUNE probably represented by 'Alretunstall' in Timperley, EPNS ii, 31. |
| 14 | BIGOT of (les) Loges in a charter of Earl Hugh; evidently connected with Roger Bigot, ancestor of the Earls of Norfolk, also from Les Loges. |
| 15,1 | COCLE. A location in Kelsall was proposed by Tait 189, EPNS iii, 161. |
| 16 | [HUGH SON OF OSBERN] MS omits the chapter heading but associates the entry for Allington with that of Eyton by use of a gallows-like section sign. |
| 16,2 | OSBERN, possibly Osbern son of Tezzo. |
| 18 | GILBERT HUNTER. Identical with Gilbert Venables, who later held these lands. |
| 19,3 | OSTEBRAND, probably for Uhtbrand. |
| 20 • | RANULF (MAINWARING). Richard Mesnilwarin (Mainwaring) gave the tithes of Blacon to St. Werbergh's in a charter of Earl Hugh in 1093. Ranulf is assumed to have been his father. |
| 20,5 | WARFORD. Located at Old Warford (SJ 805 755), EPNS ii, 83; i, 104. |
| 20,7 | CHAPMONSWICHE. Lost in the region of Peover Superior, EPNS, ii, 86. |

| | |
|---|---|
| 22,1 | The entry is scored through in the MS, evidently because the lands it records are also entered in 27,3. Farley omits the scoring in the MS of the words 'car' and 'silva'; but the intention was plainly to delete the entire entry. |
| 23 | ILBERT, father of Richard of Rullos who appears in a charter of Earl Hugh, Tait 58. |
| 26,1 | TESSELIN. 'Little Tezzo', perhaps connected with Osbern son of Tezzo. |
| 27 | The persons named are Ranulf Mainwaring, Bigot of Loges, Gilbert of Venables, Hamo of Mascy, Hugh son of Norman, Osbern son of Tezzo, Reginald Balliol and William son of Nigel. |
| 27,4 | 'sub eis    car dimid', 'and' is omitted between 'car' and 'dimid', and a blank left before 'car'. Either ½ or 1½ or 2½ are possible, but in the context 2½ is improbable. |
| S3 | NORTHWICH, an industrial enclave; the residential quarter was at neighbouring Witton (18,5), EPNS ii, 193. |
| S3,2 | SALT-BOILING. Brine drawn from wells was boiled in large leaden pans, causing salt to crystalize on the surface. |
| | FARTHING, 'minuta' not otherwise used in DB; see St. Mark s Gospel 12,42, 'duo minuta quod est quadrans' (Vulgate), two mites, which make a farthing (Authorised Version); the Old English version renders 'minuta' by 'stycas'. |
| S1 | WICH Malbank from the surname of the baron of Nantwich, EPNS iii, 30-1. |
| FD1,2 | 'RADINGTON'. A lost place near Flint in 14th century charters TaitF 15. D. Sylvester (quoted in B.M.C. Husain *Cheshire Under the Norman Earls* 17) suggested Hanmer in Maelor Saesneg, but this seems improbably distant. |
| FD3,1 | 'CLAYTON', possibly represented by Clay Hill near Aston (31 67) TaitF 17. |
| FD5,2 | OVER THE RIVER, possibly in Handbridge. |
| FD5,3 | 'EDRITONE'. The last sentence (John Morris argued), dividing the whole of the land between Osbern and Hugh, corrects the opening statement that the land was held by Richard, and implies a recent change. Since Osbern held Dodleston (in Cheshire) and Hugh held Bistre (in Flintshire), the place probably lay on the border between their holdings, and may therefore be an alternative name of Kinnerton, that is still divided by the boundary between Cheshire and Flintshire, between Dodleston and Mold. |
| FT1,1 | BRYN, later Bryn bychan (Rhuddlan). |
| FT1,7 | FULBROOK until 1535, now Greenfield TaitF 25. |
| FT2,13 | MS 'val xvi car' in error for 'val xvi solid'. |
| FT2,19 | BRETEUIL. A castle founded by King William, as duke of Normandy, in 1054, 15 miles south west of Evreux, on the border between Normandy and the dominions of the King of France. It was placed in the charge of William son of Osbern, who settled numerous traders there, and accorded them particular privileges which he subsequently used as a model for the government of the burgesses of the castles that he established in England, when he was Earl of Hereford, and of the southern Welsh march from 1066 to his death in 1070. |
| FT3,6 | MS 'wasta f..' for 'wasta fuit'. |
| FT3,7 | LOAVES.(? ). 'hestha'. The Welsh *gwestva*, tribute of food or its equivalent due to the King for the maintenance of his retinue when he was personally present; *hestcorne* and *hesterasda*, defined as oats for the King's nourishment are also recorded in the medieval traditions of John of Beverley, Archbishop of York, died 721. |
| G1 | NORTH WALES. Not controlled by Robert, but granted in anticipation of the projected conquest of Gwynedd. The conquest was not achieved. Robert was killed in 1088 by the Welsh, who in the next century recovered Rhuddlan. |
| | BISHOPRIC. In the anticipated conquest, the lands of the Welsh church were evidently to be safeguarded. |
| R 1 | ROGER OF POITOU son of Earl Roger of Montgomery. At the time of Domesday he retained some Yorkshire lands (see Y10 below), but not his main Lancashire holdings, though he subsequently recovered all or most of them. The reason is not known; he may have been deprived for supporting King William's rebellious son, Robert of Normandy. |
| R1,13 | 64d. The majority of the values in South Lancashire are given in multiples of the *ora* of 16d, see note 2,3 above. |
| R1,25 | MS Stemulf for Stenulf. |

| R1,39 | **15 MANORS**, evidently the 6 named manors of Uhtred (R1,2) and the 9 other places named as manors (R1,1;10;12;15;17;21;23;35.) disregarding the numbers of manors said to have been held in each previously. |
| R1,40 | **STAG-BEATS**, 'stabilitura', a fenced and ditched area, equipped with nets, into which huntsmen drive stags. |
| R2,1 | **ST. OSWALD'S** of Winwick. |
| | **DRENG** from the Old Norse, 'a bold, valiant, worthy man'. In Lancashire and Yorkshire men who held land by a form of free tenure combining service, money payments and military duty. |
| R3,1 | **ST. ELFIN'S** of Warrington. |
| R4,1 | **ST MARY'S** . The churches of both Blackburn and Whalley are dedicated to St. Mary. Farley 'ac ciris' misprinted for 'accipitris'. |
| R5,2 | **ST. MARY'S** of Manchester. |
| | **ST. MICHAEL'S** probably of Ashton-under-Lyne. |
| R6,5 | **PENWORTHAM** castle; a motte and bailey castle built to guard the mouth of the Ribble, probably never rebuilt in stone. |
| R7,1 | **SIX HUNDREDS**. Some of the figures given are accurate totals of those ennumerated in the previous six chapters, but others are not. |
| | **115 CARUCATES.** 'car' might alternatively mean 'ploughs', since the preceding entries commonly write 'car tre' (carucates of land), to distinguish the abbreviation car(ucatae) from car(ucae); but the entry summarises the holdings of the 'milites', granted by Roger. The previous entries total 15 men holding 125½ carucates; various alternative and ingenious calculations might deduct 6 men and 10½ carucates, and seek explanations for their omission from the total. The three 'boves' (oxen), improbably few in the context, may have been written in error for 'bovatae' (bovates). |
| Y2 | **ASCHEBI** lost in Myerscough, Ekwall 148. |
| Y4 | **SEDBERGH**. MS i.ii.c, with the first upright faint, possibly intending 2 carucates. |
| Y7 | **MARTIN**, so traditionally spelt; Marton on the Ordnance Survey maps. |
| Y8 | **'BOTHELFORD'**. Probably a lost ford over the Kent, between Natland and Helsington, EPNS i, 113. |
| Y9 | **CHERCHEBI**. Later Churchtown, a name of Cartmel village Ekwall 196. |

# APPENDIX

At the time of Domesday Book the County of Cheshire included the coast of North Wales, which the English held or claimed, and also South Lancashire. Lancashire north of the Ribble, with the southern portions of the future counties of Westmorland and Cumberland, were still included in Yorkshire. Northern Westmorland and most of Cumberland were not yet English; they were still part of the Kingdom of the Clyde, recently annexed to Scotland. The Clyde Kingdom was Welsh, its people called Cymry (anglicized Cumbri) in their own language, and the English knew it as Cumbria or Cumberland. It was permanently conquered by the English in 1092, six years after the Domesday Survey. The modern counties of Lancashire, Westmorland and Cumberland were brought into being soon after, probably in the first half of the 12th century. As a result the entries in Domesday which refer to north west England reflect the unclear political situation, and most of them were not yet arranged in the normal manner of English administration.

South Lancashire and Cheshire, like the rest of England, were organized by Hundreds. In Cheshire the majority of the Hundreds were either renamed or reorganized in the centuries after Domesday. The translation gives the later or modern name of the Hundred:

| DB Form | Modern Form | DB Form | Modern Form |
|---|---|---|---|
| Wilaveston | Wirral | Bochelau | Bucklow (East) |
| Warmundestrou | Nantwich | Tunendune | Bucklow (West) |
| Midestvic | Northwich | Risedon | Eddisbury (South) |
| Hamestan | Macclesfield | Roelau | Eddisbury (North) |
| Cestre | Chester | Dudestan | Broxton |

The boundary changes were not extensive. Picton, Upton, Guilden Sutton, Mickle Trafford and Wervin which were in Wilaveston Hundred and Claverton, Dodleston, Kinnerton (?), Lache and Marlston in Ati's Cross Hundred later became part of Broxton Hundred.
Church Minshull, Alsager and Hassall in Midestvic Hundred and Snelson and Northenden in Bochelau Hundred later became part of Nantwich Hundred.
Alpraham, Little Budworth, Rushton, Over, *Alretone, Opetone* and Thornton-le-Moors (the detached portions of Dudestan Hundred), and Weaver in Midestvic Hundred later became part of Eddisbury Hundred. These changes are not noticed in the translation but the places mentioned are starred in the map keys.

The entries relating to Wales refer to the Hundreds of Atiscross and Exestan. Bettisfield Worthenbury and Iscoyd were surveyed in the Hundred of Dudestan (Broxton). Many of the lands surveyed in 1086 were recovered by the Welsh in the 12th century. Flintshire was not created until the Statute of Rhuddlan in 1284; Denbighshire not until the 16th century. The Domesday entries are, however, arranged within the Hundreds in distinct regions which are preserved in the index and maps to this volume.
In Ati's Cross Hundred and later in Flintshire were Rhuddlan, the district around the castle and borough, Tegeingl (Englefield), along the north edge of the Dee estuary, and an area along the southern half of the Dee estuary, here called 'Deeside'. The future detached portions of Flintshire (Maelor Saesneg) are abstracted from the entries in Dudestan Hundred (Broxton).
In modern Denbighshire are the regions of Bistre (Mold) in Ati's Cross Hundred, and the Domesday Hundred of Exestan, later Maelor Cymraeg. Also included in the Cheshire folios are entries dealing briefly with parts of Gwynedd, granted in anticipation of an English conquest.

In North Lancashire beyond the Ribble and parts of the later counties of Westmorland and Cumberland Domesday Book arranges the north west similarly by regions, most of them unnamed, and grouped under the principal manor within them.
Mid Lancashire, Amounderness, had been consolidated in a single large territory administered from Preston in the possession of King Harold's brother, Earl Tosti. The area was later virtually coincident with the Lancashire Hundred of the same name.
North of Amounderness the entries are arranged in districts though not named by DB. The principal manors within each are written in capitals in the MS. Most are defined by an obvious physical unity, generally the flood plains of the major rivers or stretches of high moorland. Places in Halton are arranged around the estuary of the River Lune; in Bentham along the valley of the Wenning; in Beetham south of the Kent estuary. These regions were subsequently amalgamated or divided to form the future divisions of the modern counties of Lancashire, Westmorland and Cumberland. Recent discussion of the problems can be found in G.W.S. Barrow *The Pattern of Lordship and Feudal Settlement in Cumbria* (Journal of Medieval History 1, 1975). The Districts are here distinguished by use of chapters, and are mapped within the areas which DB describes. Boundaries, where shown, are those of obvious physical features.

# INDEX OF PERSONS

Familiar modern spellings are given when they exist. Unfamiliar names are usually given in an approximate late 11th century form, avoiding variants that were already obsolescent or pedantic. Spellings that mislead the modern eye are avoided where possible. Two, however, cannot be avoided: they are combined in the name of 'Leofgeat' pronounced 'Leffyet', or 'Levyet'. The definite article is omitted before bynames, except where there is reason to suppose that they described the individual. The chapter numbers of listed landholders are printed in italics. Persons who appear in more than one county are cross indexed; [C] Cheshire, [W] Wales and [L] Lancashire.

## CHESHIRE

| | | | |
|---|---|---|---|
| Aelfric | 2,21; 8,29; 8,34; 8,39-40 | Erlechin | 8,27 |
| Aelmer | 8,15; W; L | Erngeat | 7,1-3; 10,4; 20,4 |
| Aescwulf | 1,3; 8,7 | Ernwin | 2,18; 2,20; 8,1; 8,5; 23,1-2 |
| Aethelhard | 9,17; L | Ernwy | 1,15; 9,10; 26,7; W |
| Alfsi | 5,7; 5,9 | Ernwy Foot | 1,7 |
| Alfward | 5,6; 8,29;13,2-4; 13,6-7; 27,2 | Fran | 8,20 |
| Alfwold | 12,4 | Fulk | 2,19 |
| Alnoth | 23,2 | Gamel | 24,3; 26,9-10; L |
| Alstan | 14,11 | Geoffrey | 9,17; L |
| Ansfrid | 9,20 | Gilbert Hunter | 18 |
| Ansgot | 1,15; 14,2 | Gilbert of Venables | 16 |
| Arkell | 11,3 | Gilbert | 27,2; S1,7; L |
| Arngrim | 5,9; 8,14 | Glewin | 17,4 |
| Arni | 1,18; 9,1-3; 9,6-8; W | Godgyth | 20,5; 20, 7-8; 20,12 |
| Auti | 8,11 | Godric | 1,9; 1,28; 2,31; 8,12; 8,23; |
| Baldric | 15 | | 11,1-4; 12,5-8; 27,4 |
| Balliol, see Reginald | | Godwin | 1,12; 1,14; 1,29; 3,1; 8,32; |
| Beollan | 14,11 | | 11,3; 14,6; 14,9; 18,3-4; |
| Bernwulf | 1,27; 14,8; L | | 18,6; 19,2 |
| Bersi | 5,6 | Grim | 1,4 |
| Bigot of Loges | 14; 27,1 | Grimkel | 24,1 |
| Brictmer | 2,14 | King Gruffydd | B7; W |
| Brictric | 9,18 | Gruffydd | 9,18; 19,1 |
| Brown | 1,30; 9,28; 13,5; 14,5; 14,7 | Gunner | 3,2; 10,3 |
| Butler, see Richard | | Gunning | 8,22 |
| King Canute | 2,1; B13 | | |
| Chipping | 1,17 | Guthlac | 1,5 |
| Colben | 9,27; 26,12 | Hakon | 8,29; 8,37; 13,5 |
| Colbert | 2,21; 8,4; 8,8; 8,10 | Haldane | 8,22; 8,28; 8,42 |
| Cook, see Robert | | Hamo of Mascy | 12; W |
| David | 9,8 | Hamo | 1,22; 1,34; 27,2 |
| Dedol | 1,19; 2,25-26; 5,4 | Earl Harold | 8,21; 8,41 |
| Derch | 8,14; 8,28 | Hardwin | 9,7; 9,17 |
| Doda | 17,5 | Hasten | 9,29 |
| Dot | 1,15; 2,7; 2,17; 2,20; 6,2; | Herbert | 1,34; 3,6 |
| | 8,17; 8,23; 8,32; 8,34; 9,12; | Earl Hugh | 1 |
| | 14,4; 17,7-8; 17,10; 18,5; | Hugh of Delamere | 10 |
| | 24,8-9; L | Hugh son of | |
| Drogo | 2,7; 2,9-10; 2,17; 2,20 | Norman | 11; W |
| Dunning | 14,10; 25,1-3; 26,3; 26,6; | Hugh son of Osbern | 12; 16; W |
| Durand | 8,9 | Hugh | 1,22; 27,3-4 |
| Edric | 7,4; 8,33; 8,36 | Hugh, see Robert | |
| Edward | 9,4; 9,16; 9,22-23; 9,25; | Humphrey | 2,18; 2,21; 9,17 |
| | 24,5; 24,7; 24,9 | Hunding | 2,30; 24,4 |
| Earl Edwin | 1,1; 1,8; 1,13; 1,22; 1,24-26; | Hundulf | 2,26 |
| | 1,34; 2,1-6; 2,21; 14,1; 17,2; | Hunter, see William, Ralph | |
| | S1,1; W | Ilbert | 23 |
| Edwin | 2,7-12; 2,20; 6,1; 17,1; | Jocelyn | 1,1;19 |
| | 17,12; 24,2; W | Karl | 1,10; 8,19 |
| Egbrand | 9,11; 9,13 | Ketel | 26,1; L |
| Eli | 2,22 | Lambert | 3,2 |

Leofgeat 9,9
Leofing 8,6; L
Leofnoth 1,36; 3,3; 3,5; 3,7-10; 5,4; 5,8; 8,13; 9,24; 20,2; 20,9; 26,4; W
Leofric 1,5; 8,27; 9,19; 26,7
Leofwin 8,35; 8,38; 9,14; 10,1-2; 14,12; 20,3
Loges, see Bigot
Lothen 8,2
Luvede 7,4
Mainwaring, see Ranulf
Malbank, see William
Massey, see Hamo
Moran 26,12
Earl Morcar 2,21; 8,16; 20,11
Morfar 26,1
Mundret C24; 1,22; 1,34; 2,13; 26,3
Nigel of Burcy *25;*L
Nigel, see William
Norman, see Hugh
Odard 9,17-19; 26,2
Orde 9,26
Ording 1,23
Orm 9,17; L
Osbern son of
  Tezzo *24;*W
Osbern 24,7; 27,3
Osbern , see Hugh
Osgot 4,1-2
Osmer 5,5; 5,7; 5,10-13; 8,31; 8,35; 8,38; W
Owen 8,27; 8,31
Pat 27,2
Payne 5,4; 9,24-26
Picot 2,14
Ragenald 1,35
Ralph Hunter *21;* W
Ralph 9,9; 9,27; L; W
Ranulf Mainwaring 20
Ranulf 2,6; 27, 1-2; W
Raven 2,14; 24,6; 26,2
Ravenkel 2,21; 8,44; W
Ravenswart 9,9; 26,1; 27,4 ; W
Reginald Balliol *22;* 27,3
Restald 1,35
Rhuddlan, see Robert
Rhys 22,2
Richard Butler *6*
Richard of Vernon *5*

Richard 8,10; S1,7; W
Robert of
  Rhuddlan C25; *3;* W
Robert son of
  Hugh B13; *2*
Robert Cook *4*
Robert 1,22; L
Roger 2,14; 24,3; W; L
Sigerid 9,15
Siward 8,24; 8,30
Sten 1,16; 1,20
Stenketel 14,3
Stenulf 2,23; 14,13; 23,3; L
Sucga 27,2
Tesselin 26,1
Tezzo, see Osbern
Thored 5,1; 9,5; 16,1; 20,1; 22,1; 27,3; W
Toki 1,4; 1,6; 2,29; 5,2-3; 9,20
Uhtbrand 19,3
Uhtred 3,11; 9,20; L
Ulf 3,2; L
Ulfkel 3,6
Ulfketel 3,4; 8,25
Venables, see Gilbert
Vernon, see Richard, Walter
Walter of Vernon 7
Walter 1,22; L
Wicga 9,21
William Malbank *8;* S1,7; W
William son of
  Nigel *9;* W
William B4; A13-14; A17-18; 1,22; 2,23; 3,3-5; 3,7; 27,3; W;L
Winterlet 8,9
Woodman 2,19; 27,2
Wulfeva 2,13; 8,43; 8,45
Wulfgar, priest 12,2
Wulfgeat 1,11; 7,4; 8,18; 17,3; 17,6-7; 17,9; 17,11; 18,1-2; 20,10; 26,4; 27,1
Wulfheah 1,2; 8,3; 8,42; 15,1; W
Wulfnoth 12,1
Wulfric 1,32; 2,27-28; 5,14; 8,26; 12,3; 13,1; 26,8; 26,11;
Wulfsi 9,15; 21,1
Wulfwy 2,15-16; 2,24
Young Wulfwin 9,4

**Churches and Clergy. Bishop** of Chester *B;* 2,1-2; 2,5; S1,7; L . **Churches and Clergy** St. Chad B6; B13; 2,1; 16,2; 27,3. St. John B10; B12. St. Mary B11. St. Peter C25. St. Werbergh *A;* 1,35; 2,21. **Priests** see Ernwin, Wulfgar.

**Secular Titles and Occupational Names.** Butler *(pincerna)...* Richard. Cook (cocus)... Robert. Earl *(comes)...* Edwin, Harold, Hugh, Morcar. Hunter *(venator)...* Gilbert, Ralph

## WALES

| | | | |
|---|---|---|---|
| Aelmer | FD5,3; C; L | Osmer | FD5,2; C |
| Arni | FD2,5; FD4,1; C | Osmund | FD7,2 |
| Ascelin | FD2,3 | Ralph | FT3,4; C |
| Asgar | FD4,1 | Ralph Hunter | *FD8;* C |
| Earl Edwin | FD1,1-2; FD6,1; FT1,1; | Ranulf | FD7,1; C |
| | FT3,1; C | Ravenkel | FD3,1; FD5,3; C |
| Edwin | FD2,6; FD7,1-2; C | Ravenswart | FD5,1; C |
| Ernwy | FD3,2; C | Richard | FD3,1; FD5,3; C |
| Esbern | FD8,2 | Robert of Rhuddlan | *FD2; FT2; G;* C |
| King Gruffydd | FT3,7; C | Roger | FD2,5; C |
| Hamo of Mascy | *FD7;* C | Earl Roger | G,2 |
| Earl Hugh | *FD1; FT1;* C | Thored | FD7,1; C |
| Hugh son of | | Tual | FT2,11 |
| Norman | FD5,3; FT3,1-2; C | Warmund Hunter | FT3,3 |
| Hugh son of | | William | FT3,5; L |
| Osbern | *FD5;* C | William Malbank | *FD3;* C |
| Leofnoth | FD2,1; FD2,4; C | William son of | |
| Marchiud | FT1,9 | Nigel | *FD4;* C |
| Odin | FT1,8; FT3,1 | Wulfbert | FD2,4 |
| Osbern son of | | Wulfheah | FD8,1; C |
| Tezzo | FD5,3; *FD6;*C | Wulfmer | FD2,2 |

**Secular Titles and Occupational Names.** Earl (comes)... Edwin, Hugh, Roger.
Hunter (venator)... Ralph, Warmund.

## LANCASHIRE

| | | | |
|---|---|---|---|
| Aelmer | R1,9; C; W | Ralph | R3,1; R6,4; C; W |
| Aethelhard | R3,1; C | Robert | R1,43; R6,4; C |
| Aethelmund | R1,14 | Roger | R1,43; R1,45; R3,1; |
| Albert Grelley | R4,2 | | R6,4; C; W |
| Arnulf | Y9 | Roger of Bully | R4,2 |
| Aski | R1,11 | Roger of Poitou | Y2; *Y11-13* |
| Bernwulf | R1,4; C | Stenulf | R1,5; R1,25; C |
| Dot | R1,3; C | Teos | R1,37 |
| Dwan | Y9 | Theobald | R1,43; R3,1 |
| Ernwin, priest | Y12 | Thorfin | Y5 |
| Gamel | R5,3; R5,6; C | Thorulf | Y9 |
| Geoffrey | R1,43; R5,6; C | Earl Tosti | Y2; Y3; Y4; Y7; Y11 |
| Gerard | R6,4 | Uhtred | R1,2; R1,7; R1,13; R1,16; |
| Gilbert | R1,43;. Y12; C | | R1,22; R1,26-28; R1,31-32; |
| Gillemichael | Y8; Y11 | | R1,34; R1,36; R1,41; C |
| Godiva | R1,33 | Ulf | Y1; Y11; C |
| Ketel | R1,38; Y6; C | Walter | R6,4; C |
| Leofing | R1,20; C | Warin | R1,43; R3,1; R5,6 |
| Machel | Y11 | Wigbert | R1,29 |
| Machern | Y12 | William | R1,43; R3,1; C; W |
| Nigel | R5,6 | Winstan | R1,8 |
| Orm | Y1; Y10; C | Wulfbert | R1,18; W |
| Osmund | R3,1; W | | |

**Churches and Clergy.** St. Elfin R3,1. St. Mary R4,1; R5,2. St. Michael R5,2.
St. Oswald R2,1. **Priests** see Ernwin.

**Secular Titles and Occupational Names.** Earl (comes)... Tosti

# INDEX OF PLACES

The name of each place is followed by (i) the initial of its Hundred and its location on the Map in this volume; (ii) its National Grid Reference; (iii) chapter and section references in DB. Bracketed figures denote mention in section dealing with a different place. Unless otherwise stated, the identifications of EPNS and the spelling of the Ordnance Survey are followed for places in England; of OEB for places abroad. The National Grid reference system is explained on all Ordnance Survey maps, and in the Automobile Association Handbooks; the figures reading from left to right are given before those reading from bottom to top of the map.

## CHESHIRE

All places in Cheshire are in the 100 kilometre grid square lettered SJ. The Cheshire Hundreds are Macclesfield (M); Northwich (No); Nantwich (Na); Bucklow (East) (BE); Bucklow (West) (BW); Eddisbury (North) (EN); Eddisbury (South) (ES); Broxton (B); Wirral (W); Chester (C); Ati's Cross (A). Unidentified places are shown in Domesday Book spelling, in italics.

| | | | |
|---|---|---|---|
| Acton | Na 10 | 62 53 | 8,16; (S1) |
| Adlington | M 9 | 91 80 | 1,26 |
| Nether Alderley | M 12 | 84 76 | 14,6 |
| Over Alderley | M 13 | 86 76 | 9,28 |
| *Aldredelie* | – | – | 1,10 |
| Alpraham | ES 15 | 58 59 | 17,2 |
| 'Alretunstall' | – | – | 13,7 |
| 'Alretone' | – | – | 1,20 |
| Alsager | No 35 | 79 55 | 1,32 |
| Alvanley | EN 6 | 49 73 | 26,7 |
| Antrobus | BW 8 | 64 80 | (1,1); 1,36 |
| Appleton | BW 2 | 63 83 | 24,8 |
| Ashley | BE 11 | 77 84 | 13,6 |
| Ashton | ES 1 | 50 69 | 5,1 |
| Aston by Budworth | BW 9 | 68 80 | 9,24 |
| Aston by Sutton | BW 12 | 55 78 | A17; 9,19 |
| Aston in Newhall | Na 26 | 61 47 | 8,17 |
| Aston juxta Mondrem | Na 2 | 65 56 | 8,44 |
| Audlem | Na 34 | 65 43 | 5,12 |
| Austerson | Na 28 | 66 49 | 8,31 |
| Baddiley | Na 8 | 60 50 | 8,40 |
| Baguley | BE 5 | 81 90 | 27,2 |
| Barnston | W 13 | 27 83 | 9,9 |
| Barrow | ES 2 | 46 68 | 9,5 |
| Barthomley | Na 17 | 76 52 | 8,30 |
| Bartington | BW 16 | 60 76 | 26,3-4 |
| Basford | Na 16 | 71 52 | 8,27 |
| Batherton | Na 18 | 65 49 | 8,28 |
| Beeston | ES 17 | 53 58 | 2,24 |
| Bickerton | B 25 | 50 52 | 2,20 |
| Bickley | B 34 | 54 48 | 2,19 |
| Blacon | W 42 | 37 67 | 20,1 |
| Blakenhall | Na 30 | 72 47 | 18,6 |
| Bosley | M 26 | 91 65 | 11,5 |
| Bostock | No 10 | 67 69 | 5,11 |
| Boughton | B 1 | 42 65 | A5 |
| Bowdon | BE 7 | 75 86 | 13,3 |
| Bramhall | M 7 | 89 84 | 13,5 |
| Bredbury | M 4 | 92 92 | 5,14 |
| Brereton | No 22 | 78 64 | 18,2 |
| Broomhall | Na 27 | 63 46 | 8,36 |
| Broxton | B 24 | 48 53 | 2,14 |
| Great Budworth | BW 15 | 66 77 | 9,25 |

| | | | |
|---|---|---|---|
| Little Budworth | ES 6 | 59 65 | 1,19 |
| Buerton | Na 35 | 68 43 | 8,24 |
| Bunbury | ES 18 | 56 58 | 2,25 |
| Burton | ES 9 | 50 63 | B9 |
| Burwardsley | B 18 | 51 56 | 2,21 |
| Butley | M 11 | 91 77 | 2,30; 26,8 |
| Byley | No 11 | 72 69 | 11,3 |
| Caldecott | B 23 | 43 52 | 12,2 |
| Great Caldy | W 6 | 22 85 | 10,4 |
| Little Caldy | W 7 | 23 85 | 3,8 |
| *Calvintone* | – | – | 6,2 |
| Capenhurst | W 32 | 36 73 | 9,8 |
| Capesthorne | M 17 | 84 72 | 1,31 |
| 'Chapmonswiche' | BE 22 | 79 74 | 20,7 |
| Cheadle | M 6 | 87 88 | 26,9 |
| Chelford | M 14 | 81 74 | 1,30 |
| Chester | C 2 | 40 66 | C; A; (FD1,1) |
| Cheaveley | B 7 | 42 61 | A3 |
| Cholmondeley | B 29 | 53 51 | 2,7 |
| Cholmondeston | Na 1 | 63 59 | 8,45 |
| Chorley | Na 7 | 56 50 | 8,39 |
| Chorlton | Na 22 | 72 50 | 8,20 |
| Chowley | B 17 | 47 56 | 2,13 |
| Christleton | B 2 | 43 65 | 2,6 |
| Claverton | A 3 | 40 63 | FD5,2 |
| Clifton | BW 7 | 52 80 | A18 |
| Clive | No 13 | 67 65 | 1,33 |
| Clotton | ES 10 | 52 63 | 23,3 |
| Clutton | B 21 | 46 54 | 9,4 |
| *Cocle* | – | – | 15,1 |
| Coddington | B 20 | 44 55 | 1,15 |
| Cogshall | BW 14 | 63 77 | 5,4; 20,10 |
| 'Conersley' | EN 11 | 63 71 | 1,2 |
| Congleton | No 27 | 86 62 | 14,9 |
| Coppenhall | Na 5 | 70 57 | 8,42 |
| Cranage | M 19 | 75 68 | 2,31 |
| Crewe | Na 6 | 70 55 | 5,13 |
| Crewe Hall | B 22 | 42 53 | 2,22 |
| Croughton | W 35 | 41 72 | A8 |
| Croxton | No 15 | 70 67 | 19,2 |
| Cuddington | B 36 | 45 46 | 2,16 |
| Davenham | No 6 | 65 70 | 5,10 |
| Davenport | No 21 | 80 66 | 18,4 |
| Dodleston | A 5 | 36 61 | FD6,1 |
| *Done* | – | – | 1,11 |
| Duckington | B 27 | 49 51 | 2,11 |
| Dunham on the Hill | EN 14 | 47 72 | 1,3 |

| Place | Code | Grid | References |
|---|---|---|---|
| Dunham Massey | BE 4 | 74 88 | 13,2 |
| Dutton | BW 10 | 57 79 | 9,22; 24,7; 26,2 |
| Eanley | BW 5 | 56 81 | 9,21 |
| Eastham | W 21 | 35 80 | 1,22 |
| Eaton | B 10 | 41 60 | 1,13 |
| Eccleston | B 5 | 41 62 | 17,1 |
| Eddisbury | EN 16 | 55 69 | 1,12 |
| Edge | B 32 | 48 50 | 2,8; 2,12 |
| *Edritone*, see Kinnerton | | | |
| Elton | EN 4 | 45 75 | 1,4 |
| Farndon | B 19 | 51 54 | B3; 14,1 |
| Frith | Na 24 | 59 48 | 8,38 |
| Frodsham | EN 1 | 51 77 | 1,8 |
| Gawsworth | M 22 | 88 69 | 1,27 |
| Gayton | W 16 | 26 80 | 3,5 |
| Golborne | B 14 | 46 60 | 8,2; 24,2 |
| Goostrey | No 8 | 77 70 | 9,27; 11,4 |
| Grappenhall | BW 1 | 63 85 | 24,9 |
| Greasby | W 3 | 25 87 | 25,2 |
| Hadlow | W 25 | 33 77 | 1,24 |
| Hale | BE 8 | 77 86 | 13,4 |
| Halton | BW 3 | 53 81 | 9,17 |
| Hampton | B 33 | 49 49 | 2,9 |
| Handbridge | C 3 | 41 64 | 9,3; 10,2; 12,1 |
| Handley | B 15 | 46 57 | 24,1 |
| Hargrave | W 20 | 32 79 | 4,2 |
| Hartford | EN 10 | 63 72 | 17,5 |
| Hassall | No 33 | 76 57 | 8, 11-12 |
| Hatherton | Na 29 | 68 47 | 8,25 |
| Hatton | B 9 | 45 61 | 23,2 |
| Helsby | EN 5 | 48 75 | 1,7 |
| Henbury | M 15 | 88 73 | 1,31 |
| Heswall | W 14 | 26 82 | 3,6 |
| *Hofinchel* | — | — | 1,31 |
| Hollingworth | M 2 | 00 96 | 1,31 |
| Hooton | W 22 | 36 79 | 5,3 |
| Huntington | B 6 | 42 62 | A4 |
| Iddinshall | ES 11 | 53 62 | A6 |
| Ince | EN 2 | 44 76 | A16 |
| Kermincham | M 23 | 79 67 | 11,7 |
| Kinderton | No 19 | 72 66 | 18,3 |
| Kingsley | EN 7 | 54 74 | 26,6 |
| Kinnerton (?) | A 4 | 33 61 | FD5,3 |
| Knutsford | BE 18 | 75 78 | 9,13 |
| Lach Dennis | No 5 | 70 71 | 9,29; 26,12 |
| Lache | A 1 | 38 63 | A22 |
| *Laitone* | — | — | 1,31 |
| Landican | W 8 | 28 85 | 8,7 |
| Larkton | B 28 | 50 57 | 2,10 |
| Church Lawton | No 36 | 82 55 | 11,1-2 |
| Buglawton | No 37 | 88 63 | 11,1-2 |
| Lea nr Backford | W 34 | 38 72 | A9 |
| Lea Newbold | B 13 | 43 59 | 1,14; 1,16; 14,2 |
| Ledsham | W 29 | 35 74 | 7,3 |
| Leftwich | No 3 | 65 72 | 5,7 |
| High Legh | BE 9 | 69 84 | 17,7 |
| Little Leigh | BW 17 | 61 75 | 9,23 |
| Leighton | W 18 | 28 79 | 3,3 |
| Lymm | BE 1 | 67 86 | 17,6; 24,5 |
| Macclesfield | M 16 | 91 73 | 1,25 |
| Malpas | B 35 | 48 47 | 2,4 |
| Manley | EN 15 | 50 71 | 1,6 |
| Marbury | Na 31 | 55 45 | 8,21 |
| Marlston | A 2 | 39 63 | FD4,1 |
| Marton | M 21 | 84 68 | 1,28; 11,6 |
| Great and Little Meols | W 2 | 23 90 | 3,9-10 |
| Mere | BE 13 | 72 81 | 17,9 |
| Middle Aston | BW 13 | 55 77 | A17 |
| Middlewich | No 16 | 70 66 | S2 |
| Millington | BE10 | 72 84 | 9,12 |
| Minshull Vernon | No 30 | 67 60 | 8,13 |
| Church Minshull | No 29 | 66 60 | 8,14 |
| Mobberley | BE 17 | 78 80 | 14,4 |
| Mollington | W 39 | 39 70 | 3,1-2 |
| Mottram | M 10 | 88 79 | 26,10 |
| Moulton | No 9 | 65 69 | 5,8 |
| Nantwich | Na 11 | 65 52 | S1; (1,1;1,8; 8,16) |
| Ness | W 27 | 30 75 | 7,2 |
| Great Neston | W 23 | 29 77 | A13; 9,6 |
| Little Neston | W 24 | 30 77 | 4,1 |
| Netherleigh | C 4 | 41 65 | 9,2 |
| Newbold Astbury | No 28 | 84 61 | 18,1 |
| Newton by Chester | C 1 | 41 68 | C1; 9,1 |
| Newton in Middlewich | No 17 | 70 65 | 19,1 |
| Noctorum | W 5 | 29 87 | 8,10 |
| Norbury nr Marbury | Na 23 | 55 47 | 8,21 |
| Norbury nr Stockport | M 8 | 91 85 | 14,5 |
| Northenden | BE 6 | 83 89 | 27,1 |
| Northwich | No 1 | 65 73 | S3; (9,17; 17,5; 17,8; 20,3) |
| Norton | BW 4 | 55 81 | 9,20 |
| Occleston | No 25 | 69 62 | 1,33 |
| Ollerton | BE 19 | 77 76 | 1,9; 20,8; 26,11 |
| *Opetone* | — | — | 1,18 |
| Oulton | ES 7 | 59 64 | 25,1 |
| Over | ES 8 | 64 66 | 1,21 |
| Overleigh | C 5 | 40 65 | 10,1 |
| Overton | B 31 | 47 48 | 2,15 |
| Peckforton | ES 20 | 53 56 | 2,28 |
| Nether and Over Peover | BE 23 | 74 74 | 9,16; 17,10; 20,4; 20,6 |
| Picton | W 36 | 43 71 | 5,2 |
| Nether Pool and Over Pool | W 26 | 39 78 | 8,5 |
| Poole | Na 4 | 64 56 | (8,36); 8,37; 8,43 |
| Poulton Lancelyn | W 15 | 33 81 | 24,3 |
| Poulton | B 12 | 40 59 | 6,1 |
| Prenton | W 9 | 31 84 | 7,4 |
| Puddington | W 31 | 32 73 | 13,1 |
| Pulford | B 11 | 38 59 | A20; 12,3 |
| Raby | W 19 | 31 79 | A14; 9,7 |
| North Rode | M 25 | 88 66 | 14,7 |
| Odd Rode | No 34 | 80 56 | 27,4 |
| Romiley | M 5 | 93 90 | 1,31 |
| Rostherne | BE 12 | 74 83 | 17,11 |
| Rushton | ES 5 | 58 63 | 1,17 |
| Saighton | B 8 | 44 62 | A2 |

| | | | |
|---|---|---|---|
| Sandbach | No 31 | 75 60 | 1,33; 14,10 |
| Saughall | W 37 | 36 70 | A11; 8,6 |
| Shavington | Na 15 | 69 51 | 8,23 |
| Shipbrook | No 7 | 67 71 | 5,5 |
| Shocklach | B 30 | 43 48 | 2,17 |
| Shotwick | W 33 | 33 71 | A12 |
| Shurlach | No 4 | 67 73 | 5,6 |
| Siddington | M 18 | 84 70 | 14,7 |
| Snelson | BE 24 | 80 73 | 20,9 |
| Somerford | No 23 | 81 65 | 11,8 |
| Somerford | | | |
| Booths | M 24 | 85 66 | 26,1 |
| Sproston | No 20 | 73 67 | 8,15 |
| Spurstow | ES 21 | 55 56 | 2,27 |
| Stanney | W 30 | 41 74 | 1,35 |
| Stapeley | Na 19 | 67 49 | 8,34 |
| Stapleford | B 3 | 48 64 | 21,1 |
| Stoneley | Na 9 | 61 51 | 8,41 |
| Storeton | W 12 | 30 84 | 25,3 |
| Sunderland | BE 3 | 73 90 | 27,2 |
| Sutton | No 18 | 70 64 | 1,33; 14,11 |
| Great and | | | |
| Little Sutton | W 28 | 36 76 | A10 |
| Guilden Sutton | W 43 | 44 68 | B5; 2,29 |
| Nether Tabley | BE 15 | 72 78 | 19,3 |
| Over Tabley | BE 16 | 72 80 | 9,14 |
| Tarporley | ES 12 | 55 62 | 17,3 |
| Tarvin | ES 3 | 48 67 | B4 |
| Tattenhall | B 16 | 48 58 | 8,1 |
| Tatton | BE 14 | 74 81 | 9,11; 20,3 |
| Tetton | No 26 | 71 63 | 20,12 |
| Thingwall | W 11 | 27 84 | 8,9 |
| Thornton Hough | W 17 | 30 80 | 3,4 |
| Thornton le | | | |
| Moors | EN 3 | 44 74 | 14,3 |
| Thurstaston | W 10 | 24 83 | 3,7 |
| Tilston | B 26 | 45 51 | 2,5 |
| Tilstone | | | |
| Fearnall | ES 14 | 56 60 | 2,23 |
| Tintwistle | M 1 | 02 97 | 1,31 |

| | | | |
|---|---|---|---|
| Tiverton | ES 13 | 55 60 | 2,26 |
| Bridge Trafford | EN 12 | 45 71 | A15 |
| Mickle Trafford | W 41 | 44 69 | 1,23 |
| Wimbolds | | | |
| Trafford | EN 13 | 44 72 | 1,5 |
| Tushingham | B 37 | 52 46 | 2,18 |
| *Ulure* | — | — | 8,3 |
| Upton | W 4 | 26 87 | 8,8 |
| Upton by | | | |
| Chester | W 40 | 40 69 | 1,34 |
| Walgherton | Na 20 | 69 48 | 8,22 |
| Wallasey | W 1 | 31 92 | 3,11 |
| Warburton | BE 2 | 70 89 | 9,10; 24,6 |
| Wardle | ES 19 | 60 57 | 12,4 |
| Warford | BE 20 | 80 77 | 20,5 |
| Waverton | B 4 | 46 63 | 23,1 |
| Weaver | No 14 | 66 64 | (1,33);14,13 |
| Weaverham | EN 8 | 61 73 | 1,1 |
| Werneth | M 3 | 95 92 | 1,31 |
| Wervin | W 38 | 41 71 | A7; 8,4 |
| Weston | BW 6 | 50 80 | 9,18 |
| Wettenhall | ES 16 | 62 61 | 17,4 |
| Wharton | No 12 | 66 66 | 5,9 |
| Wheelock | No 32 | 74 58 | 20,11 |
| Whitley | BW 11 | 61 78 | 9,26 |
| *Wich*, see Nantwich, Northwich, Middlewich | | | |
| Wilkesley | Na 33 | 62 41 | 8,32 |
| Willaston | Na 13 | 67 52 | 8,18 |
| Willington | ES 4 | 53 67 | 7,1 |
| Wimboldsley | No 24 | 68 62 | (1,33); 14,12 |
| Wincham | BE 21 | 67 75 | 17,8 |
| Winnington | EN 9 | 64 74 | 20,2; 24,4 |
| Wirswall | Na 32 | 54 44 | 8,21 |
| Wistaston | Na 14 | 68 53 | 8,26 |
| 'Wisterson' | Na 12 | 66 53 | 8,35 |
| Lower | | | |
| Withington | M 20 | 81 68 | 1,29 |
| Witton | No 2 | 66 73 | 18,5 |
| Worleston | Na 3 | 68 56 | 8,29 |
| Wrenbury | Na 25 | 59 47 | 8,19 |
| Wybunbury | Na 21 | 69 49 | B8 |

**Place not named**

In BUCKLOW (West) Hundred    26,5

**Places not in Cheshire**

SHROPSHIRE   Tittenley 8,33;  Whitchurch 8,21; 8,41
*Outside Britain* (see Index of Persons)
Loges...Bigot


# WALES

All places in Wales are in the 100 kilometre grid square lettered SJ. The Welsh districts are
Rhuddlan (R); Tegeingl (T); Bistre (B); Deeside (D); Maelor Saesneg (MS); Maelor Cymraeg (MC).
Unidentified places are shown in Domesday Book spelling, in italics.

| | | | |
|---|---|---|---|
| Allington | MC 2 | 38 57 | 16,1 |
| Aston | D 9 | 30 67 | FD7,1 |
| Axton | T 12 | 10 80 | FT1,9 |
| Bagillt | D 1 | 21 75 | FD2,5 |
| Bettisfield | MS 3 | 47 37 | B13;2,1 |
| Bistre | B 4 | 27 62 | FT3,1; FT3,6-7 |

| | | | |
|---|---|---|---|
| Blorant | R 20 | 09 69 | FT1,3 |
| Bodeugan | R 14 | 05 75 | FT1,2 |
| *Boteuuarul* | — | — | FT2,2 |
| Broughton | D 12 | 33 63 | FD2,1-2; FD5,1; FD8,1 |
| Bryn | R 3 | 03 79 | FT1,1; FT2,1 |

| | | | | | | | | |
|---|---|---|---|---|---|---|---|---|
| Bryncoed | B 3 | 23 62 | FT3,3. | | Llan Elwy | | | |
| Brynford | T 20 | 17 74 | FT1,6; FT2,7 | | (St. Asaph) | R 15 | 03 74 | FT2,5 |
| Bryngwyn | R 19 | 10 73 | FT1,3 | | Llewerllyd | R 8 | 04 79 | FT1,1; FT2,1 |
| Brynhedydd | R 13 | 01 81 | FT1,1 | | Llystyn Hunydd | T 24 | 18 68 | FT1,5 |
| Bychton | T 14 | 15 80 | FT2,8 | | Llys Edwin | D 6 | 23 70 | FD7,2 |
| Caerwys | R 22 | 12 72 | FT2,5 | | Llys y Coed | T 26 | 16 65 | FT1,5 |
| Calcot | T 19 | 17 75 | FT1,8 | | Maen Efa | R 18 | 08 74 | FT1,2 |
| Carnychan | T 10 | 09 80 | FT2,12 | | Mechlas | T 25 | 19 65 | FT1,5 |
| Cefn Du | R 2 | 01 81 | FT1,1 | | *Meincatis* | — | — | FT2,6 |
| *Chespuic* | — | — | 27,3 | | *Melchanestone* | — | — | FT2,10 |
| Cilowen | R 16 | 05 72 | FT1,2 | | Meliden | T 2 | 06 81 | FT2,15 |
| 'Clayton' | D 10 | 31 66 | FD3,1 | | Mertyn | T 16 | 15 77 | FT1,8 |
| *Coiwen* | — | — | FT2,6 | | Mostyn | T 13 | 15 80 | FT2,9 |
| Coleshill | D 2 | 23 73 | FD2,6 | | *Mulintone* | — | — | FT3,1-2 |
| Cwybr | R 4 | 02 79 | FT1,1 | | *Munentone* | — | — | FT3,2 |
| Cwybr Bach | R 5 | 02 80 | FT2,1 | | *Pengdeslion* | — | — | FT2,3 |
| Cyrchynan | R 12 | 04 75 | FT2,5 | | Pentre | R 6 | 03 80 | FT1,1 |
| *Danfrond* | — | — | FT2,11 | | 'Pen y Gors' | — | — | FT2,1 |
| Dincolyn | T 1 | 06 79 | FT2,16 | | Picton | T 9 | 11 82 | FT2,10 |
| Dyserth | R 9 | 05 79 | FT1,2; FT2,2 | | Prestatyn | T 3 | 06 82 | FT2,15 |
| *Edritone,* see Kinnerton | | | | | Radington | D 3 | 24 73 | FD1,2 |
| Erbistock | MC 8 | 35 42 | 22,2 | | Radnor | MC 4 | 36 56 | 27,3 |
| Eyton | MC 7 | 35 45 | B6; 16,2 | | 'Rhiwargor' | — | — | FT2,2 |
| Fulbrook | T 17 | 19 77 | FT1,7 | | Rhos Ithel | B 5 | 23 61 | FT3,4 |
| Gellilyfdy | T 18 | 14 73 | FT1,9 | | Rhuddlan | R 1 | 02 77 | FT1,1; FT2,1; FT2,17-20 |
| Golden Grove | T 6 | 08 81 | FT2,13 | | | | | |
| Golftyn | D 5 | 28 70 | FD2,3 | | Rhyd Orddwy | R 7 | 03 81 | FT2,1 |
| Gop | T 11 | 08 80 | FT2,16 | | St. Asaph, see Llan Elwy | | | |
| Gresford | MC 3 | 35 55 | 22,1; 27,3 | | Soughton | D 8 | 24 66 | FD8,2 |
| Gronant | T 4 | 09 83 | FT2,13 | | *Sudfelle* | — | — | FT3,1 |
| Gwaunysgor | T 5 | 07 81 | FT2,12 | | Sutton | MC 6 | 41 48 | 16,2 |
| Gwesbyr | T 8 | 11 83 | FT2,11 | | *Tredveng* | — | — | FT2,1 |
| Gwysaney | B1 | 22 66 | FT3,5 | | Trefraith | R 21 | 15 73 | FT2,6 |
| Halkyn | T 22 | 20 71 | FT1,6; FT2,7 | | Trelawnyd | R 11 | 08 79 | FT2,4 |
| Hawarden | D 11 | 31 65 | FD1,1 | | Trellyniau | T 23 | 18 69 | FT1,4 |
| Hendrebiffa | B 2 | 23 03 | FT3,2 | | Tremeirchion | R 17 | 08 73 | FT1,3 |
| Hiraddug | R 10 | 07 78 | FT2,3 | | *Ulchenol* | — | — | FT1,6 |
| Hope | MC 1 | 31 58 | 17,12 | | *Weltune* | — | — | FT3,2 |
| 'Horsepool' | — | — | FT3,2 | | *Wenfesne* | — | — | FT2,14 |
| Hoseley | MC 5 | 37 55 | A19 | | Wepre | D 7 | 24 69 | A21; FD3,2 |
| *Inglecroft* | — | — | FT2,7 | | Whitford | T 15 | 14 78 | FT1,8; FT2,8 |
| Iscoyd | MS 2 | 41 50 | 2,2 | | 'Wiselei' | — | — | FT3,1 |
| Kelston | T 7 | 10 81 | FT2,11 | | *Witestan* | — | — | FT2,16 |
| Kinnerton(?) | D 13 | 32 61 | FD5,3 | | *Widhulde* | — | — | FT1,3 |
| Leadbrook | D 4 | 25 71 | FD2,4 | | Worthenbury | MS 1 | 42 46 | 2,3 |
| *Legge* | — | — | FT3,1 | | Ysceifiog | T 21 | 18 69 | FT1,4 |

**Places not in Wales**

*Elsewhere in Britain.*

HEREFORDSHIRE Hereford FT2,19

*Places outside Britain*

Breteuil FT2,19

# LANCASHIRE

Places marked with an asterix (*) are in the 100 kilometre grid square lettered SJ; all others are in square SD. The Lancashire Hundreds are West Derby (WD), Warrington (Wa), Blackburn (Bl), Salford (S), Leyland (L), and Newton (N). In North Lancashire the districts are Amounderness (A), Austwick (Au), Whittington (Wh), Beetham (Bt), Halton (H), Bentham (Bn), Ashton (As), Strickland (St) and Millom (Mi). Individual manors not included within a district are given initial letters on the maps, here within square brackets [ ]. Unidentified places are given in Domesday Book spelling, in italics.

| Place | District | | Grid | Ref |
|---|---|---|---|---|
| Aighton | A56 | 67 | 39 | Y2 |
| Ainsdale | WD 3 | 31 | 12 | R1,24 |
| Aldcliffe | H 19 | 47 | 60 | Y3 |
| Aldingham | [A] | 28 | 71 | Y9 |
| Allerton* | WD 41 | 41 | 87 | R1,15 |
| Altcar | WD 12 | 32 | 06 | R1,36 |
| Argameles | WD 2 | 33 | 18 | R1,29 |
| Arkholme | Wh 3 | 58 | 72 | Y4 |
| *Aschebi* | - | - | | Y2 |
| Ashton | As 1 | 46 | 57 | Y12 |
| Ashton on Ribble | A 26 | 50 | 30 | Y2 |
| Ashton-u-Lyne* | S 4 | 93 | 99 | R5,2 |
| Aughton | WD 17 | 39 | 05 | R1,2; R1,22 |
| Bardsea | Mi 13 | 30 | 74 | Y7 |
| Bare | H 9 | 45 | 65 | Y3 |
| Barton | WD 7 | 35 | 09 | R1,37 |
| Barton nr Preston | A 46 | 51 | 37 | Y2 |
| Birkby | [Bi] | 38 | 76 | Y10 |
| Bispham | A 5 | 32 | 41 | Y2 |
| Blackburn | Bl 5 | 68 | 28 | R4,1 |
| Bolton le Moors | [B] | 26 | 73 | Y9 |
| Bolton le Sands | H 4 | 48 | 68 | Y3 |
| Bootle* | WD 25 | 34 | 94 | R1,20 |
| Borwick | Bt 3 | 52 | 73 | Y10 |
| Broughton | A 47 | 52 | 35 | Y2 |
| Broughton, in Furness | Mi 6 | 21 | 87 | Y7 |
| Burn | A 2 | 33 | 45 | Y2 |
| Nether Burrow | Bn 8 | 61 | 75 | Y1 |
| Over Burrow | Wh 11 | 61 | 76 | Y4 |
| Cantsfield | Wh 5 | 62 | 72 | Y4 |
| Carleton | A 4 | 33 | 39 | Y2 |
| Carnforth | H 3 | 49 | 70 | Y3 |
| Cartmel | [C] | 38 | 78 | Y9 |
| Caton | Au 14 | 53 | 64 | Y5 |
| Catterall | A 43 | 49 | 42 | Y2 |
| Childwall* | WD 36 | 42 | 89 | R1,17 |
| Chipping | A 58 | 62 | 43 | Y2 |
| Claughton | A 43 | 53 | 42 | Y2 |
| Claughton nr Lancaster | Au 13 | 56 | 66 | Y5 |
| Clifton | A 24 | 46 | 30 | Y2 |
| Cockerham | [C] | 46 | 52 | Y10 |
| Crimbles | A 38 | 45 | 57 | Y2 |
| Crivelton | Mi 15 | 20 | 71 | Y7 |
| Great and Little Crosby | WD21;24 | 31 | 99 | R1,2; R1,41 |

| Place | District | | Grid | Ref |
|---|---|---|---|---|
| Dalton nr Wigan | WD 14 | 49 | 08 | R1,26; R1,4 |
| Dalton, in Furness | Mi 14 | 22 | 74 | Y7-8 |
| Dendron | [D] | 24 | 70 | Y9 |
| West Derby* | WD 32 | 39 | 94 | R1 |
| Dilworth | A55 | 62 | 37 | Y2 |
| Downholland | WD 13 | 34 | 08 | R1,35 |
| Great Eccleston | A 32 | 42 | 40 | Y2 |
| Little Eccleston | A 33 | 41 | 39 | Y2 |
| Ellel | As 2 | 48 | 56 | Y10 |
| Elswick | A 35 | 42 | 38 | Y2 |
| Farleton | Bn 4 | 57 | 67 | Y6 |
| Fishwick | A 54 | 56 | 24 | Y2 |
| Fordbootle | Mi 19 | 22 | 70 | Y7 |
| Formby | WD 8 | 30 | 07 | R1.23 |
| Forton | A 40 | 48 | 51 | Y2 |
| Freckleton | A 23 | 42 | 28 | Y2 |
| Garstang | A 42 | 49 | 45 | Y2 |
| Gleaston | Mi 21 | 25 | 70 | Y7 |
| Goosnargh | A 50 | 55 | 36 | Y2 |
| Greenhalgh | A 14 | 40 | 35 | Y2 |
| Gressingham | Wh 4 | 57 | 69 | Y4 |
| Grimsargh | A 53 | 58 | 34 | Y2 |
| Haighton | A 51 | 56 | 34 | Y2 |
| Halsall | WD 6 | 37 | 10 | R1,38; R1,4 |
| Halton | H 1 | 50 | 65 | Y3 |
| Hambleton | A 31 | 37 | 42 | Y2 |
| Hart | Mi 22 | 26 | 67 | Y7 |
| Heaton | Mi 12 | 22 | 75 | Y7 |
| Heaton nr Lancaster | H 13 | 40 | 11 | Y3 |
| Heysham | H 14 | 41 | 61 | Y3 |
| Hillam | H 17 | 45 | 52 | Y3 |
| Holker | [H] | 36 | 77 | Y10 |
| Hornby | Bn 5 | 58 | 68 | Y1 |
| Huncoat | Bl 3 | 77 | 30 | R4,2 |
| Hurlston | WD 5 | 40 | 10 | R1,32 |
| Hutton | H 23 | 48 | 63 | Y3 |
| Huyton* | WD 34 | 44 | 91 | R1,3 |
| Ince Blundell | WD 19 | 32 | 03 | R1,10 |
| Inskip | A 37 | 46 | 37 | Y2 |
| Ireby | Wh 9 | 65 | 75 | Y4 |
| Kellet | H 2 | 50 | 68 | Y3 |
| Killerwick | Mi 9 | 21 | 75 | Y7 |
| Kirkby* | WD 26 | 41 | 98 | R1,2 |
| Kirkby Ireleth | Mi 20 | 23 | 78 | Y7 |
| Kirkdale* | WD 31 | 35 | 94 | R1,7; R1,4 |
| Kirkham | A 19 | 42 | 33 | Y2 |

| Place | Code | Grid | Ref |
|---|---|---|---|
| Kirk Lancaster | H 21 | 48 62 | Y3 |
| Knowsley* | WD 30 | 43 95 | R1,2 |
| Lancaster | H 20 | 47 61 | Y3 |
| Lathom | WD 10 | 46 19 | R1,31 |
| Layton | A 8 | 32 37 | Y2 |
| Lea | A 26 | 47 32 | Y2 |
| Leck | Wh 10 | 64 76 | Y4 |
| Leece | Mi 23 | 24 69 | Y7 |
| Leyland | L 2 | 54 22 | R6,1 |
| Down Litherland | WD 27 | 33 97 | R1,9 |
| Up Litherland | WD 23 | 37 07 | R1,28 |
| Lonsdale | [L] | 43 54 | Y10 |
| Lydiate | WD 16 | 36 04 | R1,34 |
| Lytham | A 21 | 34 27 | Y2 |
| Maghull | WD 20 | 37 02 | R1,2 |
| Manchester* | S 3 | 83 98 | R5,2 |
| Martin | Mi 8 | 24 77 | Y7 |
| Marton | WD 4 | 42 12 | R1,32 |
| Great and Little Marton | A 10 | 32 35 | Y2 |
| Melling | Bn 6 | 59 71 | Y1 |
| Melling nr Liverpool | WD 25 | 39 00 | R1,33 |
| North Meols | WD 1 | 34 19 | R1,42 |
| Raven Meols | WD 11 | 27 05 | R1,12 R1,30 |
| Middleton | H 15 | 42 59 | Y3 |
| Mythop | A 12 | 36 35 | Y2 |
| Newsham | A 45 | 51 36 | Y2 |
| Newsham in Skerton | H 7 | 51 36 | Y3 |
| Newton in Cartmel | Mi 26 | 40 83 | Y7 |
| Newton in Lancaster | H 22 | 50 64 | Y3 |
| Newton nr Preston | A 24 | 44 31 | Y2 |
| Newton in Whittington | Wh 2 | 60 75 | Y4 |
| Newton-le-Willows * | N 1 | 59 95 | R2,1 |
| Orgrave | Mi 10 | 24 76 | Y7 |
| Overton | H 16 | 43 58 | Y3 |
| Oxcliffe | H 12 | 45 62 | Y3 |
| Pendleton | Bl 1 | 75 39 | R4,2 |
| Pennington | Mi 7 | 26 77 | Y7 |
| Penwortham | L 1 | 51 28 | R6,5 |
| Field Plumpton | A 15 | 38 33 | Y2 |
| Wood Plumpton | A 47 | 50 34 | Y2 |
| Poulton le Fylde | A 6 | 34 39 | Y2 |
| Poulton le Sands | H 11 | 44 65 | Y3 |
| Preesall | A 29 | 36 47 | Y2 |
| Preese | A 11 | 37 36 | Y2 |
| Preston | A 28 | 54 29 | Y2 |
| Priest Hutton | Au 11 | 53 74 | Y5 |
| Radcliffe | S 2 | 78 07 | R5,2 |
| Rawcliffe | A 32 | 47 42 | Y2 |
| Ribby | A 18 | 40 31 | Y2 |
| Ribchester | A 55 | 65 35 | Y2 |
| Roby* | WD 33 | 43 91 | R1,2 |
| Rochdale | S 1 | 89 13 | R5,3 |
| Roose | Mi 24 | 22 69 | Y7 |
| Rossall | A 1 | 37 45 | Y2 |
| St Michael's On Wyre | A 36 | 46 41 | Y2 |
| Salford* | S 5 | 82 98 | R5; R6,2 |
| Salwick | A 20 | 51 31 | Y2 |
| Scotforth | As 3 | 48 59 | Y10 |
| Sefton | WD 23 | 35 01 | R1,16 |
| Singleton | A 7 | 38 38 | Y2 |
| Skelmersdale | WD 15 | 46 06 | R1,27 |
| Skerton | H 8 | 47 63 | Y3 |
| Slyne | H 6 | 47 66 | Y3 |
| Smithdown* | WD 40 | 38 88 | R1,14 |
| Sowerby | Mi 17 | 18 71 | Y7 |
| Sowerby nr Preston | A 38 | 47 39 | Y2 |
| Speke* | WD 44 | 42 83 | R1,16 |
| Staining | A 9 | 34 36 | Y2 |
| Stainton | Mi 16 | 24 72 | Y7 |
| Stalmine | A 30 | 37 45 | Y2 |
| Stapleton Terne | H 5 | 49 66 | Y3 |
| *Suntun* | Mi 18 | c 21 71 | Y7 |
| Swainseat | A 41 | 54 53 | Y2 |
| Tarbock* | WD 38 | 46 87 | R1,13 |
| Tatham | Bn 3 | 60 69 | Y6 |
| Thirnby | Wh 12 | 61 78 | Y4 |
| Thornton | A 3 | 35 42 | Y2 |
| Thornton nr Liverpool | WD 22 | 34 02 | R1,11 |
| Threlfall | A 49 | 57 39 | Y2 |
| Thurnham | H 18 | 45 54 | Y3 |
| Torrisholme | H 10 | 46 64 | Y3 |
| Toxteth* | WD 39 | 37 88 | R1,4-5 |
| Treales | A 16 | 36 34 | Y2 |
| Tunstall | Bn 7 | 60 73 | Y6 |
| Ulverston | [U] | 28 78 | Y9 |
| Upholland | WD 18 | 52' 05 | R1,25 |
| Walton | Mi 25 | 37 79 | Y7 |
| Walton-le-Dale | Bl 4 | 55 28 | R4,2 |
| Walton on the Hill* | WD 29 | 36 95 | R1,8 |
| Warrington* | Wa 1 | 60 88 | R3,1 |
| Wart | Mi 11 | 24 75 | Y7 |
| Warton | Au 12 | 50 72 | Y5 |
| Warton nr Preston | A 22 | 49 72 | Y2 |
| Wavertree* | WD 35 | 37 89 | R1,20 |
| Weeton | A 13 | 38 34 | Y2 |
| Wennington | Bn 2 | 61 70 | Y1; Y6 |
| Westby | A 17 | 38 31 | Y2 |
| Whalley | Bl 2 | 73 36 | R4,1 |
| Wheatley | A 58 | 62 39 | Y2 |
| Whittingham | A 52 | 54 36 | Y2 |
| Whittington | Wh 1 | 60 76 | Y4 |
| *Wibaldslei* | WD 42 | c42 87 | R1,18 |
| Winwick* | N 2 | 60 92 | R2,1 |
| Little Woolton* | WD 37 | 43 87 | R1,13 |
| Much Woolton* | WD 43 | 42 86 | R1,19 |
| Yealand | Bt 2 | 50 74 | Y10 |

# CUMBERLAND and WESTMORLAND

Places marked with an asterix (*) are in the 100 kilometre grid square lettered SD, and also in Cumberland; all other places are in square SD and in Westmorland. The districts are Austwick (Au), Millom (Mi), Strickland (St), Whittington (Wh) and Beetham (Bt).

| | | | | | | | | | |
|---|---|---|---|---|---|---|---|---|---|
| Barbon | Wh 15 | 63 | 82 | Y4 | Kirksanton* | Mi 4 | 13 | 80 | Y7 |
| Beetham | Bt 1 | 50 | 80 | Y13 | Levens | Bt 6 | 49 | 86 | Y5 |
| Bootle* | Mi 2 | 10 | 88 | Y7 | Lupton | Au 8 | 56 | 81 | Y5 |
| 'Bothelford' | St 5 | c51 | 89 | Y8 | Mansergh | Au 5 | 60 | 83 | Y5 |
| Burton | St 9 | 53 | 76 | Y8 | Middleton | Au 4 | 62 | 86 | Y5 |
| Casterton | Wh 14 | 63 | 80 | Y4 | Millom* | Mi 1 | 17 | 80 | Y7 |
| Dalton | St 10 | 54 | 77 | Y8 | Millom Castle* | Mi 3 | 17 | 81 | Y7 |
| Farleton | Bt 4 | 53 | 81 | Y13 | Mint | St 3 | 52 | 94 | Y8 |
| Helsington | St 6 | 50 | 89 | Y8 | Patton | St 2 | 55 | 96 | Y8 |
| Heversham | Bt 5 | 50 | 83 | Y13 | Preston | | | | |
| Hincaster | Bt 7 | 51 | 85 | Y13 | Patrick | Au 7 | 56 | 85 | Y5 |
| Holme | Au 9 | 52 | 79 | Y5 | Preston | | | | |
| Old Hutton | St 8 | 56 | 89 | Y8 | Richard | Bt 8 | 53 | 84 | Y13 |
| Hutton Roof | Wh 13 | 57 | 78 | Y4 | Stainton | St 7 | 52 | 86 | Y8 |
| Kendal | St 4 | 52 | 93 | Y8 | Strickland | St 1 | 50 | 97 | Y8 |
| Kirkby | | | | | Whicham* | Mi 5 | 13 | 82 | Y7 |
| Lonsdale | Au 6 | 61 | 79 | Y5 | | | | | |

**Places not in Lancashire, Westmorland or Cumberland**

YORKSHIRE  Austwick Y5; Barnoldswick Y4;  Burton Y4-5; Clapham Y5; *Heldetune* Y5; Sedbergh Y4; Thornton Y1.

# MAPS

West Cheshire

East Cheshire

Wales

South Lancashire

Mid Lancashire

North Lancashire with Westmorland and Cumberland I

North Lancashire with Westmorland and Cumberland II

The **Abbreviations** used for the Hundreds and Districts are

## West Cheshire

| | |
|---|---|
| W | Wirral |
| BW | Bucklow (West) |
| EN | Eddisbury (North) |
| ES | Eddisbury (South) |
| B | Broxton |
| Na | Nantwich |
| A | Ati's Cross |
| C | Chester |

## East Cheshire

| | |
|---|---|
| BE | Bucklow (East) |
| M | Macclesfield |
| No | Northwich |
| Na | Nantwich |

## Wales

| | |
|---|---|
| R | Rhuddlan |
| T | Tegeingl |
| D | Deeside |
| B* | Bistre |
| MC | Maelor Cymraeg |
| MS | Maelor Saesneg |

## South Lancashire

| | |
|---|---|
| Wa | Warrington |
| N | Newton |
| S | Salford |
| L | Leyland |
| WD | (West) Derby |

## Mid Lancashire

| | |
|---|---|
| A | Amounderness |
| Bl | Blackburn |

## North Lancashire with Westmorland and Cumberland II

| | |
|---|---|
| Mi* | Millom |

## North Lancashire with Westmorland and Cumberland I

| | |
|---|---|
| Au* | Austwick |
| Wh* | Whittington |
| Bt* | Beetham |
| H | Halton |
| Bn* | Bentham |
| As | Ashton |
| St | Strickland |

A star (*) marks a district divided by a modern county boundary.

In the map keys, places not numbered are not mapped, since their location is not known.

The National Grid is shown in the map border, at 10 km. intervals.

# WEST CHESHIRE

## WIRRAL Hundred

1 Wallasey
2 Meols
3 Greasby
4 Upton
5 Noctorum
6 Great Caldy
7 Little Caldy
8 Landican
9 Prenton
10 Thurstaston
11 Thingwall
12 Storeton
13 Barnston
14 Heswall
15 Poulton Lancelyn
16 Gayton
17 Thornton Hough
18 Leighton
19 Raby
20 Hargrave
21 Eastham
22 Hooton
23 Great Neston
24 Little Neston
25 Hadlow
26 Netherpool and
   Overpool
27 Ness
28 Great and Little Sutton
29 Ledsham
30 Stanney
31 Puddington
32 Capenhurst
33 Shotwick
34 Lea nr Backford
35 Croughton
36 Picton*
37 Saughall
38 Wervin*
39 Mollington
40 Upton nr Chester*
41 Mickle Trafford*
42 Blacon
43 Guilden Sutton*

## CHESTER

1 Newton
2 Chester
3 Handbridge
4 Netherleigh
5 Overleigh

## NANTWICH Hundred

## EDDISBURY (North) Hundred

1 Frodsham
2 Ince
3 Thornton le Moors
4 Elton
5 Helsby
6 Alvanley
7 Kingsley
8 Weaverham
9 Winnington
10 Hartford
11 'Conersley'
12 Bridge Trafford
13 Wimbolds Trafford
14 Dunham on the Hill
15 Manley
16 Eddisbury
*Aldredelie*
*Done*
*Opetone*

## EDDISBURY (South) Hundred

1 Ashton
2 Barrow
3 Tarvin
4 Willington
5 Rushton
6 Little Budworth
7 Oulton
8 Over
9 Burton
10 Clotton
11 Iddinshall
12 Tarporley
13 Tiverton
14 Tilstone Fearnall
15 Alpraham
16 Wettenhall
17 Beeston
18 Bunbury
19 Wardle
20 Peckforton
'Alretone'
*Cocle*
*Ulure*

## ATI'S CROSS Hundred

1 Lache*
2 Marlston*
3 Claverton*
4 Kinnerton(?)*
5 Dodleston*

*The map key is given facing the map of East Cheshire*

A star (*) denotes places subsequently in different Hundreds,
see Appendix.

## BROXTON Hundred

1 Boughton
2 Christleton
3 Stapleford
4 Waverton
5 Eccleston
6 Huntington
7 Cheaveley
8 Saighton
9 Hatton
10 Eaton
11 Pulford
12 Poulton
13 Lea Newbold
14 Golborne
15 Handley
16 Tattenhall
17 Chowley
18 Burwardsley
19 Farndon
20 Coddington
21 Clutton
22 Crewe Hall
23 Caldecott
24 Broxton
25 Bickerton
26 Tilston
27 Duckington
28 Larkton
29 Cholmondeley
30 Shocklach
31 Overton
32 Edge
33 Hampton
34 Bickley
35 Malpas
36 Cuddington
37 Tushingham
*Calvintone*

## BUCKLOW (West) Hundred

1 Grappenhall
2 Appleton
3 Halton
4 Norton
5 Eanley
6 Weston
7 Clifton
8 Antrobus
9 Aston by Budworth
10 Dutton
11 Whitley
12 Aston by Sutton
13 Middle Aston
14 Cogshall
15 Great Budworth
16 Bartington
17 Little Leigh

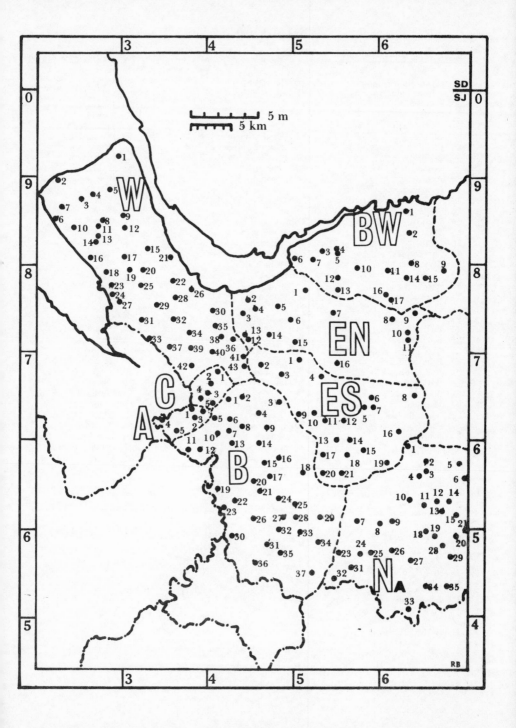

# EAST CHESHIRE

## NANTWICH Hundred

1 Cholmondeston
2 Aston juxta Mondrem
3 Worleston
4 Poole
5 Coppenhall
6 Crewe
7 Chorley
8 Baddiley
9 Stoneley
10 Acton
11 Nantwich
12 'Wisterson'
13 Willaston
14 Wistaston
15 Shavington
16 Basford
17 Barthomley
18 Batherton
19 Stapeley
20 Walgherton
21 Wybunbury
22 Chorlton
23 Norbury
24 Frith
25 Wrenbury
26 Aston
27 Broomhall
28 Austerson
29 Hatherton
30 Blakenhall
31 Marbury
32 Wirswall
33 Wilkesley
34 Audlem
35 Buerton

## BUCKLOW (East) Hundred

1 Lymm
2 Warburton
3 Sunderland
4 Dunham Massey
5 Baguley
6 Northenden*
7 Bowdon
8 Hale
9 High Legh
10 Millington
11 Ashley
12 Rostherne
13 Mere
14 Tatton
15 Nether Tabley

16 Over Tabley
17 Mobberley
18 Knutsford
19 Ollerton
20 Warford
21 Wincham
22 'Chapmonswiche'
23 Peover
24 Snelson*
'Alretunstall'

## MACCLESFIELD Hundred

1 Tintwistle
2 Hollingworth
3 Werneth
4 Bredbury
5 Romiley
6 Cheadle
7 Bramhall
8 Norbury
9 Adlington
10 Mottram
11 Butley
12 Nether Alderley
13 Over Alderley
14 Chelford
15 Henbury
16 Macclesfield
17 Capesthorne
18 Siddington
19 Cranage
20 Lower Withington
21 Marton
22 Gawsworth
23 Kermincham
24 Somerford Booths

## NORTHWICH Hundred

1 Northwich
2 Witton
3 Leftwich
4 Shurlach
5 Lach Dennis
6 Davenham
7 Shipbrook
8 Goostrey
9 Moulton
10 Bostock
11 Byley
12 Wharton
13 Clive
14 Weaver*
15 Croxton
16 Middlewich
17 Newton
18 Sutton
19 Kinderton
20 Sproston
21 Davenport
22 Brereton
23 Somerford
24 Wimboldsley
25 Occleston
26 Tetton
27 Congleton
28 Newbold Astbury
29 Church Minshull*
30 Minshull Vernon
31 Sandbach
32 Wheelock
33 Hassall*
34 Odd Rode
35 Alsager*
36 Church Lawton
37 Buglawton

A star (*) denotes places subsequently in different Hundreds, see Appendix.

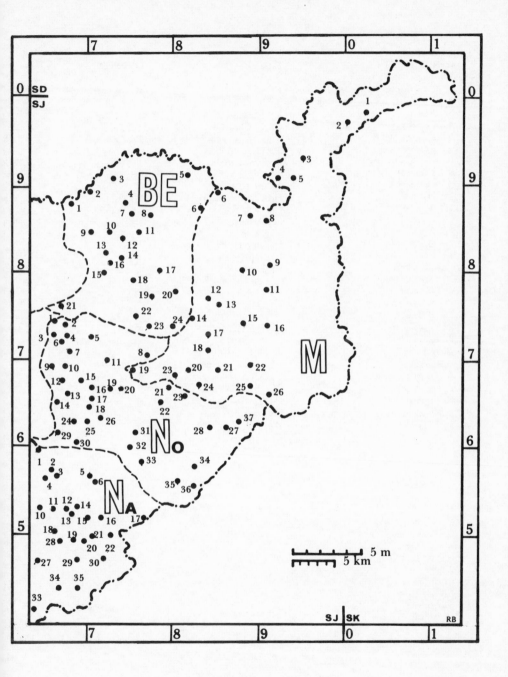

# WALES

## RHUDDLAN

1 Rhuddlan
2 Cefn Du
3 Bryn
4 Cwybr
5 Cwybr Bach
6 Pentre
7 Rhyd Orddwy
8 Llewerllyd
9 Dyserth
10 Hiraddug
11 Trelawnyd
12 Cyrchynan
13 Bryn Hedydd
14 Bodeugan
15 Llan Elwy (St. Asaph)
16 Cilowen
17 Tremeirchion
18 Maen-Efa
19 Bryngwyn
20 Blorant
21 Trefraith
22 Caerwys
*Boteuuarul*
*Coiwen*
*Meincatis*
*Pengdeslion*
*Tredveng*
*Widhulde*

## BISTRE

1 Gwysaney
2 Hendrebiffa
3 Bryncoed
4 Bistre
5 Rhos Ithel
*Legge*
*Mulintone*
*Munentone*
*Sudfelle*
*'Wiselei'*

## TEGEINGL

1 Dincolyn
2 Meliden
3 Prestatyn
4 Gronant
5 Gwaunysgor
6 Golden Grove
7 Kelston
8 Gwesbyr
9 Picton
10 Carn-ychan
11 Gop
12 Axton
13 Mostyn
14 Bychton
15 Whitford
16 Mertyn
17 Fulbrook
18 Gellilyfydy
19 Calcot
20 Brynford
21 Ysceifiog
22 Halkyn
23 Trellyniau
24 Llystyn Hunydd
25 Mechlas
26 Llys y Coed
*Danfrond*
*Melchanestone*
*Wenfesne*
*Witestan*
*Inglecroft*
*Ulchenol*

## MAELOR SAESNEG

1 Worthenbury
2 Iscoyd
3 Bettisfield

## DEESIDE

1 Bagillt
2 Coleshill
3 Radington
4 Leadbrook
5 Golftyn
6 Llys Edwin
7 Wepre
8 Soughton
9 Aston
10 'Clayton'
11 Hawarden
12 Broughton
13 Kinnerton (?)

## MAELOR CYMRAEG

1 Hope
2 Allington
3 Gresford
4 Radnor
5 Hoseley
6 Sutton
7 Eyton
8 Erbistock
*Chespuic*

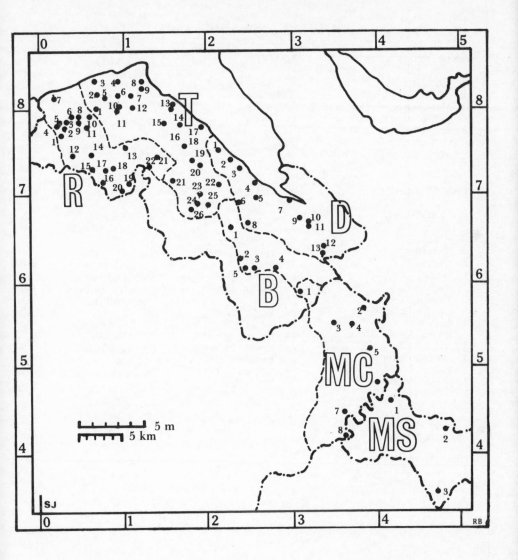

# SOUTH LANCASHIRE

## SALFORD

1 Rochdale
2 Radcliffe
3 Manchester
4 Ashton-under-Lyne
5 Salford

## NEWTON

1 Newton
2 Winwick

## LEYLAND

1 Penwortham
2 Leyland

## WARRINGTON

1 Warrington

## (WEST) DERBY

1 North Meols
2 Argameols
3 Ainsdale
4 Marton
5 Hurlston
6 Halsall
7 Barton
8 Formby
9 Up Litherland
10 Lathom
11 Raven Meols
12 Altcar
13 Downholland
14 Dalton
15 Skelmersdale
16 Lydiate
17 Aughton
18 Upholland
19 Ince Blundell
20 Maghull
21 Great Crosby
22 Thornton
23 Sefton
24 Little Crosby
25 Melling
26 Kirkby
27 Down Litherland
28 Bootle
29 Walton
30 Knowsley
31 Kirkdale
32 West Derby
33 Roby
34 Huyton
35 Wavertree
36 Childwall
37 Little Woolton
38 Tarbock
39 Toxteth
40 Smithdown
41 Allerton
42 *Wibaldslei*
43 Much Woolton
44 Speke

## BLACKBURN

*Blackburn Hundred is shown on the map of Mid-Lancashire*

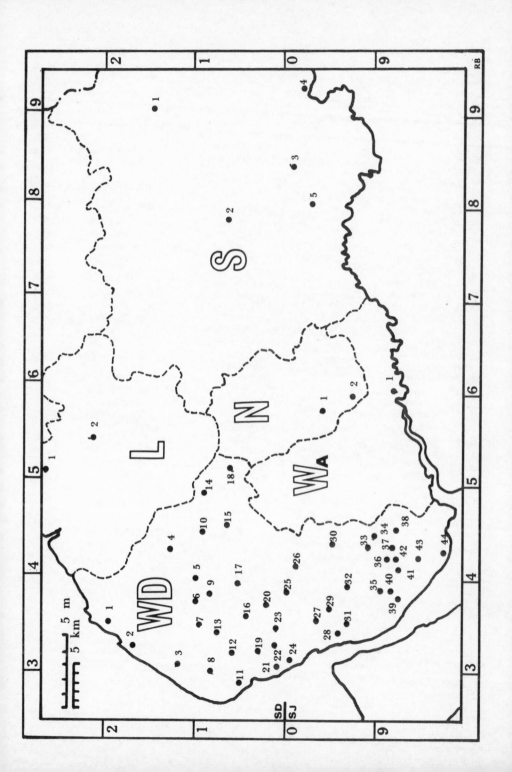

# MID LANCASHIRE

## AMOUNDERNESS

1 Rossall
2 Burn
3 Thornton
4 Carleton
5 Bispham
6 Poulton-le-Fylde
7 Singleton
8 Layton
9 Staining
10 Great and Little Marton
11 Preese
12 Mythop
13 Weeton
14 Greenhalgh
15 Field Plumpton
16 Treales
17 Westby
18 Ribby
19 Kirkham
20 Salwick
21 Lytham
22 Warton

23 Freckleton
24 Newton
25 Clifton
26 Lea
27 Ashton
28 Preston
29 Preesall
30 Stalmine
31 Hambleton
32 Rawcliffe
33 Great Eccleston
34 Little Eccleston
35 Elswick
36 St. Michael's-on-Wyre
37 Inskip
38 Sowerby
39 Crimbles
40 Forton
41 Swainseat
42 Garstang
43 Catterall
44 Claughton

## BLACKBURN

1 Pendleton
2 Whalley
3 Huncoat
4 Walton
5 Blackburn

45 Newsham
46 Barton
47 Wood Plumpton
48 Broughton
49 Threlfall
50 Goosnargh
51 Haighton
52 Whittingham
53 Grimsargh
54 Fishwick
55 Ribchester
56 Dilworth
57 Aighton
58 Wheatley
59 Chipping
*Aschebi*

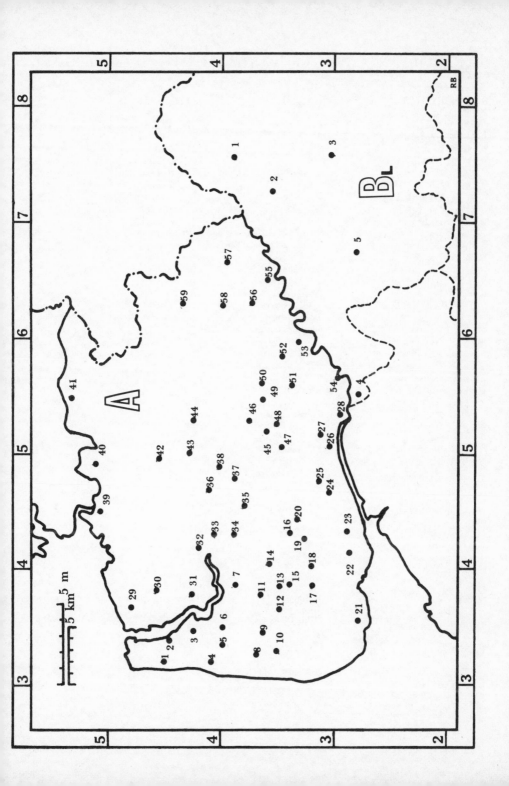

# NORTH LANCASHIRE with WESTMORLAND and CUMBERLAND I

## AUSTWICK

1* Austwick [Y]
2* *Heldetune* [Y]
3* Clapham [Y]
4 Middleton†
5 Mansergh†
6 Kirkby Lonsdale†
7 Preston Patrick†
8 Lupton†
9 Holme†
10 Burton†
11 Priest Hutton
12 Warton
13 Claughton
14 Caton

## WHITTINGTON

1 Whittington
2 Newton
3 Arkholme
4 Gressingham
5 Cantsfield
6 Burton [Y]
7 Barnoldswick [Y]
8 Ingleton [Y]
9 Ireby
10 Leck
11 Over Burrow
12 Thirnby
13 Hutton Roof†
14 Casterton†
15 Barbon†
16 Sedbergh [Y]

## BEETHAM

1 Beetham†
2 Yealand
3 Borwick
4 Farleton†
5 Heversham†
6 Levens†
7 Hincaster†
8 Preston Richard†

## HALTON

1 Halton
2 Kellet
3 Carnforth
4 Bolton-le-Sands
5 Stapleton Terne
6 Slyne
7 Newsham
8 Skerton
9 Bare
10 Torrisholme
11 Poulton-le-Sands
12 Oxcliffe
13 Heaton
14 Heysham
15 Middleton
16 Overton
17 Hillham
18 Thurnham
19 Aldcliffe
20 Lancaster
21 Kirk Lancaster
22 Newton
23 Hutton

## BENTHAM

1 Bentham [Y]
2 Wennington
3 Tatham
4 Farleton
5 Hornby
6 Melling
7 Tunstall
8 Nether Burrow
9 Thornton [Y]

## STRICKLAND

1 Strickland†
2 Patton†
3 Mint†
4 Kirkby (Kendal)†
5 'Bothelford'†
6 Helsington†
7 Stainton†
8 Hutton†
9 Burton†
10 Dalton†

## ASHTON

1 Ashton
2 Ellel
3 Scotforth

A dagger (†) denotes places subsequently in Westmorland.

An asterix (*) denotes places not mapped, in Yorkshire

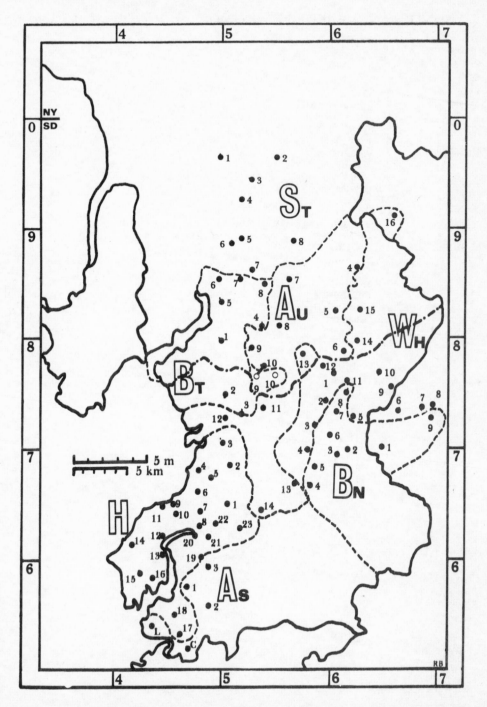

The detached portions of Strickland (9, Burton; 10, Dalton) are shown by open circles.

## MILLOM

1 Millom†
2 Bootle†
3 Millom Castle†
4 Kirksanton†
5 Whicham †
6 Broughton
7 Pennington
8 Martin
9 Killerwick
10 Orgrave
11 Wart
12 Heaton
13 Bardsea
14 Dalton
15 Crivelton
16 Stainton
17 Sowerby
18 *Suntun*
19 Fordbootle
20 Kirkby Ireleth
21 Gleaston
22 Hart
23 Leece
24 Roose
25 Walton
26 Newton

C  Cartmel
A  Aldingham
U  Ulverston
B  Bolton
D  Dendron
H  Holker
Bi  Birkby

A dagger (†) denotes places subsequently in Westmorland.

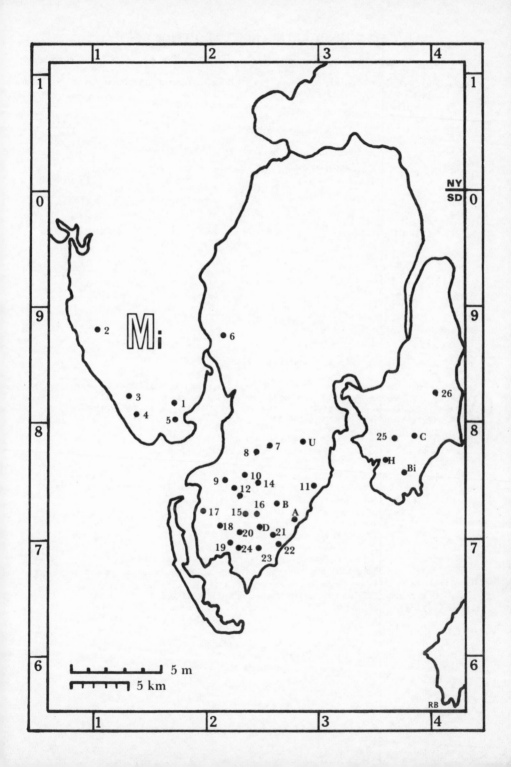

# SYSTEMS OF REFERENCE TO DOMESDAY BOOK

The manuscript is divided into numbered chapters, and the chapters into sections, usually marked by large initials and red ink. Farley however did not number the sections. References in the past have therefore been to the page or column. Several different ways of referring to the same column have been in use. The commonest are:

| (i) | (ii) | (iii) | (iv) | (v) |
|---|---|---|---|---|
| 152a | 152 | 152a | 152 | 152ai |
| 152b | 152 | 152a | 152.2 | 152a2 |
| 152c | 152b | 152b | 152b | 152bi |
| 152d | 152b | 152b | 152b.2 | 152b2 |

The relation between Vinogradoff's notation (i), here followed, and the sections is

| | | | | | |
|---|---|---|---|---|---|
| 262c | C1 - C18 | 266a | 8,43 - 9,16 | 269a | FT1,1 -FT2,8 |
| d | C18 - C25 | b | 9,17 - 9,29 | b | FT2,9 - G3 |
| 263a | B1 - B13 | c | 10,1 - 13,4 | c | R1,1 - R1,39 |
| b | A1 - A19 | d | 13,5 - 16,2 | d | R1,40 - R3,1 |
| c | A20 - 1,9 | 267a | 17,1 - 18,4 | 270a | R4,1 - R6,5 |
| d | 1,10 - 1,25 | b | 18,5 - 21,1 | b | R7,1 |
| 264a | 1,26 - 1,36 | c | 22,1 - 24,9 | 301c | Y1 |
| b | 2,1 - 2,9 | d | 25,1 - 26,12 | d | Y2 - Y7 |
| c | 2,10 - 2,26 | 268a | 27,1 - S3 | 302a | Y8 - Y9 |
| d | 2,27 - 4,2 | b | S1 - S2 | 327c | Y10 |
| 265a | 5,1 - 6,2 | c | blank column | 332b | Y11 |
| b | 7,1 - 8,12 | d | FD1 - FD9 | | |
| c | 8,13 - 8,27 | | | | |
| d | 8,28 - 8,42 | | | | |

## TECHNICAL TERMS

Many words meaning measurements have to be transliterated. But translation may not dodge other problems by the use of obsolete or made-up words which do not exist in modern English. The translations here used are given in italics. They cannot be exact; they aim at the nearest modern equivalent.

BEREWIC. An outlying place, attached to a manor. *o u t l i e r*

BORDARIUS . Cultivator of inferior status, usually with a little land. *s m a l l h o l d e r*

CARUCA. A plough, with the oxen who pulled it, usually reckoned as 8. *p l o u g h*

CARUCATA. Normally the equivalent of a *hide*, in former Danish areas. *c a r u c a t e*

FEUUM. Old English *feoh*, cattle, money, possessions in general, compare Latin *pecunia* and German *Vieh;* in later centuries, *feoff*, 'fief' or 'fee'. *h o l d i n g*

FIRMA. Old English *feorm*, provisions due to the King or lord; a sum paid in place of these and other miscellaneous dues. *r e v e n u e*

GELDUM. The principal royal tax, originally levied during the Danish wars, normally at an equal number of pence on each *hide* of land. *t a x*

HIDE. A unit of land measurement, reckoned at 120 acres. *h i d e*

HUNDRED. A district within a shire, whose assembly of notables and village representatives usually met about once a month. *H u n d r e d*

LEUGA. A measure of length, usually about a mile and a half. *l e a g u e*

PRAEPOSITUS, PRAEFECTUS. Old English *gerefa*, a royal officer. *r e e v e*

TAINUS, TEGNUS. Person holding land from the King by special grant. formerly used of the King's ministers and military companions. *t h a n e*

T.R.E. *tempore regis Edwardi*, in King Edward's time. *b e f o r e 1 0 6 6*

VILLANUS. Member of a *villa. v i l l a g e r*

VIRGATA. A fraction of a *hide,* usually a quarter, notionally 30 acres. *v i r g a t e*